POLICIES FOR DEVELOPMENT

Policies for Development

Essays in Honour of Gamani Corea

Edited by
Sidney Dell
Senior Fellow
United Nations Institute for Training and Research

M
MACMILLAN
PRESS

First published 1988

Published by
THE MACMILLAN PRESS LTD
Houndmills, Basingstoke, Hampshire RG21 2XS
and London
Companies and representatives
throughout the world

Printed in Hong Kong

British Library Cataloguing in Publication Data
Policies for development: essays in honour of Gamani Corea.
1. Developing countries—Economic conditions
I. Corea, Gamani II. Dell, Sidney 330.9172′4 HC59.7
ISBN 0–333–43861–2

Contents

Notes on the Contributors

Parvin Alizadeh is a DPhil graduate from the Institute of Development Studies at the University of Sussex. She has been teaching economics and has also undertaken a number of consultancies for UNCTAD and the ILO.

Dragoslav Avramovic is an Economic Adviser, Bank of Credit and Commerce International SA. He is a Yugoslav national; government official 1945–53 and lecturer in economics, University of Belgrade 1947–53; World Bank economist 1954–77; Director, Brandt Commission Secretariat 1978–9; UNCTAD economist 1974–5 and 1980–4. His publications include *Economic Growth and External Debt*; *Common Fund: Why and What Kind*.

Sidney Dell is a Senior Fellow in the United Nations Institute for Training and Research (UNITAR). He has spent nearly forty years as an economist at the United Nations and has written books and articles on trade, economic integration and the international monetary system.

Gerald K. Helleiner is Professor of Economics at the University of Toronto. He is the author of numerous books and articles on international development issues and editor of *The IMF and Africa* and *For Good or Evil: Economic Theory and North–South Negotiations*. He has served as a consultant to many development organisations, including the World Bank, UNCTAD, ILO, the Group of Twenty-four, the Commonwealth Secretariat, and the Brandt Commission.

Johan Kaufmann is visiting scholar at the Netherlands Institute of Advanced Studies, has been Netherlands Ambassador to the United Nations in Geneva and New York, and Professor at the University of Leiden and at the International University of Japan.

Alfred Maizels is a Senior Fellow at the World Institute for Development Economics Research, Helsinki. Previously, he held a number of economic research posts at the London School of Economics, the Economic Commission for Europe and the National Institute of Economic and Social Research in London. He later became Deputy Director of UNCTAD's Commodities Division and subsequently

Director of its Policy Evaluation and Co-ordination Unit. He is the author of several books and numerous articles on international trade in commodities and manufactures.

H. M. A. Onitiri graduated with a BSc Economics at the London School of Economics with first-class honours and later obtained an MA from Yale and a PhD from London. He was Director of the Nigerian Institute of Social and Economic Research before joining UNDP in 1980. He has served on the United Nations Committee for Development Planning.

Ignacy Sachs is Professor at the EHESS (École des Hautes Études en Sciences Sociales), Director of the CIRED (International Research Centre on Environment and Development) as well as of the Research Centre on Contemporary Brazil (CRBC), and Programme Director at the United Nations University. He is a French citizen of Polish origin, an economist with degrees from a Brazilian, an Indian and a Polish university, author of several books including *The Discovery of the Third World*, *Studies in Political Economy of Development*, and *Développer les champs de planification*.

H. W. Singer is Professor of Development Economics and Fellow of the Institute of Development Studies in Sussex. He had previously worked on the Pilgrim Trust Unemployment Enquiry, as lecturer at the Universities of Manchester and Glasgow, and as senior economist in the British Ministry of Town and Country Planning. He had twenty-two years' service with the United Nations, ending as Director of the Economic Division of UNIDO. He led, jointly with Richard Jolly, the ILO Employment Mission to Kenya.

Harsha V. Singh is an economist in the GATT secretariat. He has been a consultant to UNCTAD, ILO and the Bureau of Industrial Costs and Prices, Government of India. He has worked on topics related to technology, trade and industrial organisation.

John Spraos is Emeritus Professor of Political Economy, University College, University of London. Since September 1985, he has been Chairman of the Greek Council of Economic Advisers. Has written extensively on trade and payments including a book entitled *Inequalizing Trade*. He has also written on the economics of the cinema.

Frances Stewart is a Fellow of Somerville College and Senior Research Officer at Queen Elizabeth House, Oxford. She has recently completed a year at UNICEF as Special Adviser. She has written widely on Third World development and North–South relations. Publications include *Technology and Underdevelopment* and *Planning to Meet Basic Needs in the Third World.*

Paul Streeten is the Director of the World Development Institute at Boston University. He was a Special Adviser to the Policy Planning and Programme Review Department of the World Bank. He was Warden of Queen Elizabeth House, Director of the Institute of Commonwealth Studies, and a Fellow of Balliol College, Oxford. He was Professor of Economics at the University of Sussex, a Fellow of the Institute of Development Studies at the University of Sussex and Deputy Director-General of Economic Planning at the Ministry of Overseas Development.

Jan Tinbergen is Professor Emeritus of Development Planning at Erasmus University, Rotterdam. In recent work he has advocated the integration of security policy into economic policy. He is a Nobel Prize winner in economics.

Preface

This volume of essays on *Policies for Development* is dedicated to Dr Gamani Corea on the occasion of his retirement as Secretary-General of UNCTAD. The distinguished analysts contributing to the volume have chosen this way of honouring a great citizen of the world, and, by this means, of voicing their support for the path of international co-operation that he used his high office to uphold with great skill, determination and eloquence.

Despite all the manifestations of rapidly growing international interdependence, so obvious to all, co-operation among nations has fallen to an extraordinary low ebb. Military confrontation has reached the limits of human capacity to control it, and threatens to pass those limits, if it has not already done so. Threats of trade and currency wars are heard with growing frequency, and hostilities may be said to have begun already in many areas. For the United Nations, conflict and confrontation are by now a relatively old story, though constantly reaching new peaks of disruptiveness. What is remarkable in more recent times is the erosion of support for the Bretton Woods institutions and GATT even among those countries that may be said to occupy privileged positions in them, and which had hitherto regarded them as linchpins of the international monetary, financial and trading systems.

One of the most important functions of UNCTAD has been as a forum for North–South dialogue in precisely these areas of international money, finance, and trade. The dialogue has often been tense, and yet it has made contributions of great importance to international understanding. UNCTAD has pointed to the need for change in international economic relationships and policies with a view to bringing about greater equality of opportunity to countries and peoples worldwide. Although it was always argued in UNCTAD that this would be in the common interests of North and South, it was, perhaps, inevitable that resistance to change would be fierce and prolonged. From the very beginning UNCTAD was viewed with misgivings by the industrial countries, especially since in an international institution with unweighted voting, the North was bound to be in a permanent minority.

Gamani Corea always stressed the negotiating role of UNCTAD, while recognising that if negotiations were to be successful, and if they were to be followed by effective action, the North would have to be convinced and not merely voted down. There was, in fact, less and less recourse to voting in UNCTAD and it is significant that Johan Kaufmann, a major figure from the industrial country side in the North–South dialogue, has the following comment in the course of his essay in this volume.

> In United Nations organs occasional hasty voting on important texts has created, rightly or wrongly, an amount of resentment with a minority. Some of the resolution texts emanating from the Group of 77 have been thus criticised. The criticism, as a generalisation, seems to be exaggerated, because there are many examples of important texts on which the Group of 77, although it had the obvious majority, showed patient willingness to engage in informal negotiations.

Gamani Corea gave brilliant leadership to UNCTAD, exerting great influence in the key areas with which UNCTAD was concerned, though in none more, perhaps, than in the commodity field. This is by far the most difficult area of UNCTAD's work in a policy as well as in a technical sense, and for some years a unified approach to this fragmented subject was lacking. The conceptual breakthrough achieved by Dr Corea in this respect in his Integrated Programme for Commodities and the Common Fund was among the finest of his achievements. There was general recognition that the commodity-by-commodity approach had not yielded the results that had been hoped for. In these circumstances, Dr Corea saw the need for

> a new approach which did not deny the importance of dealing with the specific problems of individual commodities on a case-by-case basis, but which would at the same time present the commodity issue as a single problem with many common facets . . . and . . . treat [it] within a common framework of principles, goals, objectives and instruments in which a number of commodities were treated more or less as part of a single programme of action. Gamani Corea, *Need for Change* (Pergamon Press, 1980) pp. 8–9.

Though much impressed by Keynes's proposal for a commodity organisation capable of helping to stabilise commodity prices, Dr Corea recognised that the establishment of such an organisation would not be practicable within the foreseeable future. He felt, however, that there was a good prospect of gaining acceptance for the creation of a financing institution – the Common Fund – that would not intervene directly in commodity markets, but which would provide finance to commodity bodies and other agencies authorised to deal in commodity markets under the control of producers and consumers of commodities. If such an institution were established with adequate resources – estimated at $US6 billion to cover commodities produced by developing countries and suitable for stocking – its very existence might help to break the deadlock impeding movement towards commodity agreements.

Dr Corea did not see the Integrated Programme and the Common Fund as providing the final and total answer to the commodity problem, which could, in his view, ultimately be solved only through economic transformation of the producing countries, notably through industrial development. The new measures would, however, constitute an important and even decisive phase in the evolution of the commodity problem designed to give greater strength and stability to the developing countries as producers of major commodities. The Common Fund came much closer to realisation than is commonly understood. It was, in fact, accepted in principle by the OECD countries, including even those that had previously been critical of the idea (particularly the Federal Republic of Germany, Japan, UK and USA). And while the form of the Fund agreed upon in June 1980 was much less ambitious than the original proposals had been, and might not, in itself, have gone very far towards strengthening world commodity markets, it would have been an important step forward towards that goal and something on which the future could have built. Subsequent ratifications of the Agreement on the Common Fund came within a few percentage points of the minimum requirement, but the fact that the United States and the USSR did not ratify was a setback to the enterprise, at least for the time being.

It is, perhaps, not far-fetched to think that in a more favourable international political climate, the two super-powers would have attached higher priority to the objective of international commodity price stabilisation, and would have wished and been able to bring the Common Fund to fruition. And although it has more recently become fashionable to deride the Common Fund and to argue that solutions to the commodity problem must be sought in other directions, the fact remains that no other solutions have been proposed, or are available. Meanwhile, the threat to the world economy posed by weak commodity prices has grown even worse than before as prices have fallen to their lowest post-war levels in real terms, making it impossible for debtor countries in the Third World to meet their debt service obligations. Gamani Corea's ideas continue to offer the international community an option for dealing with the commodity problem, as well as a stimulus and guide to the search for solutions.

Mention should also be made of Dr Corea's contributions in the international monetary field, for which his experience as Deputy Governor of the Central Bank of Sri Lanka had prepared him. He was chairman of two UNCTAD expert groups in the 1960s that stated a reasoned case for the creation of an international reserve asset that would make it possible to bring the management of international liquidity under multilateral control. Issuance of the new asset on a basis of universality was advocated, contrary to views expressed at the time by the Group of Ten (G-10). The G-10 eventually gave way on this score, in response to the strong position on this matter taken by the developing countries with the enlightened support of the then IMF Managing Director, Pierre Paul Schweitzer.

Another extraordinarily successful initiative on Dr Corea's part was the proposal to undertake a retroactive adjustment of the terms of official development assistance so as to bring the relatively hard terms applied to old loans into line with current norms. At the Ministerial Meeting of the UNCTAD Trade and Development Board in March 1978, it was agreed that this adjustment should be made for the low-income countries, and virtually all DAC governments subsequently announced specific actions towards this end. It has been estimated that the total nominal value of the measures adopted by these governments has amounted to close to $US 6 billion, of which more than one-half has taken the form of debt cancellation, while most of the remainder has consisted of 'equivalent action', including repayment of part of the debt service in local currency. UNCTAD also succeeded in stimulating the IMF to liberalise the Compensatory Financing Facility (CFF) which, though not a substitute for the Integrated Programme for Commodities, did provide modest assistance at low conditionality to countries experiencing export shortfalls for reasons beyond their control.

More recently the G-10 has begun to question the need for an internationally managed reserve asset, and at their insistence the CFF has been deprived of most of its significance through being transformed, in effect, into a fifth credit tranche. Will this persistent retreat from multilateralism continue indefinitely? It seems hardly conceivable that it can, though it must be admitted that at times in recent years it has seemed that almost anything could happen. The United States proposal of October 1985 for dealing with the international debt problem – a proposal often referred to as the Baker plan – offers a model for multilateral action in that field, though realisation of the opportunities thereby opened up will depend on whether creditor countries accept the full resource implications of the plan.

It was one of Gamani Corea's many strengths as Secretary-General of UNCTAD that he never became cynical or embittered about the North–South deadlock that faced him continually, and he always retained his confidence in the power of persuasion and in the ultimate victory of reason over unreason. It is in tribute to his resilience and steadfastness in support of the United Nations and world development that these essays are offered to him and to the public at large in all countries.

SIDNEY DELL

Part I

Intergenerational Responsibilities

1 Intergenerational Responsibilities or Our Duties to the Future

Paul Streeten

GROWTHMEN VERSUS ENVIRONMENTALISTS

It is, on the face of it, odd that growthmen (who embrace, of course, growthwomen) and environmentalists, who share a concern for future generations, should be so much at loggerheads. The need to accumulate physical and human capital for greater output and enjoyment later, at the expense of current enjoyment, is at the heart of high growth strategies. Sometimes we hear of the objective of 'maximising growth'. This, strictly interpreted, would mean that we should tighten our belts to the bare minimum consumption for productive survival, accumulate the difference between production and consumption, and the last generation before doomsday could then indulge in an infinite consumption orgy. While the strategy is nonsensical, what greater concern could there be for the future? But even more sensible growth strategies aim at higher levels of income and consumption for future generations. On the other hand, conservationists, environmentalists and ecologists wish to preserve a decent natural environment and an adequate supply of raw materials for subsequent generations. They, too, have the welfare of future generations at heart. What then are the issues of disagreement? We might identify five.

1. First, growthmen and environmentalists disagree on the form that provision for the future should take. Growthmen emphasise reproducible capital, and education and training (human capital), anti-growth environmentalists emphasise exhaustible resources – minerals, open space, virgin land, clean air, safe water. They are worried lest rapid growth destroy these and leave future generations worse off. If environmentalists take exhaustibility seriously, the advocacy of zero growth is no remedy. Even zero growth requires replacement of existing capital, and leads eventually to exhaustion, though exponential growth does so sooner. The difference is merely a

matter of time. The strategy would lead to the advocacy not of zero growth but zero consumption. But if the present generation would have to be extinguished in order to leave resources over for future generations, there would be no future generations. If, on the other hand, the environmentalists assert that technical substitutes for exhaustible raw materials can be found, so that the issue is a battle between technology and resources, the difference becomes an empirical question about the length of time and the appropriate policies. It is anybody's guess how long it would take for technological innovation to substitute for exhaustible materials. If it were the case that the rate of our technical progress exactly offsets the rate of depletion, pollution and risk creation, intergenerational responsibilities would be met according to both growthmen and environmentalists.

2. A second difference is the degree of probability that the two groups attach to a sudden drastic change for the worse, such as irreversible pollution, or complete exhaustion of an essential resource, or complete dislocation of life that would spell disaster. Growthmen tend to attach rather small or zero probabilities to such events and view progress as a more continuous process, while environmentalists attach higher probability to such disasters, if current policies are continued.

3. A third difference may be the rate of time discount that the two groups attach to the welfare of future generations, perhaps together with different estimates of when a disaster might occur. Assume that both groups agreed that it is possible, or even probable, that a disaster will occur in 5 million years. Anti-growthmen may have a longer time horizon, so that they attach greater negative weights to such a prospect, whereas growthmen may discount the very distant future at a higher rate. This higher discount rate has to be distinguished from their greater faith in the 'technical fix', the human ingenuity of avoiding the disaster, which is a separate point, more fully discussed below.

It may also be that the two schools apply different time discount rates to the not so very distant future. The view that we owe special responsibilities to those near to us would fully take into account the lifetime of our children and their children, but might give decreasing weights to the welfare of subsequent generations. We may reply to this that if we love our children and those who they in turn love, the love chain presumably extends into the indefinite future. In fact, however, we attach less weight to an extra dollar accruing to our greatgreatgreatgrandchildren than to that of our grandchildren. On the other hand, even if we agree that the special relationship of kinship calls for stronger weights to be given to the welfare of those near to us in kinship or space or by some other bonds, it does not call for even lower weights the further they are away in time. Once the special relationship has levelled off, say with our grandchildren, the same weights would apply. And, moreover, we do attach the same weights, irrespective of kinship or other relationships, to the infliction of some forms of damage. We believe, for instance, that it is wrong to harm intentionally not only our children but any human being anywhere, and at any time.

It could also be that there are some who would want us to apply a negative discount rate to future benefits, so that we should wish to sacrifice more than a dollar now for an extra dollar accruing to a member of a subsequent generation. A value system that attaches great value to the continued existence of the human race might support such negative discount rates.

4. A fourth difference is in their estimate of the costs incurred in slowing down economic growth, where such slow-down is favourable to conserving exhaustible resources and reducing pollution. These costs comprise not only the costs of present forgone consumption, and the consumption forgone in the near future, but also the social and psychological consequences of a slowly growing or stagnating economy. All sorts of adjustment, between occupations, between regions, etc. are much easier in a rapidly growing economy, where shrinkage of certain sectors takes the form of redeploying only new entrants, than in a stagnant or slowly growing economy, where dismissal, unemployment and dislocation have to be suffered. Rapid growth makes adjustment not only less difficult and less painful, but whatever adjustments have to be made become easier to bear. More resources are there to maintain the unemployed at a higher level of income, and retrain and relocate them. Anti-growthmen, on the other hand, accept these costs and pains of slower growth as an insurance premium that we have to pay in order to avoid the risks of future dislocation or disaster, which they regard as more likely with rapid growth.

5. A fifth and final difference lies in the confidence the two schools have in a 'technical fix'. In the past, technical ingenuity has often substituted for exhaustible natural resources, but what guarantee is there that the future will be like the past? Anti-growthmen, who emphasise discontinuities, may quote the story of the man who fell out of the window of the 30th floor, and, when he reached the 14th,

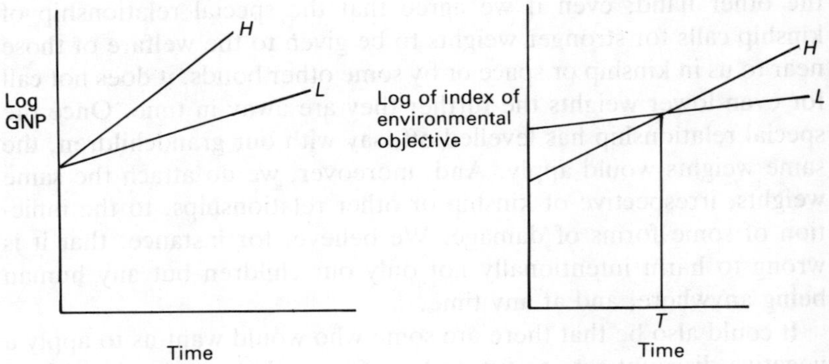

Figure 1.1

said, 'so far, so good'. In contemporary relations we do not regard it as legitimate to take detrimental actions on the presumption that the potential victims will invent ways of getting out of the scrape. Why should we rely on it in intergenerational relations? Given our ignorance and uncertainty surrounding the future, a sensible moral strategy would be to compare the costs of having relied on a technical fix when it did not turn up, with the costs of having sacrificed options and benefits now for the sake of avoiding such reliance, when in fact it did turn up.

It should also be remembered that growth can be complementary with environmental protection. If we count industrial anti-pollution devices and the technology that produces them and innovations that economise in exhaustible materials, as part of GNP (but for a different approach see the next paragraph), it is possible that a certain type of growth, consisting of many of these inventions, contributes positively to our environmental objectives. Even so, there is probably some trade-off between environmental objectives and economic growth in the short run. The diagram (Figure 1.1) illustrates temporal paths of GNP growth and something to be measured by an index of the preservation of the environment and the conservation of resources. *H* is the high-growth path, *L* the low-growth path. We are measuring the log of the GNP and of the environmental index on the vertical axes, in order to show equiproportional increases as equidistant. Until time *T* the high-growth strategy sacrifices the environment. But for ever after *T*, high growth promotes a purer and safer environment. Which path is chosen depends on the rate of discount for environmental objectives, compared with that for GNP. Since the marginal utility of consumption declines with rising income, whereas the relative value of reducing pollution rises with rising income, the rate of discount for environmental objectives is likely to be lower than that for GNP. (Some have even argued for a zero or negative rate.) If this is so, those who lay much store by the environment and by the welfare of future generations ought to advocate a *higher*, not a lower, growth strategy than that dictated by optimising consumption over time. Only then can devices to protect the environment (a growth industry), the technology that develops anti-pollution techniques, processes, products, and innovations that economise in the use of exhaustible materials develop sufficiently rapidly.

GOOD AND ANTI-BADS

Another way of approaching the differences and reconciling them is from the point of view of measurement. Growthmen, after all, are concerned with the annual percentage growth of an aggregate of heterogeneous goods and services. Since we do not aggregate these according to their weight or size, but their prices, which are supposed to reflect human valuations, a way to reconciling some of the conflicts is by adjusting the measurement of GNP and its growth. Now it is largely a measure of production, and, as the name says, it is gross, not net. We might approach the collection by trying to measure welfare, and to measure it net, rather than production, measured gross. Some might think that such a revision would bring together growthmen and environmentalists. If, for example, it were to be found that what we had been measuring was not goods, but anti-bads, produced in order to combat the bads produced by the process of growth, we might all agree that economic growth was not all that wonderful. But before discussing these issues, a more fundamental difference might exist. If the divergence between private costs, reflected in market prices, and social costs is so pervasive that it is not the exception (as in the smoke emitted by a factory that raises other people's laundry bills) but the rule, conventional accounting methods might fail us. Environmentalists might justifiably ask: can the choice between fresh air and unspoilt land on the one hand, and the motor-car with all its implications on the other, be brought under the calculus of the pricing system? The choice between different total life styles, it may be said, cannot be subjected to the measuring rod of money.

Let us next assume that we do not have to accept such a radical critique of income measurements, and that shadow pricing can capture all divergencies between private and social costs and benefits. But we might still concede that we should not include in our income and welfare measure what have been called 'regrettable necessities', or anti-bads. Perhaps growthmen and environmentalists might then agree that the growth of properly measured economic welfare is desirable.

Bads derive from three distinct sources: enemies, nature, and the economic system itself. Anti-bads made necessary by the activities of our enemies would cover expenditure on the army and the police. Anti-bads made necessary by nature are such things as the provision of shelter, clothing and heating against cold, or of airconditioning against heat. Carried to logical consistency, almost all goods and services are intended to remove some void. We eat because our physiology requires food for survival, and we sleep for the same reason. So food and beds could be regarded as anti-bads against the bads created by our nature. Only the most superfluous frills would, on this approach, be counted as 'goods' (it would be an anti-Marxist definition of national income), and even they fulfil some whim, the removal of which could be considered as an anti-bad. But one can drive logical consistency too far. The most relevant bads in the present context are those created by the process of production itself. If production pollutes and we then produce an anti-pollution device, say a scrubber, it is an anti-bad that combats a bad produced in the course of producing other goods.

The anti-bads made necessary by our enemies and by nature are not relevant in the present context, but those made necessary by the production process itself are, as is the appropriate evaluation of exhaustible natural resources, because they affect the fate of future generations. But it does not follow that we must then opt for a lower rate of correctly measured economic growth, i.e. growth of income from which anti-bads are subtracted. For although we might opt for fewer goods, if they brought with them more bads and the need for anti-bads, we might also opt for even more goods, compensated by more anti-bads (the solution suggested on the diagram). Or we might opt for technical innovation that produces different types of goods, perhaps with fewer of the attractive qualities of goods, but also with fewer complementary bads. What we should avoid doing is just producing more goods that produce bads (e.g. pollution), without either the anti-bads or the redesign. Some of the differences between growthmen and environmentalists can be reduced by a proper redefinition and measurement of net national income as a measure of welfare and its growth.

Future generations are particularly exposed to our creation of bads. As Sidney Holt has argued,[1] they are not only without a voice, without votes in the present, but in addition, they are 'downstream' (in time) and therefore vulnerable to any harmful effects we may be inflicting on them, like people who have to live downstream from a polluting factory. They are therefore both powerless and vulnerable. It is from this awareness that the claim to appoint a trustee or guardian for the interests of future generations has sprung. What may be needed is a society for the propagation of anti-bads, especially for the protection of future generations.

But deducting anti-bads from a measure of net economic welfare raises more fundamental problems. We have so far concentrated on bads such as pollution that require anti-bads such as scrubbers. The economic system also creates certain desires (or voids), the satisfaction of which calls for scarce resources. Had it not been for this creation, the resources could have been left unused, or used for purposes of satisfying 'natural' not 'artificially created' desires. Advertisers persuade us that, unless we keep ourselves dandruff-free, we shall not be rechosen by our loved ones at breakfast. Or they create in us the fear that if we do not use the deodorants and mouthwashes they sell we shall be shunned by our friends and neighbours. The fear of not being sociably acceptable or loved may have been there all the time, but its focus on specific deficiencies that can be removed by buying the advertised product is generated by those producing and selling the product. Is this situation not parallel to the emitter of smoke who imposes the need to install a scrubber? Should we not eliminate from our welfare calculations goods bought only to remove created fears? The situation is like that of a blackmailer or kidnapper or protection racketeer who creates a nuisance for the removal of which he then extracts a payment. Such payments, it might be argued, bring us back to square one, they do not add to our welfare.

Yet, the problem is not so simple. Not only some of the nastiest feelings of jealousy, competitiveness and fear of ostracism can be artificially created, or stimulated, but also some of the highest desires: the desire for beauty, truth and goodness, the wish to buy and enjoy books, paintings and music, is not 'natural' but the result of an often painful process of education. Those of us who are university teachers know. It is not a question whether the created desires are artificial or natural that should guide us, but whether they are bad or good. We need a value judgement before we can decide whether an item should be included in or excluded from our measure of economic welfare. Not all artificially created 'bads' call for 'anti-bads' that we should want to exclude from our measure.

The only reason for not including all goods and services responding to the 'artificially created' desires of education is that some have to be excluded from net income as replacements of human capital. As older people retire from the labour force, and as skills become obsolete, their replacement calls for educational efforts which are of the same nature as those items of physical capital that replace worn-out plant and equipment.

The main conclusion of this discussion is that we cannot identify 'bads' with voids generated by the society (and not 'naturally' given), but that we must exercise value judgements before we can evaluate the net national income as a measure of economic welfare. This leaves then an area for possible disagreement between those who put a higher value on resource-using or polluting activities that add to current welfare and those who put a lower value in favour of the welfare of future generations.

THE TIME DISCOUNT RATE

Why should I do anything for the future? The frivolous and facetious question: what has the future done for me? may, as Wilfred Beckerman has pointed out,[2] have an important content worth further exploring. Positive discount rates are powerful instruments of downgrading the future. At a discount rate of 10 per cent, a given increase in welfare next year counts for ten times as much as the same increase in twenty years, and at 5 per cent, next year's benefit counts for more than a thousand times as much as the same benefit in 200 years.

Some people regard it as irrational to discount the future at all. Many of the apparent reasons for discounting the future are based on principles other than the passage of time, though some are loosely related to time flow. Events in the future are uncertain, and this would require that we attach probabilities of less than one to them. A special case of the reduced probability of a harmful event in the future is the case where the same event if it occurred now would be very damaging, but we believe that inventiveness will produce later a technology that will enable future generations to overcome the problem. An example would be the disposal of nuclear waste. But the reason for discounting such damaging events is then not that they are in the future, but that their occurrence will be less probable. Although there is a relationship between the future and uncertainty, events do not grow more uncertain the more distant they are in time. Indeed, in some cases it is easier to predict events in the more distant future.

Future generations may be better off than we are now, and the marginal utility of an extra dollar to a richer man is less than to a poorer man. Or his moral desert of getting an extra dollar may be smaller. We should not permit a member of our generation to go hungry in order to add a second car to a member of a future generation. But, again, the reason for discounting his benefit is not future time, but higher income. If someone in the future were to be poorer than we are now, his marginal utility or desert would be greater, and the appropriate 'discount rate' would be negative.

Derek Parfit discusses additional apparent reasons for discounting the future, which he rejects.[3] One is the argument from opportunity costs. Earlier benefits can be used to yield greater benefits later. An investment next year can yield much more over the next ten years than had we made the investment after ten years. Delaying the investment therefore imposes opportunity costs. But once again, the reason for putting a premium on nearer events is not time, but their yield. This can be seen when we consider benefits that are not invested but consumed. Parfit uses the example of the enjoyment of a beautiful landscape that results from not building an airport. This enjoyment is the same next year and in ten years' time, and should not be discounted. It is also true that if, for example, we were to compensate for certain genetic deformities, a sum invested now would yield more money for compensation than the same sum invested later. But Parfit argues, correctly, that it is not the distance in time of the later deformity that matters, but the investment and compensation. Were we not to compensate, this would become irrelevant.

Parfit also discusses what he calls the argument from democracy. Since most people care less about the future, the government, reflecting the views of the electorate, should discount it. But unless we believe that what the electorate wants is *ipso facto* right (vox populi, vox dei), the question of whether we should or should not care less about the future has to be answered independently of what the majority wants.

Another argument considered by Parfit is the argument from excessive sacrifice. Without a discount rate, any small increase in benefit that extends indefinitely in time could demand any amount of sacrifice in the present, because in time the benefits outweigh the costs. But, once again, the objection to the argument is that no generation can be required to make excessive sacrifices for future generations. Parfit illustrates this by supposing that, at the same costs to us now, we could prevent either a minor catastrophe in the nearer future or a major catastrophe in the further future. 'Since preventing the major catastrophe would involve no extra cost, the Argument from Excessive Sacrifice fails to apply.'

Finally, Parfit discusses the argument from special relations. We have greater responsibilities to certain people to whom we stand in special relations: our children, parents, students, patients, clients, fellow citizens. And future generations do not stand in any of these relations. But first, it is the distance in the relationship, which may be correlated to distance in space or in time, rather than the distance in time that matters. Second, the discount rate according to special relationships levels off, and does not increase with time. Our obligations to the tenth generation are no less than to the ninth or eighth. Third, the duty to avoid inflicting grave harm applies to *all* people, now and in the future.

People who argue that we should not discount the future at all would attach the same weight to enjoyment by myself now, in a few years' time, and by all future generations. The refusal to do this has been called by A. C. Pigou the lack of telescopic faculty, and by Roy Harrod the conquest of reason by passion. It must be concluded from the previous arguments that there is no case for a positive time discount rate.

OUR RESPONSIBILITIES TO FUTURE GENERATIONS

What does intergenerational justice demand? A utilitarian approach might suggest that we owe future generations the same level of utility that we are enjoying now. Since we do not know and cannot determine the size of future generations, this must apply to total utility, distributed among their numbers according to a different set of principles. But there are well known difficulties in distributing utility, happiness or welfare equally, and Brian Barry has argued convincingly[4] that it is opportunities, not welfare, that should be distributed equally over generations. For energy this would mean that we should leave future generations the same productive capacity and therefore the same opportunities to produce that we enjoy. If we deplete some exhaustible resource, we would have to compensate for this by some technological innovation or capital accumulation that makes any given amount of oil or coal yield more energy, or substitutes by some other source for the depleted resource. But compensating for depletion presupposes our knowing how much we should have left to future generations without the depletion. Would it be just if we consumed all the capital we inherited from previous generations and only compensated for the depletion of natural resources we caused? Or would it be just if we added to man-made capital as much as the previous generations had added? Or should we leave the same amount of man-made capital that we inherited, plus compensation for the depletion we caused? These are difficult questions and no answer will be attempted here.

Brian Barry discusses the question, 'what does adequate compensation in practice mean?' If we develop a technology that enables us to raise the rate of extraction by the same proportion that we have used up the resource, that would be adequate compensation. Or if we invent a technology that gives us as much more power as we have used up, maintaining effectively performance, that also would qualify. Such guidelines take us some way, but not all the way, for different forms of energy have different benefits and costs, which it is not easy in practice to bring to a common denominator.

All this presupposes that humanity should survive. Yet, as Wilfred Beckerman and others have shown, the assumption that we should perpetuate mankind is not logically justified. What is the loss of people who were never conceived and born (say, as a result of contraception or abstention or annihilation of the human race)? Who, if anybody, is worse off because these people have not been born, compared with their potential existence?

We have to turn to the basis of our moral obligation to others and specifically to future generations. Different answers have been given. The facetious question raised above suggests that future generations cannot benefit us. But they also cannot harm us. And one tradition in moral philosophy bases moral obligation on the ability to do harm. Hobbes talked about 'convenient articles of peace', which prevent us from harming other people in order to avoid being harmed ourselves by them.[5] If this is the social basis of moral law, we would have no obligations towards future generations, for they are not capable of harming us.

Another basis for moral obligations is Locke's theory of entitlement, according to which a man can do whatever he wishes with his own, if he has legitimately acquired it. The main current expositor of his view is Robert Nozick. From it follow no obligations at all to future generations. If we wished to destroy everything we own, or ask our executors to do so after we die, this would be fully consistent with our moral obligations. A third theory is that of Rousseau, who bases moral obligations on our sense of community. But here again, it is hard to see how we can postulate a sense of community with numerous as yet unborn members of future generations.

So neither the approach and tradition of Hobbes, nor that of Locke, nor that of Rousseau help us in formulating moral duties for the welfare, interest or benefit of persons not yet, or never born. And it is this that we are concerned with when we talk of future generations. Can it be in a person's interest, or, for that matter, against the person's interest, to have been born? Beckerman and Parfit argue that the answer is No. For if we say it is in a person's interest to have been conceived, we say that this person has benefited from receiving life. But to benefit is to be made better off than he would otherwise have been. But if he had not been conceived, he would not 'otherwise have been'. However happy his life would have been, had he been born, he does not miss this happiness, not having been born. It is therefore meaningless to say that people benefit from having been conceived and born. The argument is taken one step further by Beckerman. He suggests that even happy people should commit suicide. They will not miss their happiness and might miss some unhappiness that they might suffer later.

Does the same apply to being worse off for having been born? Some time ago there was a lawsuit of an utterly disabled, miserable person against a doctor's inefficient sterilisation of that person's mother. Beckerman argues that the situation may not be symmetrical, and that it might be possible to say that a person would be better off not having been born. (There is a tradition in literature going back to Sophocles asserting that 'not to be born is best'.) But if we accept the argument that we cannot say that a person is better off than if he had never been born (or conceived), we destroy any claims of future generations on our concern.

Is there not a contradiction in maintaining that there is no case for a positive discount rate and that there is no case for assuming the desirability of the existence of future generations? Can we argue simultaneously that the enjoyment of future generations should count the same as our enjoyment, and that their existence is not desirable? I think the contradiction is only apparent. The argument is that *if* future generations exist, their enjoyment should not be discounted, but there is no case for the perpetuation of the human race.

Parfit suggests an example. Let us assume that we choose a policy with benefits to us that leads to a catastrophe after two centuries. Had we chosen a safe policy and sacrificed these benefits, the catastrophe would have been avoided. But the people who are harmed by the dangerous policy are different people from those who would have existed had we chosen the safe policy. The timing of the meeting of parents, and of the conception is different, and therefore different people are born into the world. According to Parfit, the dangerous policy is not worse for anyone who ever lives.

Various attempts have been made to escape this conclusion. For example, we might 'look in the opposite direction'.[6] Our duties are not to future generations, but to our ancestors, who laboured to make us better off, but not only us: subsequent generations as well. This view fits the view that we are only trustees of the environment which we inherit, and should hand it on in at least as good a condition as the one in which we received it. But the value of the traditions handed on to us by our ancestors has to be independently assessed. Some of the heritage has been bad, and has to be rejected, like slavery or imperialism. So 'looking in the opposite direction' for a moral justification may add strength to duties independently regarded as valid, but it does not provide a basis for our responsibilities.

One way out of the repugnant conclusion that there is no basis for our responsibilities to future generations is to say that particular persons not being made worse off by our actions is not the only reason why these actions can be morally condemned. Assume our action produces the result that the population of people, though themselves not worse off, is worse off than an alternative, hypothetical population of the same number, who would have enjoyed greater benefits had we abstained from our action. Derek Parfit and Douglas MacLean have argued that our action may then be regarded as wrong, even although nobody is made worse off by it. Sidney Holt appears to argue along similar lines when he writes that

> to the extent that humanity, past, present and future, is perceived as one with the rest of the nature – or, at least, with the living world, the biosphere – so discussion of the rights of animals is inseparable from discussion of the rights of humanity.[7]

Others, on the other hand, think that a policy that makes nobody worse off cannot be morally wrong, even if the fate of people who might have lived, but never did, would have been improved by a different policy.

Even if there were no reason in terms of people's interests for accepting responsibility for the fate of future generations, there may be other reasons. Brian Barry ends his article on 'Justice Between Generations' by saying that

> if I try to analyse the source of my own strong conviction that we should be wrong to take risks with the continuation of human life, I find that it does not lie in any sense of injury to the interests of people who will not get born but rather in a sense of its cosmic impertinence – that we should be grossly abusing our position by taking it upon ourselves to put a term on human life and possibilities.[8]

In spite of the logical difficulty of justifying the continuation of the human race, we shall in the following accept Brian Barry's view and assert instinctively or genetically or on the basis of a new, extended ethics, not based on benefits and harm to the interests of people, the desirability to perpetuate it.

SOME SPECIFIC PROBLEMS

Sometimes the concern for social justice among contemporaries and between generations is presented as a conflict: why be concerned with future generations when we have so many poor and so much inequality among us now? Trade unionists and the unemployed advocate large projects such as hydroelectric dams and call the ecological opponents 'gentlemen's kids'. The ecologists blame industrialists for greed and causing future ecological disasters.

But there is no such conflict. In principle, having decided upon how much we owe to future generations, the remainder can be distributed in as egalitarian a manner as we wish. Any anti-poverty strategy must have a temporal dimension, and it would be as wrong to remove all poverty now by aggravating poverty later, as it would be to starve ourselves in order to provide plenty for the future. Indeed, since it is the present high-income consumers who use up most exhaustible resources, justice requires that compensation be paid both to low-income consumers and to future generations.

A specific obstacle to exercising our responsibility to future generations arises from an institutional lag, or deficiency. Let us suppose that national governments have assumed responsibility for future generations and, as a result, have adopted policies to conserve exhaustible raw materials and avoid excessive pollution. This assumption is not quite unrealistic, for many governments have in fact adopted such policies. Indeed, it could be argued that it is precisely one of the functions of government to take on these responsibilities through public action, because any one individual, however eager he was on achieving the objective, could not give force to his desires in the absence of coordination or even enforcement of other individuals. It is what economists call a public good.

Having achieved the right policies at the national level, the danger arises that the damage will be exported. Resources outside the national boundaries will then be excessively exploited and the air and water beyond the frontiers will be happily polluted. It is likely that these forms of transnational damage would be even greater than if the national government had taken no action. The growing dispersal of acid rain outside national frontiers as a result of high chimney stacks, imposed to avoid national pollution, and the danger of the extinction of whales are examples.

The greater concern shown for future generations inside the national boundaries has led to a situation in which the same concern outside these boundaries is reduced. The reason for this is that we do not have a world government, a global authority, that would enact the appropriate rules. Even if each nation state were, individually, concerned about the future of the world community, and not only about future generations inside its borders, it would not be able to give effect to this. The result is a prisoner's dilemma situation in which each nation is made worse off by the impact of the actions of others. There are also difficulties in getting coordinated action on the part of a group of nation states. For each state will hope to benefit from the actions of others, were these to show global concerns, without itself contributing to the costs and restraints. It is the free rider problem, superimposed upon the prisoner's dilemma. The solution lies in a surrender of national sovereignty to a supranational authority with power to impose laws and regulations that safeguard the interests of future generations of the global community.[9]

What kinds of moral obligations to future generations may arise? If an action now has no consequences affecting future generations, or entirely beneficial ones, no problem arises. But there are two kinds of other actions. First, actions which benefit us may have harmful consequences for future generations, and, second, actions which impose a sacrifice on us may have beneficial consequences. In addition to these choices, there may be actions, whether beneficial or harmful to us, that have different impacts on different future generations, beneficial to some, harmful to others.

It should, however, be noted that in many cases actions that impose an apparent sacrifice turn out, on closer inspection, to be profitable, so that the conflict can be avoided. A company called 3M established a programme that it called 3P, which stands for 'Pollution Prevention Pays'[10] Once product and process innovation are included in the analysis, it turns out there are many unexplored and unexploited profit opportunities that manifest themselves in response to the challenge of pollution control. If the costs of these innovations are less than the new profits to be earned, the whole operation turns out to be economical even from the firm's point of view. In this case no conflict between present and future interests arises.

Let us take as the first illustration the exploitation of exhaustible and irreplaceable natural resources, such as fossil fuels, mineral reserves, ocean fisheries, tropical forests, etc. It is quite possible for the reductions in these nature-given resources to exceed the accumulation of man-made capital. If this is so, we are using up a capital that we have inherited and leaving future generations worse off. Even if there is a net addition to the sum of natural and man-made capital, not making full allowances for the exploitation of natural resources in our national income accounts would lead to overstatements of the amount we leave to future generations.

Let us take as another illustration the dangers to future generations that arise from nuclear power. First, there are the technical dangers of accidents in the extreme case of a core melt in a reactor. But there is also great uncertainty about the dangerous effects, some possibly genetic, and over a long period, of milder exposure to radiation.

Secondly, there is a danger that material may be stolen from a plant and used for the fabrication of nuclear bombs.

A proliferation of such bombs, particularly in the hands of terrorists or other extremists who would not hesitate to use it, constitutes a considerable danger.

Third, there is a danger of sabotage at the plant by enemies or opponents of certain policies. Fourth, there is a danger of an attack in war or civil war on the plant and the consequential release of radiation. Fifth, there is the problem of nuclear waste disposal. Such waste has a very long half-life and risks continue for hundreds of years, while all the benefits accrue to the present generation.

A very serious, not much discussed sixth risk to future generations arises from the need to protect the plant against terrorists, saboteurs and enemies. The guards that police these stations have to be armed and given a high degree of discretion with regard to the use of their weapons. Armed private armies are a new phenomenon in democracies and constitute a threat to our civil liberties. It may well be that this social and political threat is more serious than the technical risks of breeder reactors.

The crash of an airliner in which 40 people are killed makes headline news, but the death of 40 motor-car accident victims in different places does not. Spatially concentrated death from a nuclear accident or sabotage is judged worse than random or dispersed death. This reinforces the argument that risks of a disaster befalling simultaneously groups of people are worse than risks in which the same number of victims is distributed over time.

To this must be added another element: death caused by the actions of others is judged worse than that caused by our own acceptance of risks. We accept the same risks caused by our rock climbing or driving motor-cars that we would not accept if they were inflicted on us involuntarily. And risks from nuclear power are among those that are 'downstream'. Future generations are both powerless and vulnerable.

SUMMARY AND CONCLUSIONS

After examining five points of disagreement between growthmen and environmentalists, both of whom are concerned with protecting the future, the chapter has discussed some problems of measurement of economic welfare. The conclusion is that value judgements are necessary in order to know which 'anti-bads' should be counted positively, and which as 'regrettable necessities'. It was then argued that there is no case for a positive (or negative) time discount rate. Apparent arguments in its favour are based on grounds other than pure time discount. The next section discussed the moral basis for our obligation to future generations. It cannot be in a person's interest to be born (or not to be born), because a comparison with the alternative implies judging how well that person would otherwise have been, and he would not have otherwise been. It is concluded that no case can be made out for our responsibilities on grounds of benefits and harm to people, but the search for a different moral basis will continue. The apparent contradiction between the case for a zero time discount rate and against the continuation of the human race is cleared up. The final section attempts to clarify some specific problems concerned with our responsibilities to the future. The principles previously discussed are applied to these cases.

Notes

1. Sidney Holt, 'Towards Ensuring the Rights of Future Generations: Scientific Aspects', UNESCO Paper (September 1982) p. 4.
2. Wilfred Beckerman, 'Human Resources: Are They Worth Preserving?', in *Human Resources, Employment and Development*, vol. 2, *Concepts, Measurement and Long-Run Perspective* (edited by Paul Streeten and Harry Maier, for the International Economic Association, Macmillan, 1983).
3. Derek Parfit, 'Energy and the Further Future: The Social Discount Rate', in Douglas MacLean and Peter G. Brown (eds), *Energy and the Future*, Maryland Studies in Public Philosophy, chapter 2.
4. Brian Barry, 'Intergenerational Justice and Energy Policy', in Douglas MacLean and Peter G. Brown (eds), *Energy and the Future*, Maryland Studies in Public Philosophy (New Jersey: Rowman and Littlefield, 1983).
5. Brian Barry, 'Justice Between Generations', in P. M. S. Hacker and J. Raz (eds), *Law, Morality and Society*, Essays in honour of H. L. A. Hart (Oxford, 1977).
6. Douglas MacLean, 'A Moral Requirement of Energy Policies', in Douglas MacLean and Peter G. Brown (eds), *Energy and the Future*, Maryland Studies in Public Philosophy (New Jersey: Rowman and Littlefield, 1983) p. 187.
7. Sidney Holt, 'Towards Ensuring the Rights of Future Generations: Scientific Aspects', UNESCO Paper (September 1982) p. 2.
8. Brian Barry, 'Justice Between Generations', in P. M. S. Hacker and J. Raz (eds), *Law, Morality and Society*, Essays in honour of H. L. A. Hart (Oxford, 1977).

9. See Peter Inglott, 'The Rights of Future Generations: Some Socio-Political Considerations', UNESCO Paper, unpublished.
10. Joseph T. Ling, vice-president, environmental engineering and pollution control, *Pollution Prevention Does Pay*, 3M Company, USA. *Industry and Environment*, vol. 7, no. 2, United Nations Environment Programme, 17 rue Margueritte, 75017 Paris.

Part II

Overcoming the External Constraints

2 African Recovery and Development

H. M. A. Onitiri

1 INTRODUCTION

The Special Session of the United Nations General Assembly on the Critical Economic Situation in Africa ended with the adoption, without dissent, of a United Nations Programme of Action for African Economic Recovery and Development. It was a unique occasion in many ways. First, it was a crucial stage in the series of international actions prompted by the African economic crisis – crucial in the sense that the Session was devoted specifically to addressing the fundamental economic issues of the African crisis rather than to the organisation of emergency supplies of food to feed the hungry. Second, it was the first time that a special session had been held on the economic problems of a particular region of the world, rather than on the problems of developing countries as a whole. Third, the fact that such a special session was held midway through the Third United Nations Development Decade gave rise to several questions about the state of implementation of the Decade programme and the state of the New International Economic Order. Fourth, it gave rise to some discussion about Africa's relations with the rest of the developing world.

The purpose of this chapter is to examine the various questions arising from the uniqueness of the Special Session, and to consider how the experience would be most likely to influence African economic development and Africa's relations with the rest of the world. The chapter is divided into eight sections. Section 2 puts the Special Session in broad historical perspective. Section 3 analyses the results of the Special Session and the United Nations Programme of Action for African Development. Section 4 considers the problems of implementation of the programme against the background of current trends in African economies and the recent experience of several African countries with the implementation of policy reforms and structural adjustment measures, particularly under the IMF conditionality programme. Section 5 examines the implications of the

Special Session for the New International Economic Order and the programme for the Third United Nations Development Decade. Section 6 discusses the present state of the debate on some key economic issues such as primary commodity prices and debt, in the light of the discussions during the Special Session and the conclusions of the Session. Section 7 examines the implications of the Special Session for Africa's relations with other developing regions of the world. Section 8 concludes with a brief review of the future perspectives for African development in the light of the conclusions of the Special Session.

2 HISTORICAL PERSPECTIVES

African economic problems have been the subject of special debates within the United Nations system since the African economic crisis became particularly critical in 1984, as a result of two years of severe drought. It will be recalled that in March 1984, a United Nations Conference on the Emergency Situation in Africa was held in Geneva to mobilise international support for the countries most affected by the drought. In the same connection, the Secretary-General of the United Nations established the Office for Emergency Operations in Africa to facilitate and co-ordinate the mobilisation and disbursement of emergency assistance.

As the crisis intensified, African countries held a major economic summit in July 1985 to prepare an agenda for emergency, short-term and long-term actions to cope with the situation. The Summit adopted the African Priority Programme for Economic Recovery 1986–1990 (APPER)[1] which consists of short-, medium- and long-term measures to cope with the symptoms of the crisis as well as the fundamental causes. While the programme was presented in general rather than in quantitative terms, it was evident that its successful implementation would require a higher level of international support than was then evident, to supplement the substantially increased effort that African countries themselves would be making to implement the Priority Programme. It was on the basis for this awareness that a request was made to the Secretary-General of the United Nations by the Organisation of African Unity to convene a special session of the General Assembly to consider the critical economic situation on the continent.

The basic philosophy underlining APPER was the firm belief that the food crisis which had aroused so much international concern and sympathy was, in fact, a symptom of deeper and more fundamental causes which needed to be addressed if such crises were not to become an endemic condition in a majority of African countries. In the Declaration on the Economic Situation in Africa adopted by the same Summit,[2] African leaders stressed that:

> the current battle to save lives and reduce the impact of hunger and famine should not be the only focus of international support and co-operation. Otherwise, the international community will be unwittingly contributing to making the emergency a permanent phenomenon. On our part, we are determined not only to cope more efficiently with current and future emergencies but are also determined to go beyond emergency and get to the root of Africa's food and agriculture crisis. We recognize that effective mobilization and judicious exploitation of our national and collective potentials, on the basis of well-formulated development strategies and plans, are vital to the eradication of famine and for the control of drought and desertification and for the rehabilitation of agriculture in Africa.

Although the APPER had drawn attention to the dramatic increase in the volume of Africa's external debt, and the heavy debt service burden, the real analysis of the fundamental causes of the African crisis was left for Africa's submission to the Special Session. The submission was notable in many ways. First, it presented what came to be acknowledged as a balanced picture of internal and external causes of the crisis, drawing attention in particular to shortcomings in domestic economic policies, the collapse of primary commodity prices, the decline in concessional assistance, and the effect of high interest rates on the burden of external debt. All these were recognised as further aggravating the unbalanced economic structures inherited from colonial regimes.

Second, it was recognised that the central issue of Africa's structural crisis was pervasive low productivity, particularly in the agricultural sector. Third, it called for 'commitment to a common point of reference' as the basis for mutually agreed responsibilities. In return for commitments by the African countries to undertake policy reforms and a reordering of development priorities, the developed countries would undertake to fill the gap in external resources required to finance the Priority Programme, as well as take steps to ease the external constraints to African development. Finally, the

African submission proposed a follow-up mechanism that, among other things, would involve at the national level joint monitoring of the implementation of the agreed commitments.

While the African submission to the Special Session did not break new ground in its proposals on the key economic issues with which it was concerned, the proposals provided a constructive framework for the discussion at the Special Session.

3 THE UNITED NATIONS PROGRAMME OF ACTION

As was to be expected, the session itself proved to be a difficult negotiating process. From the outset, there was an understanding that it was neither going to be a pledging conference nor a forum for a general declaration on the African economic crisis. However, it was more difficult to define where the outcome would fit between these points. In the event, the negotiating process became an exercise in pushing the pendulum one way or the other, with the rich countries reaching for a general declaration while the African countries strived to obtain as firm a commitment as possible to the goals and priorities of APPER, and some form of endorsement of the financial estimates that they had presented.

Another vital feature of the protracted negotiations was the attempt of the rich countries to hold down the African side to even more firmer commitments to domestic policy reforms than was evident in the African submission. In fact, at one stage in the endless footwork between formal and informal negotiations, the expression 'the necessity to change their economic systems' had crept into one of the countries draft proposals floating around the smoke-filled, tightly packed negotiating rooms. The crisis which it generated was an evidence that the quest for the mutual monitoring of agreed commitments had not dulled the sensitivities about national sovereignty and the right of every nation to choose its own path to national development.

While the outcome of the session is itself open to different interpretations, the following elements in the agreed package, adopted without dissent, are worthy of note.

The Status of APPER

The developed countries had argued that, while they were fully appreciative of the frank tone of APPER and were in general sympathy with its orientation, they could not underwrite the goals and priorities embodied in it in very specific terms, still less make precise financial commitments for its implementation. The compromise agreed was that the key elements of APPER, including the financial estimates, would become one of the two central elements of the United Nations Programme of Action for African Economic Recovery and Development 1986–1990,[3] while the second central element would be the response and commitment of the international community to support and complement the African development efforts.

Commitment to a Common Point of Reference

Given that the two principal elements of the United Nations Programme were, on the one hand, the priorities of the African countries as stated in APPER and, on the other, the commitment of the international community to assist the implementation of APPER, there was considerable debate as to whether it was still necessary to have a section dealing with 'commitment to a common point of reference'. In their submission to the Special Session, the Africans had intended that this section would contain a balanced mix of commitments on both sides – commitment by Africans to APPER priorities and commitment by the international community to assist the implementation of APPER. Once the developed countries had shrunk from endorsing APPER in firm and specific terms, largely because of the financial estimates to which they were unwilling to commit themselves, the Africans were unable to pursue this strategy. However, it was the developed countries who were now interested in retaining this section, although they were still not prepared to commit themselves to any financial targets. As it turned out, what came out from the long drawn out negotiations on this section was little more than a restatement of those elements of the African priorities that the developed countries would particularly like to see implemented.

The section begins with the statement 'Africa is committed to provide the necessary framework to launch long-term programmes for self-sustaining socio-economic development and growth. The international community is committed to assist Africa to achieve this objective.' It then goes on to list the African priorities which should be included in the 'framework of understanding'.

Responses and Commitment of the International Community

Undoubtedly the most important part of the United Nations Programme – indeed, what the Special Session was all about – is the response and commitment of the international community. If indeed the session was not meant to be a pledging session where specific financial commitments would be made by donor governments, then it must be agreed that the Africans had actually succeeded in obtaining undertakings and commitments from the developed countries which they could exploit successfully to implement their Priority Programme. However, this would depend on three conditions:

(i) sustained effort on their part to follow up the agreed commitments by the developed countries, and their skill in negotiating specific concessions within the broad commitments;
(ii) determined effort to begin to implement the priorities of APPER in a most purposeful manner; and,
(iii) close consultations with their partners in other developing regions, most especially through the Group of 77, on the fine details of the specific concessions to be negotiated to ensure that they are broadly consistent with the overall negotiating positions of the developing countries as a whole, on the major issues of international economic relations.

If those conditions are fulfilled, the response and commitment of the international community contains much that could provide real assistance and support in the implementation of APPER. Three key elements of the response provide a general introduction to the main details. They are as follows:

(i) The international community is aware that the process of development being initiated by the African countries as reflected in Africa's Priority Programme for Economic Recovery, has to be supplemented by complementary actions of the international community through intensified co-operation and substantially increased support. In this context, it is also realized that lasting solutions to the serious exogenous constraints, over which Africa has no control, will have to be found since their persistence will impede the efforts of the African countries;
(ii) The international community recognizes that the African countries need additional external resources. In this context, it com-

mits itself to making every effort to provide sufficient resources to support and supplement the African development effort; it also appreciates that the realization of Africa's development efforts would be greatly eased if the flows of external resources were predictable and assured;

(iii) The international community recognizes the magnitude of Africa's debt and the severe and restrictive burden which this has placed on many African countries. It realizes that measures have to be taken to alleviate this burden and to enable those countries to concentrate on the full implementation of priorities. In addressing problems arising from such debt, existing mechanisms should respond flexibly and be improved as appropriate.

Further details were spelt out in three areas: improving the quality and modality of external assistance and co-operation; improvement in the external environment; and support for Africa's policy reforms. These include greater emphasis on programme support, improvement of procurement policies and delivery of production inputs, speedier disbursement of funds; increased concessionality in development assistance; use of indigenous competence and expertise in the implementation of assistance programmes; assistance with meeting the recurrent and local costs of programmes and projects in certain circumstances; and improvements in the effectiveness of technical assistance.

As regards the flow of resources, the response and commitment include agreement to enable multilateral development institutions to increase their concessional assistance to African countries; to work towards the rapid implementation of the IMF Structural Adjustment Facility; to urge the speedy eighth replenishment of IDA and the fifth ADF at levels which should take into account the need to fully support African recovery and development; increased support for IFAD's Special Programme for African countries affected by drought and desertification; increased support for LDCs within the framework of the Substantial New Programme of Action for the Least Developed Countries; and firm invitation to all countries to give priority consideration to the implementation of resolution 165 (S-IX) of UNCTAD. One measure which deserves special mention is the agreement to 'strive to ensure that no individual bilateral donor, during the period 1986–1990, becomes a net recipient of official capital flows from African countries that undertake adjustment programmes'.

As regards the improvement in the external environment, two broad concessions were made by the developed countries. One concerns

> the elimination of protectionism, particularly non-tariff barriers, in accordance with existing commitments, the adoption of measures which encourage African export and diversification programmes, and improved market access, especially for tropical products, within the framework of the General Agreement on Tariffs and Trade.

The other is an undertaking

> to deal urgently with commodity issues, taking into account the special interests of the African countries, in the framework of an overall approach, embracing commodity agreements/arrangements, adequate compensatory financing, and also to increase the capacity of African countries to process, market, distribute and transport their exports; and, in this context, to stress the importance of sufficient ratifications of the Agreement of the Common Fund for Commodities, for it to quickly become operational.

The Programme of Action also contains a major statement on South–South co-operation in which the

> international community reaffirms its belief in the strategy for collective self-reliance among developing countries and reiterates its conviction that economic and technical co-operation among these countries should constitute a key element in the economic recovery of Africa and to the mutual benefit of third world countries giving due regard to the Caracas Programme of Action and to the Plan of Action for Africa adopted by the Non-Aligned Movement.

It goes on to identify a number of specific areas where such co-operation could make an effective contribution to the urgent needs of African countries. These include: water management and small-scale irrigation technology; dry-land farming, training in agricultural support services, including extension services for animal husbandry; institution building development and management in the area of farm co-operatives; small-scale rural industrial development; rural energy production, including the development of new and renewable sources of energy; and agricultural research. Other areas of South–South co-operation identified include co-operation in the development of human resources, and joint participation in the implementation of self-sustaining, self-generating and self-financing development projects.

Follow-up Evaluation Machinery

The follow-up machinery agreed at the national level will amount very largely to a continuation of the present arrangements – consultative group meetings and round tables or similar arrangements, where these do not already exist. Follow-up action at the regional level is entrusted to existing mechanisms. In all probability, this will mean an expanded role for the Permanent Steering Committee of the OAU, with substantial assistance from the Economic Commission for Africa and other United Nations agencies. At the global level, the Secretary-General of the United Nations is requested to

> co-ordinate the assistance and support of the organizations and agencies of the United Nations system for the effective implementation of the United Nations Programme, to monitor the process of implementation, and to report thereon to the forty-second and forty-third sessions of the Assembly.

4 THE PROBLEMS OF IMPLEMENTATION

In this kind of difficult and protracted negotiation, it was to be expected that the arguments, observations and casual remarks which were aired in the corridors outside the formal meeting rooms would be just as important as the niceties of the formal negotiations. In this case, the air outside the formal negotiation forums was heavy with doubts and scepticism. Will the Africans really implement APPER? Do they have the absorptive capacities? Will they be able to mobilise the domestic resources that they have committed themselves to mobilise? Will they now approach the issue of regional and subregional co-operation as seriously as they have indicated? Can we now expect them to mobilise the required political will to enhance the effectiveness of their regional and subregional institutions, on which so much depends in such a fragmented continent? What about the commitment to encourage wider popular participation in the processes of development planning and plan implementation? How well will the pursuit of this objective fit into existing political structures in many African countries, and current attitudes to freedom of expression in some of the countries.

These are some of the questions that were raised informally and in rather subdued voices, from the side of the developed countries. But the doubts were not entirely on one side. African delegates wondered whether any commitments from the developed countries that did not include at least some indicative figures of concessional financial flows, should be taken seriously. They were disappointed with the formal statements of some of the donor governments which they thought were little more than formal lectures about the virtues of private enterprise and free markets. They would have been happier if there had been some dramatic gestures on such matters as debt relief, support for UNCTAD's Common Fund for Commodities, and substantially increased concessional assistance, at least to the poorest countries. Though, as we have seen, the session ended on a note of agreement and expressions of mutual confidence, the lingering doubts on both sides make it even more important that the task of implementation should be approached with great seriousness.

At the regional level, the central institutions that will undoubtedly be involved in the implementation of the United Nations Programme are the Permanent Steering Committee of the Organisation of African Unity (OAU), and the secretariat of the Economic Commission for Africa (ECA). The OAU Permanent Steering Committee is a committee of fifteen Foreign Ministers established by the OAU Economic Summit in July 1985, among other things, to monitor the implementation of APPER, and to pay permanent attention to issues concerning African economic development. The committee is tailor-made to occupy the centre stage in promoting and monitoring the implementation of the United Nations Programme, and in mobilising the necessary support from international agencies. Many people, in fact, expect that the committee will function more or less like the OECD, and that it will also facilitate the establishment of an African Common Market and Economic Community which is one of the long-term aims of the Lagos Plan of Action and the Final Act of Lagos. However, if the Permanent Steering Committee is to succeed in steering the implementation of APPER and the United Nations Programme, it would have to be very active in persuading and encouraging African countries to take a number of immediate steps:

(i) strengthen national machineries that will be involved in negotiating with their development partners. Many of them, in fact, have had experience in holding consultative group meetings and round tables but, in many cases, the national machineries for the preparation for such meetings have been very weak. In fact the World Bank proposes in its new report on Sub-Saharan Africa to establish, for the purpose of consultative group meetings, joint secretariats of donors and recipient countries, manned by the Bank. However, a preferable alternative would seem to be strong national mechanisms, assisted, as may be required, by bilateral and international agencies. There is no reason why such mechanisms cannot service the 'joint committees or joint bilateral commissions' that have been proposed in the United Nations Programme for monitoring the implementation of the agreed commitments;

(ii) strengthen or create national institutions and arrangements to promote wider popular participation in the processes of development planning and plan implementation. Although this is bound to be a sensitive political issue in some countries, the goal should no longer be in dispute, as it has been agreed in APPER and endorsed in the United Nations Programme. Indeed, the successful pursuit of this objective should contribute to a more rational determination of development priorities, and make it easier for governments to mobilise public support for the hard decisions that may have to be taken to deal with difficult economic situations;

(iii) promote arrangements for the co-ordination of national development plans and sectoral programmes at subregional levels, as a means of strengthening the present instruments for subregional co-operation.

The real initiative for the promotion of the implementation of the United Nations Programme should lie with African governments. It is they who have to articulate their plans and programmes, on the basis of the priorities that they have established in APPER, and confront their development partners with the economic realities that they have to face. It is only in this way that they can demonstrate their new resolve to address the pressing economic problems now facing them and dramatise the constraining effects of external factors on their development.

5 IMPLICATIONS FOR AFRICA'S RELATIONS WITH OTHER DEVELOPING REGIONS

While the other developing regions were generally in sympathy with the African case as presented to the Special Session, they had some reservations about strategy which were aired more in informal consultations with the African Group than during the formal negotiating sessions. In the first place, although they went along with the decision to hold the Special Session, they had lingering doubts as to the value of such sessions when held to consider problems of long-term development. While the need for a special United Nations Conference on the Emergency Situation in Africa held in Geneva in March 1984 was easier for them to understand, they remained doubtful about the value of a special session to consider the problems of long-term development of a particular region of the world.

They were particularly concerned about the discussion of national economic policies within the organs of the United Nations, as they feared that this might provide avenues for the developed countries to control and direct the course of national development in the developing countries. In the second place, they were concerned that the developed countries could use the occasion of such special sessions to break the ranks of the Group of 77 and the Non-Aligned Movement on critical economic issues in global negotiations. They believed firmly that the discussion of such global issues, as they pertain to particular regions, could weaken global negotiations on the same issues, within the framework of the New International Economic Order, and the International Development Strategy for the Third United Nations Development Decade. Finally, they were concerned that on any particular issue, the Africans should not demand something less favourable than the concessions that were in the process of being negotiated at the global level.

The concerns of the developed countries were in direct opposition to those of the other developing regions. The developed countries were particularly concerned that other developing regions should not find it easier to extract from them at the global level whatever concessions they had made to Africa at the Special Session. Indeed, a review of the commitments made by the 'international community' against the background of these varying concerns would lead to the conclusion that the Least Developed Countries as a group should be able to exploit several of these commitments to widen the present scope of concessions made by the developed countries within the framework of the Substantial New Programme of Action for the Least Developed Countries. Furthermore, other developing regions may be able to gain from the commitment of the developed countries to 'deal urgently with commodity issues' and 'to stress the importance of sufficient ratifications of the Agreement on the Common Fund for Commodities, for it quickly to become operational'.

While still on this topic, it is worth noting one important area which receives some attention in the response by the international community, that is South–South co-operation: this may turn out to be far more important in the future evolution of Africa's international economic relations than it would seem at the moment. The African submission to the Special Session had made reference to this issue only in a very small way. However, thanks to the influence of the Group of 77, the coverage in the United Nations Programme is far more extensive than in the African submission, and it provides a really major platform on which the present rather slow action in this important area can be speeded up.

6 THE UNITED NATIONS PROGRAMME OF ACTION AND THE NEW INTERNATIONAL ECONOMIC ORDER

In the course of the negotiations at the special session, there was a noticeable sensitivity by the developed countries to any references to the New International Economic Order, and the Programme for the Third United Nations Development Decade, in the agreed documents. However, the fundamental importance of these basic international programmes was clearly evident from many formal speeches, most especially by the developing countries, and in several of the observations during the ensuing debates. Clearly, the explanation of the African crisis cannot be complete without some reference to the failure to implement the global strategies that might have addressed the unbalanced economic structures inherited from colonial regimes, and make it possible for the weakest and poorest countries to find a just place in an international community of unequal partners. The Brandt Commission, in its first report,[4] had drawn attention to this failure and had proposed that:

> An action programme must be launched comprising emergency and longer-term measures, to assist the poverty belts of Africa and Asia and particularly the least developed countries. Measures

would include large regional projects of water and soil management; the provision of health care and the eradication of such diseases as river-blindness, malaria, sleeping sickness and bilharzia; afforestation projects; solar energy development, mineral and petroleum exploration; and support for industrialization, transport and other infrastructural investment.

Such a programme would require additional financial assistance of at least $US4 billion per year for the next two decades, at grant or special concessional terms, assured over long periods and available in flexibly usable forms. New machinery is required on a regional basis to coordinate funding and to prepare plans in cooperation with lending and borrowing countries. Greater technical assistance should be provided to assist such countries with the preparation of programmes and projects.

However, these measures were not translated into substantially increased assistance to those areas of the world. On the contrary, the instability in the prices of primary commodities, and the decidedly downward trends in the prices of those commodities during the past fifteen years, have drained those countries of a substantial part of what would have been their legitimate earnings from the few commodities that they produce for exports. In its edition of 30 November 1985, in a leading article entitled 'Poor Man's Gift', *The Economist* had the following comment:

> Just as yesterday's dearer oil twice brought stagflation to the rich countries, so today's cheaper raw materials can now help them kill inflation and boost economic growth. Unless they also want to cause a banking crash, however, they must make sure that the mainly poor countries which depend on selling commodities can still pay for their imports and service their debt.
>
> Most of the rich countries have not yet understood the nature of their anti-inflationary opportunity, nor how much of it is a gift from poor countries. In the past 12 months, the world price of food – raw stuff like wheat and cocoa beans, not sliced bread and after dinner chocolates – has fallen by 10 per cent. That fall is in terms of Special Drawing Rights (SDRs), a five-currency-basket that avoids the muddles from valuing commodities in dollars or pounds. The SDR price of metals has dropped by 15 per cent that of oil by $5\frac{1}{2}$ per cent. These declines, applied to their respective chunks of world trade, mean that consumers are now paying about $US65

billion a year less for the same amount of raw materials than they did 12 months ago.

The situation in the primary commodity market has further deteriorated since that article was written, and the current estimate of real income that has been transferred from poor to rich countries over the past two years will be even more staggering.

The consequences of extremely low levels of income, and the rigidities of economic structures, were again manifest in the severe impact of the world recession on those countries, and most tragically, in the devastation, misery and deaths which accompanied the drought and famine in Africa. Even now, the effects of that recession linger on in the weakest countries when the rest of the world has mostly recovered from its consequences. The critical question that needs to be answered – and which some members of the Group of 77 were airing in the private consultations with the African Group is whether even the measures that will now be taken to deal with the fundamental causes of the African crisis will have maximum impact without simultaneous progress on some of the basic global measures proposed in the New International Economic Order and in the International Development Strategy for the Third United Nations Development Decade. This is, perhaps, a most opportune time to recall three of the basic elements in the Declaration on the Establishment of a New International Economic Order[5] which provided the basis for the Programme of Action on the establishment of the New Order: They are as follows:

(1) The greatest and most significant achievement during the last decades has been the independence from colonial and alien domination of a large number of peoples and nations which has enabled them to become members of the community of free peoples. Technological progress has also been made in all spheres of economic activities in the last three decades, thus providing a solid potential for improving the well-being of all peoples. However, the remaining vestiges of alien and colonial domination, foreign occupation, racial discrimination, apartheid and neo-colonialism in all its forms continue to be among the greatest obstacles to the full emancipation and progress of the developing countries and all the peoples involved. The benefits of technological progress are not shared equitably by all members of the international community. The developing countries,

which constitute 70 per cent of the world's population, account for only 30 per cent of the world's income. It has proved impossible to achieve an even and balanced development of the international community under the existing international economic order. The gap between the developed and the developing countries continues to widen in a system which was established at a time when most of the developing countries did not even exist as independent States and which perpetuates inequality.

(2) The present international economic order is in direct conflict with current developments in international political and economic relations. Since 1970, the world economy has experienced a series of grave crises which have had severe repercussions, especially on the developing countries because of their generally greater vulnerability to external economic impulses. The developing world has become a powerful factor that makes its influence felt in all fields of international activity. These irreversible changes in the relationship of forces in the world necessitate the active, full and equal participation of the developing countries in the formulation and application of all decisions that concern the international community.

(3) All these changes have thrust into prominence the reality of interdependence of all the members of the world community. Current events have brought into sharp focus the realisation that the interests of the developed countries and those of the developing countries can no longer be isolated from each other, that there is a close interrelationship between the prosperity of the developed countries and the growth and development of the developing countries, and that the prosperity of the international community as a whole depends upon the prosperity of its constituent parts. International co-operation for development is the shared goal and common duty of all countries. Thus the political, economic and social well-being of present and future generations depends more than ever on co-operation between all the members of the international community on the basis of sovereign equality and the removal of the disequilibrium that exists between them.

The real lesson that the world has to learn from the African crisis is that it would be far less costly in human and material terms to approach the problems of international inequality within the framework of a purposeful and consistent international strategies than to wait to respond to crises and disasters that could either have been prevented by those strategies, or whose impact would have been substantially mitigated. All the recent humanitarian efforts, as generous and timely as they undoubtedly have been, may turn out to have had little of lasting value if this fundamental lesson has not been learnt.

7 SOME BASIC ECONOMIC ISSUES

In a way, the African submission to the General Assembly was a contribution to the on-going debate about the priorities of economic policy in Africa and the policy instruments that would be appropriate in the pursuit of those policies. That debate had become important in the context of the controversies that had been generated by the difficult negotiations between the IMF and a number of African countries under the IMF's financial programmes requiring agreement on structural adjustment measures by the borrowing countries.

The debate is no longer just an academic exercise. During the years 1982–5, the Fund supported the adjustment programmes of 23 African countries, so that quite a few countries have now had some years of experience with the IMF package. Indeed, some evaluations of these experiences are now available, and should provide important lessons for future policy. The experience of those countries that are judged to have been particularly successful in implementing adjustment measures will no doubt be closely studied for valuable information on the measures and instruments that are most appropriate to the structural conditions faced by many African countries.

In the relatively more pragmatic atmosphere in which this debate is now being conducted, the lingering doubts about specific components of adjustment measures, and the special difficulties encountered by African countries with respect to particular instruments of adjustment, are now being discussed in a more realistic manner. For example, the case studies of the 'success stories' presented in recent IMF and World Bank reports have been notable as much for their emphasis on the positive results as for the frankness with which the problems and difficulties that will have to be surmounted have been discussed.

As regards those components of adjustment measures relating to management improvement, budgetary restraint, greater role for the private sector, removal of food subsidies, and shifting the terms of trade in favour of rural communities, there has never been any serious controversy. The real bone of contention has centred on the efficacy of changes in the exchange rates, given the structural conditions faced by many African countries.

In the evaluation of the country experiences made so far, what is undoubtedly the most positive result of devaluation is the higher producer prices for farmers that it has made possible, and the consequent expansion of output of export crops that has resulted from the price incentives. However, the overall judgement of the positive impact of devaluation must depend on what happens to the value of exports. In this regard, the World Bank has taken great pains, in its last three reports on sub-Saharan Africa, to draw attention to the problems faced by African countries. The report, *Sub-Saharan Africa: Progress Report on Development Prospects and Programs*,[6] notes that:

> Developments since 1980 warrant a greater degree of concern about the external economic circumstances confronting African countries. Over the past few years, the externally determined foreign exchange situation has become a major constraint on almost all African countries. Falling export prices, aggravated in some instances by restrictions on market access, have undermined attempts by governments to improve their balance of payments. For instance, in Sudan, major changes in macro and sectoral policies have been introduced by the Government in recent years to improve cotton production for exports. These policy reforms contributed to a 35 per cent increase in output in 1981 and to a further 10 to 20 per cent increase in 1982. However, due to the fall in the world market price, the increased foreign exchange earnings which could have been expected from increased cotton production have essentially been wiped out. In Senegal, an increase in incentive prices for groundnuts was followed by a greater-than-anticipated fall in the world market price which upset the effort to restore budgetary equilibrium. In Kenya, the implementation of a major programme for reforming the protective system in order to improve both the industrial and agricultural incentive structure is being slowed down because of the desperate shortage of foreign exchange earnings from traditional exports especially tropical beverages. Similar developments have taken place in other countries as a consequence of the drastic and persistent falls in export prices, aggravated by rising debt service commitments.

In the same manner, the report, *Toward Sustained Development in Sub-Saharan Africa*[7] notes that:

> For export crops, Africa's total volume expanded by about 1 per cent a year over the 1980–82 period – an improvement over the decline during 1970–80. However, for most crops, the fall in world market shares that started in the 1970s continued in the 1980s. The declines have occurred in commodities in which Africa has a comparative advantage and which are likely to remain its main potential source of foreign exchange earnings.

The most recent report, *Financing Adjustment with Growth in Sub-Saharan Africa, 1986–90*,[8] is not more optimistic about future prospects. It observes that 'movements of the terms of trade are hard to predict, but the long-term projection is for renewed deterioration' (p. 7).

While there are uncertainties on the export side about the impact of devaluation, this is not so with imports. In almost all the cases that have been evaluated, the rise in local prices of imports resulting from devaluation has caused sharp declines in the volume of imports. And the standard case usually advanced for reducing imports in this way, rather than through import licences and foreign exchange restrictions, is that it gives less room for the few favoured groups in the society to make windfall gains from their access to import licences and foreign exchange allocations, apart from the administrative inefficiency, bureaucratic delays, and wanton corruption usually associated with such controls. It is a very powerful case; but even here, there may be need for some flexibility. A two-tier exchange rate regime, for all its administrative difficulties may be more suited to the African situation than a single-tier system. As some of the recent experiences with foreign exchange auctions have shown, to treat luxuries and essential imports in the same way as regards access to foreign exchange in an open auction market, is to put the latter imports at serious disadvantage. An evaluation of the experience of Uganda in this connection will be awaited with keen interest. While the IMF and World Bank have favoured a two-tier system of foreign exchange only as a temporary transition to a unified sytem, they may have to review this policy in the light of the experience of African countries. In this regard, it is instructive to ponder the following observation in the latest World Bank report *Financing Adjustment with Growth in Sub-Saharan Africa, 1986–1990*,[9] and consider whether the situation thus described could not be attributed, in large measure, to the lack of discrimination, as between luxury imports and imports of essential items, in using a single price for foreign exchange to determine access to the limited foreign exchange resources available.

Budget restraint, reflected in lower public employment, is desirable in much of Africa, but in some cases it has led to excessive cuts in financing for equipment, maintenance, operating costs, and materials. The result has been a steady deterioration in the quality of public services and further declines in the productivity of public employees. The impact is plain when road maintenance crews lack fuel and bitumen to accomplish their work, when teachers lack books, chalk, and even classrooms for their students, and when health workers have no medicines to distribute. This deterioration in public services is especially disruptive for programmes designed to deal with the basic constraints on development. Unless a better balance is established between personnel and other expenditures, these programmes are in jeopardy. To maintain non-wage expenditures, most countries must reduce government employment and, in some instances, civil service wages. What is posed as a problem of budget restraint can also certainly be attributed to the high cost of foreign exchange resulting from massive devaluation in those countries where essential commodities are not given preferential treatment in the allocation and pricing of foreign exchange.

The real problem that makes it so very difficult for Africa to enjoy the full benefits of exchange rate adjustments is the structural rigidities of African economies and the pervasive low level of productivity. This reduces the scope for expanding the production of more diversified exports and for shifting resources into the production of import substitutes, when relative prices change as a result of devaluation. This is why it is important that these structural problems should be addressed more vigorously within the new framework provided by the United Nations Programme of Action for African Economic Recovery and Development. In the meantime, it would be important to put into effect, as quickly as possible, the commitment of the international community as regards the stabilisation of commodity prices or to set up a compensatory financing arrangement on the model of the EEC Stabex, but with more substantial resources. In this way, African countries would at least be confident that their efforts to expand the production and exports of their traditional export commodities will not be defeated by falling prices in the world market.

As regards the liberalisation of imports, there is one pertinent question that needs to be answered. Given the serious shortage of foreign exchange resources, and considering the current drive to find domestic substitutes for imported food and the raw materials used in the production of a wide range of consumer goods, the liberalisation of imports will certainly not advance this policy. In fact, some countries have had to ban the importation of rice in order to encourage consumers to return to the consumption of local foodstuffs that are reputed to be more nutritious and, sometimes, even cheaper. The International Institute for Tropical Agriculture (IITA) in Ibadan, Nigeria, is reported to have discovered a method for making bread out of cassava flour. How successfully will the new product be promoted if the free importation of wheat flour is not restricted? Even now, as Africa finds it difficult to obtain enough foreign exchange to buy spare parts for transportation equipment, and power generating plants, and to provide educational materials, medicines and laboratory equipment for hospitals, to mention only a few, substantial foreign exchange resources are being devoted to the importation of malt for beer brewing, essence for the production of beverages that have no food value whatever, and can even be harmful, and a wide range of fanciful manufactured foods for which far better domestic substitutes are available, if only they will enjoy the same promotional advantages as the imported products. Food aid has undoubtedly contributed to this preference for foreign foods, but it is only one factor, since the same preference can be detected in countries that have not been large recipients of food aid.

It has been argued that overvaluation of the exchange rate is one reason why imported foods tend to be cheaper than local food products. That statement is valid only where the government provides importers of such foods with foreign exchange at the official exchange rate. Where this is not the case, imported foods could be effectively controlled by outright banning, as some countries have done, or by prohibitively high rates of import duties.

Another basic economic issue that needs to be tackled more decisively is the creation of larger markets through regional and sub-regional economic co-operation. More than any other area of the world, Africa suffers from a fragmented market, although serious efforts have been made in the past decade to promote subregional groupings. There are now in existence the Economic Community of West African States (ECOWAS), the Southern African Development Coordination Conference (SADCC), the Preferential Trade Area of Eastern and Southern Africa (PTA), the Economic Community of Central African States (ECCAS) and the Economic Community of the Great Lakes Countries (GEPGL). In addition to these, preliminary work is under way to implement the decision in the Lagos Plan of Action and Final Act of Lagos, that an African Economic Community should be established by the year 2000. The difficulties of nursing existing institutions are immense, but there is now a greater determination that they should succeed and pave the way for the continental community envisaged by the turn of the century. Nothing will bring foreign investment back to Africa in a big way more than a demonstrated capacity to make these institutions work and to co-ordinate more effectively the exploitation of the continent's rich resource potential.

8 CONCLUSION: WHERE DO WE GO FROM HERE?

The next five years are not going to be easy for African countries, but they can be one of the most decisive periods in African history if the determination that runs through Africa's Priority Programme for Economic Recovery, and Africa's submission to the Special Session of the General Assembly can be sustained, and if the international community holds fast to its commitment to assist Africa's efforts. A good deal of painstaking work will be required to sort out unimportant details from the main thrust of the policy changes that African countries have committed themselves to undertake and a good deal of understanding will be required on the part of the international community in judging the pace of change in a continent where there is so much to be done to cope with structural problems and serious deficiencies of economic and social infrastructure. For example, the commitment by African countries to give a greater role to the private sector, and to allow more scope for market forces, should not be used as a pretext for insisting that the baby should be thrown out with the bath water. Even as they honour these commitments, African governments will still need to strengthen their capabilities to manage and regulate the main arteries of their economic and social life, and provide a strong foundation for the achievement of self-reliant and self-sustaining development, which is the fundamental goal of the

Lagos Plan of Action and the Final Act of Lagos, carried through into APPER, and now endorsed by the United Nations Programme of Action for African Economic Recovery and Development.

Notes

1. *Africa's Priority Programme for Economic Recovery 1986–1990*, adopted by the Twenty-first Ordinary Session of the Assembly of Heads of States and Government of the Organisation of African Unity, 18–20 July 1985.
2. Ibid.
3. United Nations Programme of Action for African Economic Recovery and Development 1986–1990, adopted by the Thirteenth Special Session of the General Assembly on 31 May 1986.
4. *North–South: A Program for Survival* (The Report of the Independent Commission on International Development Issues, under the chairmanship of Mr Willy Brandt) (Cambridge, Mass., MIT Press, 1980).
5. United Nations General Assembly, Sixth Special Session, Resolution 3201(S.VI), Declaration on the Establishment of a New International Economic Order, and Resolution 3202(S.VI), Programme of Action on the Establishment of a New International Economic Order.
6. *Sub-Saharan Africa: Progress Report on Development Prospects and Programs* (The World Bank, Washington DC, September 1983).
7. *Toward Sustained Development in Sub-Saharan Africa – A Joint Programme of Action* (The World Bank, Washington DC, September 1984).
8. *Financing Adjustment with Growth in Sub-Saharan Africa 1986–1990* (The World Bank, Washington DC, 1986).
9. *Financing Adjustment with Growth in Sub-Saharan Africa 1986–1990* (The World Bank, Washington DC, 1986).

3 External Constraints and Endogenous Development: Reflections on the Brazilian Case

Ignacy Sachs

UNCTAD was founded on the expectation that it would help to reshape international economic relations into a positive-sum game for all the partners. In a world characterised by an extremely uneven distribution of economic power, a fairer distribution of gains from trade and financial flows would not be achieved by the free interplay of market forces, requiring a set of correcting institutional mechanisms, codes of conduct and mutually agreed policies. UNCTAD was the appropriate forum to prepare, negotiate and implement such measures.

In spite of the efforts deployed by the UNCTAD secretariat under the able guidance of Raúl Prebisch, Manuel Perez Guerrero and Gamani Corea, the prospect, as seen from Third World countries, is today more dismal than ever. Confronted by the 'economic totalitarianism of industrialized countries'[1] they are the big losers in the game, trapped in the vicious circle of indebtedness, collapse of commodity prices, restricted access to markets of developed countries, outflow of resources to the North,[2] slow growth or even stagnation and maldevelopment.

Evidence is growing that these are not merely conjunctural problems. The great disorder in the world economy reflects deep structural and adverse trends occurring in the economy of industrialised countries. As pointed out by Peter F. Drucker, within the last decade or two, three fundamental changes have affected the very fabric of the world economy:

> The primary products economy has come 'uncoupled' from the industrial economy. In the industrial economy itself, production

has come 'uncoupled' from employment. Capital movements rather than trade (in both goods and services) have become the driving force of the world economy. The two have not quite come uncoupled, but the link has become loose, and worse, unpredictable.[3]

Raw material prices are at their lowest, reflecting the working of a steady technological trend which reduces the material inputs per unit of industrial output.[4] As a consequence of this marginalisation of primary products in the industrial economies, the very foundations of traditional development theories and policies are shattered. It becomes ever more difficult to use commodity trade as an 'engine of growth'. Significantly, Drucker acknowledges the pioneering contribution of the late Raúl Prebisch to the understanding of this emerging situation.

Likewise the falling share of labour in the costs of industrial production (and the increasing share of capital) forecloses to the Third World countries the option of an outward-looking industrialisation, based on their competitive advantage for 'cheap labour' goods. Accordingly, leap-frogging into the 'high-tech' industries or else an inward-looking industrialisation would appear as the only alternatives left, at least for some large and medium-sized Third World countries.[5]

The condition to this is that they will find ways of protecting themselves from the disrupting effects of the 'decoupling' between the capital movements, exchange rates and credit flows and the real economy – the flow of goods and services. The growth of 'fictitious capital'[6] which defies all controls – national or international – is a threat to them, as much as to the rest of the world.[7] Several Third World countries were lured into the foreign debt trap by the availability of international credits fuelled *inter alia* by the recycling of petrodollars through Western banks.[8] What had seemed first as a bargain, became through the mechanism of variable rates of interest, a drain of resources impossible to sustain in the long run.

Brazil is one of such countries. Her foreign debt amounts to 100 billion dollars. The interest paid on it took in 1985 roughly half of her exports and produced a net outflow of capital amounting to about 5 per cent of GNP. Servicing of foreign debt (which is mainly public) requires from the Government buying over 10 billion dollars per year from private exporters. This, in turn, fuels the internal debt that has been snowballing and pushing up the internal rates of interest to a level at which honest, productive investment becomes impossible; thus capital flows to financial, foreign exchange, land and real estate speculation,[9] while inflation reaches unprecedented heights.[10] Conventional adjustment policies, intended to slow down inflation and to cope with the servicing of the foreign debt, pushed the country into a severe 'inflationary recession' from 1981 to 1983, generating mass unemployment among industrial workers and depressing still more the already low living standards of the great majority of the Brazilian working class.[11]

Reducing the burden of foreign debt, and loosening (if not severing) the ties with the international financial market in its present form, is thus for Brazil – as much as for other heavily indebted Third World countries – a *conditio sine qua non* for further steady and socially more responsive growth.

Given the ominous trends described above, the chances for Third World countries to develop through trade as an 'engine of growth' are very thin indeed, notwithstanding the advice they get from some international institutions. The inward-looking strategy should not be seen as an ideological choice but as the only realistic option which remains open to most of them in the absence of a serious action to strengthen their 'collective self-reliance'.

Nor should it be mistaken for an unconditioned plea for autarky, a costly and unworkable proposition even for the largest countries. The two key concepts for an inward-looking strategy are: priority, but by no means exclusivity, to the development of the internal market and selectivity in external relations, which is not tantamount to their neglect, quite to the contrary. Countries with a small share of foreign trade in their GNP are the most 'import-sensitive' ones. They must learn accordingly to make the most efficient use of the limited amount of foreign exchange in their command – the 'joker' of the planning game – while ensuring that reasonable opportunities of increasing exports are not being foregone.[12]

In the real world, the choices are seldom dichotomic. They rather consist in establishing a proportion between the postulated amount of import substitution and export promotion; agricultural and industrial investment, etc. The planners may even arrive at a fairly precise evaluation of the range of available opportunities (subject, of course, to the exogenous variation of foreign prices) by calculating the net domestic cost per unit of foreign exchange saved through import substitution or earned through exports.

However, import substitution or export promotion belong to the realm of *instrumental* choices. Under no circumstances they should become a goal *per se*, just like growth is necessary to sustain development, but cannot be mistaken for it. Import substitution may be 'good' or 'bad', depending on how it fits in the development strategy and how it serves the *substantive* social goals put forward. Import substitution of luxury goods, hitherto purchased abroad but deemed of low priority, will be counterproductive in a development strategy aimed at the satisfaction of the basic needs of the low-income strata of the population. The resources released by banning the imports of such luxuries should be instead channelled into the production of other high priority items, be they producer goods or essential consumer goods. The same argument applies to proceeds from exports. They can be spent to purchase high priority items or else be wasted in importing luxuries (or producer goods and inputs required to produce them).

Likewise, a given society in a given period of time could engage in different inward-looking strategies equally successful in growth terms, some of them deemed 'good' and others 'bad' when examined in the light of substantive social objectives. In order to evaluate the development/maldevelopment performance of a country it is thus necessary to address two questions: the social distribution of gains and costs from the growth process, as well as the ecological costs entailed.

Finally, another useful dichotomy[13] is the distinction between, on the one hand, endogenous development, understood as a national project responding to the specific cultural, ecological and historical conditions and needs of a country and, on the other hand, mimetic growth transplanting exotic lifestyles, production patterns and technologies with little concern for their fitting the setting of the importing country. Endogenous development calls for cultural capacity to unfold the national project, political will and administrative skills to carry it out and an integrated techno-economic structure to sustain it. Only very few countries have this potential as of now.

How does Brazil fare when assessed against these criteria?

The country's outstanding performance in terms of growth has been already mentioned: almost half a century of growth at an average rate close to 7 per cent per year has very few parallels in the world. By conventional standards Brazil also achieved a spectacular modernisation.

The industrialisation process gained momentum in the 1930s, when the country was deeply immersed in the Great Depression. The absolute shortage of foreign exchange[14] forced Brazil into an import

Table 3.1 Brazil: Gains of foreign exchange from sectorial programmes of industrialisation (in billion US dollars)

	1981	*1982*	*1983*	*1984*
Oil	1.05	1.90	2.35	4.40
Non-ferrous metals	0.02	0.14	0.37	0.35
Paper and cellulose	0.09	0.17	0.19	0.38
Iron and steel products	0.15	0.08	0.36	0.64
Fertilisers	0.35	0.22	0.31	0.33
Chemicals	1.03	1.21	1.31	1.31
Capital goods	0.75	1.8	1.7	2.2
Total	3.44	5.52	6.59	9.61

Estimates of Antonio Barros de Castro.

substituting process continued through the Second World War, stepped up under President Kubitschek's 'Plano de Metas' (1956–60) aimed at 'making-up for half a century in five years' and, finally, deepened after the 1973 'oil shock'.

Throughout this whole period the Brazilian economy managed to work with a fairly low import coefficient.

A quelque chose malheur est bon. In an important book significantly called 'The forced march of the Brazilian Economy' Barros de Castro and Pires de Souza[15] contend that as a response to the 1973 'oil shock' which severely hit Brazil,[16] the country embarked on an ambitious programme of import-substituting heavy industrialisation: 'the rapid, horizontal and technologically passive growth of the years 1968–1973 ended abruptly in 1974. From now on the economy would climb in a *forced march* the ramp of capital-intensive and technology intensive industries' (p. 76). The implementation proved too costly in economic and, most certainly, social terms. But as a result of this structural adjustment, Brazil enjoys today a situation in which it can sustain a high rate of growth with a very low import coefficient. The size of the country, its resource endowment, the diversification of the economy and the level of technological development warrant a comparison with the United States which, from 1930 to 1970, had an import coefficient between 3.2 per cent and 4.6 per cent (p. 198).

Barros de Castro's estimates of the additional potential for import substitution obtained through the 1974–5 vintage of industrial projects are impressive indeed (Table 3.1).

The 10 billion dollars gained in this way in 1984 should be compared with the 7.4 billion dollars spent on imported fuels or the 13

Table 3.2 Brazil: coefficients of imports and exports

	Imports/GDP (in %)	*Exports/GDP (in %)*
1970	*8.8*	*8.3*
1971	*9.5*	*7.5*
1972	*10.5*	*8.5*
1973	*11.1*	*9.7*
1974	*16.1*	*9.3*
1975	*12.9*	*8.4*
1976	*10.7*	*8.0*
1977	*9.0*	*8.2*
1978	*8.5*	*7.2*
1979	*9.6*	*7.6*
1980	*11.7*	*9.4*
1981	*10.4*	*10.0*
1982	*9.1*	*8.4*
1983	*7.5**	*9.4**
1984	*6.8**	*11.1**
1985	*5.6**	*9.7**

* Our preliminary estimates.
Source *Anuario Estatistico do Brasil 1983* for the years 1970–82.

Table 3.3 Brazil: imports as share of supply of manufactured goods (percentage)

1949	*1964*	*1967*	*1970*	*1974*	*1979*	*1984*
13.9	6.1	7.1	8.0	11.9	6.8	3.5

Source Barros de Castro and Pires de Souza, *A Economia Brasileira em Marcha Forçada*, p. 71.

billion dollar surplus in the trade balance which made it possible for Brazil to continue to sevice the foreign debt.

These conclusions are further substantiated by looking at the evolution of the input coefficients (Table 3.2) and, even more, at the share of imports in the supply of manufactured goods (Table 3.3).

The years 1949, 1967 and 1983 are end years of a recession and are therefore comparable. In both periods, the input coefficient was reduced by half.

The years 1982–5 deserve a closer look.

The recovery from the 1981–3 recession was clearly export led, but

Table 3.4 Brazil: exports and imports (millions of US dollars)

	1982	*1983*	*1984*	*1985*
Exports	20 213	21 900	27 005	25 639
Imports	19 396	15 428	13 937	13 189

Source *Conjuntura Economica*.

Table 3.5 Brazil: indexes of growth

	1982	*1983*	*1984*	*1985*
GNP	100	96.8	101.2	109.6
Exports	100	108.3	133.6	126.8
Imports	100	79.6	71.9	68.0

Source Calculated from *Conjuntura Economica*.

the country could achieve again a very high rate of growth in 1985 with record low imports (Tables 3.4 and 3.5).

The import coefficient dropped to less than 6 per cent, roughly half of it taken by oil.

According to Barros de Castro and Pires de Souza, Brazil has now reached a stage in which the huge export surplus has become structural (and should be used for a better purpose than servicing the debt to the tune of 5 per cent of GNP). Their conclusion may be too optimistic, as the new investment cycle did not start as yet. Even allowing for an underestimate, on their part, of future import coefficients and capital/output ratios, Brazil stands as an example of a successful inward-looking industrialisation strategy, which ends up by giving a competitive edge to the newly set industries. The two goals of import substitution, first, and export promotion, next, are indeed complementary and not antithetic; they follow one from the other – Japan's example is there. The concept of competitiveness should, however, be used carefully, especially in Brazil. Too often it is achieved by underpaying the labour and underselling the raw materials incorporated in the industrial product.

The Brazilian case thus contradicts the neo-liberal prescription at least on two points: it did not follow the outward-looking pattern and it relied heavily on public intervention.

What then are the limitations of the Brazilian experience?

Table 3.6 Options for structural adjustment to the oil shock

A. *At the supply level* (to increase the supply)
1. Increasing the domestic production of oil.
2. Substituting other domestically produced liquid fuels for oil: (a) sugar-cane alcohol; (b) other biomass fuels.
3. Substituting other fuels for oil.

B. *At the demand level* (to reduce the demand)
1. Promoting energy conservation and recovery programmes: (a) in the industrial sector; (b) in the urban economy; (c) in the households.
2. Restructuring the transportation system: (a) long distance; (b) intra-urban.
3. Restructuring and integrating the local and regional economies (to reduce the demand for the long haul of products).
4. Restructuring the production structure (shifting to less oil-intensive products and technologies): (a) in industry; (b) in agriculture.
5. Shifting to less oil-intensive lifestyles and consumption patterns.

C. *At the foreign trade level* (to increase import capacity)
1. Releasing foreign exchange by building up import substitution capacities in: (a) industry; (b) agriculture.
2. Earning foreign exchange by increasing exports: (a) of primary goods; (b) of manufactured goods.

The structural adjustment after the 1973 oil shock, analysed by Barros de Castro and Pires de Souza, left unexplored several options that were theoretically open to the Brazilian planners. These options are summarised in Table 3.6.

The Brazilian strategy concentrated on the supply side much more than on the demand side and, as far as import substitution is concerned, on heavy industries, in sharp contrast with the neglect of food production for the internal market.

The main options explored were:

A.1 increasing the domestic production of oil;
A.2(a) substituting sugar-cane alcohol for oil;
C.1(a) building import substituting capacities in industry;
C.2 stepping up exports.

Some results were achieved in the field of energy conservation (B.1(a) and B.1(b)).

The situation was allowed to deteriorate in agriculture, where an energy-intensive and labour-saving model inappropriate to the

Brazilian case, was chosen (B.4(b)) and food production was neglected to the point of allowing per capita production of staples to fall[17] (C.1(b)).

Opportunities were foregone in:

A.2(b) biomass fuels other than alcohol, in particular those that could be produced by peasants instead of large landowners;
B.2 restructuring of the transportation system based on the preeminence of road transport and private cars;
B.3 restructuring of local economies;
B.5 change in lifestyles and consumption patterns;
C.1(b) substituting the produce of the peasant farm sector for imported foods.

These choices – both positive and negative – add up into a coherent picture. The structural adjustment did not purport to change the development style often described as 'conservative modernisation' or 'growth through inequality'.[18] It stopped short of a land reform that could have drastically changed the situation with respect to the food and biomass energy production. It accommodated instead the converging interests of the motor-car industry and of the large sugar-cane planters by lavishly subsidising the alcohol programme.[19] It clearly underestimated the potential for energy conservation and energy recovery from agricultural and urban wastes (and, more generally, the possibility of growing through better maintenance and management rather than by new investment).

Above all, it allowed still further deterioration to take place in the already appalling income distribution, which makes of Brazil an emerging industrial power with social indicators comparable to those of much poorer Asian and African countries and accounts for the fact that over half of Brazilian families live below the 'poverty line' (and over one quarter below the 'destitution line').[20]

On all counts, the social costs and destructiveness of the Brazilian growth process have been very high indeed.[21] Both the 'debts' – the social and the ecological – are today acknowledged by the Republica Nova and the priority for the new plan set accordingly.

Thus, the gap between the economic structure and the social performance of Brazil has widened as a result of the last round of industrialisation. The country emerged from the crisis *per fas or nefas* with a modern and integrated industrial economy, in striking contrast with the prevailing socio-economic conditions. Its potential for endogenous development has been greatly enhanced. The capital and intermediate goods sectors are versatile enough to be redirected to serve as a support for a need-oriented development strategy instead of only catering for the sector turning out luxuries. The low import requirements and the structural export surplus (to the extent to which it will maintain itself) strengthen the bargaining power of Brazil in renegotiating the foreign debt.

The huge reserve of land offers a unique possibility of sustained growth of agricultural and rural industrial employment and settlement of several million people in the rural areas on the double condition of engaging in a genuine land reform and a thoughtful choice of production systems and technologies adapted to the diversity of ecosystems and socio-cultural settings.[22]

In other words, to engage on the path of endogenous development Brazilian people need political determination as well as cultural, scientific and technical creativity. In order to develop, many countries – Japan is an outstanding example – had to overcome a severe lack of natural resources. Brazil's problems are instead to eliminate wastefulness and to invent an original agro-industrial civilisation making the most of the country's diversified resource endowment. The Constituent Assembly that was elected on 15 November 1985 has a heavy responsibility ahead.

Notes

1. The expression is of former Venezuelan President, Carlos Andrés Pérez (see UNCTAD, *The Development Dialogue in the 1980s – Continuing Paralysis or New Consensus?* (1985, United Nations, New York), p. 15).
2. In 1985 the flow of resources from the South to the North has been about 167 billion dollars, while the flow of resources from the North has amounted only to 36 billion. The net interest paid on external debt servicing amounted to 54 billion dollars, while the outflow on foreign direct investment amounted to 13 billion. Declining commodity prices, including the price of oil, have resulted in substantial gains to developed countries estimated at over 100 billion dollars.
3. P. F. Drucker, 'The Changed World Economy', *Foreign Affairs* (Spring 1986) pp. 768–91.
4. Lamartine Yates already made this observation in a book published in the 1950s, see P. L. Yates, *Forty Years of Foreign Trade* (London, 1959). A reinforcing factor is the rapid demographic growth in commodity producing countries in contrast with the commodity buying countries. See I. Sachs, *Foreign Trade and Economic Development of Underdeveloped Countries* (Bombay: Asia Publishing House, 1965).

5. Drucker is more pessimistic, as far as the leap-frogging into the 'high-tech' industries is concerned, because of the required infrastructure of knowledge and education, although he acknowledges South Korea's progress. He does not consider in his article the possibility of an inward-looking industrialisation.
6. I prefer this term, borrowed from Marx, to Drucker's 'symbol' economy.
7. The transactions at the London Eurodollar market amount to 75 trillion dollars per year, at least 25 times more than the world trade. In addition, foreign exchange transactions run at about 35 trillion dollars per year – twelve times the world trade in goods and services.
8. The present debt crisis is thus, in some respect, a perverse effect of a positive event: OPEC's 1973 decision to assert the sovereignty of a group of Third World countries on a strategic natural resource: oil. However, the opportunity to use the accumulated reserves of petrodollars to strengthen the South–South linkages was missed.
9. Antonio Barros de Castro speaks suggestively of the 'international flight of capital', A. Barros de Castro and F. E. Pires de Souza, *A Economia Brasileira em Marcha Forçada* (Rio de Janeiro: Paz e Terra, 1985).
10. This was the situation before the reform of the cruzado, introduced on 28 February 1986. The reform succeeded in eliminating the 'inertial inflation' and curbing financial speculation; however, the main structural problems confronting the Brazilian economy remain yet to be tackled.
11. Between 1940 and 1980 Brazilian economy grew at an average of 7 per cent per year. Yet the purchasing power of the legal minimum wage decreased between 1940 and 1985 roughly by one-half. The legal minimum wage of about 60 dollars per month is very low indeed for a country whose GNP per capita is about 2000 dollars.
12. See I. Sachs, *Foreign Trade and Economic Development of Underdeveloped Countries* (*op. cit.*); and I. Sachs, *Studies in Political Economy of Development* (Oxford, Pergamon Press, 1979).
13. So long as they are used as heuristic constructs and not as watertight taxonomic categories.
14. The industrial take-off was made possible by a Keynesian policy *avant la lettre;* 'buying and burning coffee surpluses left coffee planters with money to finance industries to cater for their needs hitherto covered by imports. On this point, see Celso Furtado, *Formaçao Economica do Brasil* (Sao Paulo: Editora Nacional, 1956).
15. A. Barros de Castro and F. E. Pires de Souza, *A Economia Brasileira em Marcha Forçada* (Rio de Janeiro: Paz e Terra, 1985).
16. In 1972 fuels accounted for 11.1 per cent of Brazilian imports, in 1974 for 23.4 per cent, in 1980 44.4 per cent, reaching the peak of 55.8 per cent in 1983. In 1985 (data for January–October) their share was still 47.7 per cent (*Conjuntura Economica*, March 1986).
17. In 1984 the per capita production of five staples was 15.1 per cent lower than in 1977, F. Homem de Melo, *Prioridade Agricola: Successo ou Fracasso?* (Sao Paulo: Pioneira, 1985).
18. I. Sachs, 'Growth and Poverty: Lessons from Brazil', paper prepared for the UNU/WIDER, Helsinki (1986).

19. See I. Sachs, D. Maimon and M. T. Tolmasquim, 'The Social and Ecological Impacts of Pro-Alcool', *The IDS Bulletin* (1986) forthcoming.
20. See Jaguaribe *et al.*, 'Pesquisa para un novo pacto social', Rio de Janiero (1986) (mimeo). The poverty line has been set at two minimum legal wages, the destitution line at one minimum legal wage.
21. See I. Sachs, 'Les quatre dettes du Brésil', *Problèmes d'Amérique Latine*, No. 78 (4ème trimestre 1985).
22. Ademar Ribeiro Romeiro (unpublished doctoral dissertation, EHESS, Paris, 1986) estimates that 2.5–3 million families could be settled on 60 million hectares of fertile and idle land (15 per cent of the total cultivated area not including most of the Amazon Region). The theoretical limit of agricultural employment, assuming a land/man ratio ten times higher than in Asia and the present level of technology, is 66.6 million people, roughly 250 million together with their families, twice the total population of the country!

4 Import Substitution Revisited in a Darkening External Environment

H. W. Singer and Parvin Alizadeh

SUMMARY

In the 15 to 20 years after the Second World War, import substitution (IS) was the dominant method of industrialisation, both in theory and in practice. In the subsequent fifteen years or so, say from 1965 to 1980, import substitution was heavily criticised and held responsible, particularly by the emergent neoclassical school, for many of the ills and distortions in developing countries. More recently, with the world recession, balance-of-payments crises, debt crises and rising protectionism in industrial countries, a definite reassessment of import substitution is clearly noticeable. The chapter argues that such a re-evaluation of import substitution should not be in the nature of a combination or synthesis of IS and EO – the export orientation (EO) heavily recommended and praised by the more recent critics of IS. The chapter argues that the Republic of Korea provides a good model of the right kind of synthesis, rather than the market-oriented 'neutrality' between IS and EO now preached by the neoclassicals.

The chapter argues that the main trouble with the IS strategy was not inherent in the strategy itself, but due to the way in which it was implemented. Recent empirical evidence has shown that since the onset of the first world recession of 1973, the countries which have relied on IS rather than EO have not done any worse, and for the most recent years the presumption must be that they have done better. The examination of this last proposition should be a high priority for research.

IMPORT SUBSTITUTION AND ITS CRITICS

Development economists in the 1940s and 1950s put great emphasis on the necessity of a deliberate, intensive and guided effort to promote and encourage industrialisation in LDCs. A number of authors, including Rosenstein-Rodan, Nurkse, Prebisch, Hirschman and Dobb, while concerned with a variety of issues, argued that a radical transformation of backward economies with limited or no industrial base requires a deliberate and conscious industrial strategy because the market mechanism, notably in the context of LDCs, is an inadequate means of ensuring rapid industrial development.

The theoretical rationale for a deliberate industrial strategy, as discussed by those authors, rested on a number of grounds including infant industry, external economies and, broadly speaking, the dynamic benefits associated with industrialisation. The tautological use of 'advanced', 'developed' and 'industrial' countries indicated that industrialisation was not only the end-result but also the 'engine' of development.

Another closely related argument favouring a deliberate industrialisation strategy rested upon the existing structural rigidity in the composition of LDCs' exports and its implication for growth in terms of trade. The Prebisch–Singer (PS) thesis (1949–50) of a secular decline in terms of trade for primary exporters implied that market forces can work to the secular disadvantage of the poorer countries (identified as exporters of primary commodities) and to the advantage of the more advanced industrial countries (identified as exporters of manufacturers) in international trade and investment. It was argued that gains from international trade and specialisation are not equally distributed between the LDCs and advanced industrialised countries because of unfavourable demand, inferior market power and price conditions facing primary product producers while the opposite condition prevails in the case of exporters of manufactures.[1] 'Unequal exchange' and 'dependency' schools were the direct offshoots of the PS thesis.

This thesis argued that unregulated free markets work to the disadvantage of LDCs so that regulation or other intervention (including measures to reduce fluctuations in commodity prices, compensatory financing, or more generally a greatly expanded flow of soft aid to LDCs etc.) are needed to achieve a more equitable and sustainable international system. The failure to establish the ITO appeared to members of this school as a fatal gap in the Bretton Woods system, never filled. Moreover, the thesis by implication called for a deliberate industrialisation strategy as a means of altering the existing pattern of LDCs' specialisation within the international economy.

While the PS thesis was strenuously opposed by 'mainstream' economists it provided the intellectual mainspring for the foundation of UNCTAD in 1964 as well as a general conceptual framework which greatly influenced the 'development dialogue' between rich and poor countries (Maizels, 1984).[2]

Industrialisation in the context of this early literature implied import substitution. It was difficult in 1950 to visualise large exports of manufactured goods from LDCs when they lacked an industrial base and the age of the transnational corporations had only just dawned. Moreover, import substitution with the help of protective tariffs was the traditional and proved policy for infants (latecomers) in industrialisation. The 'infant industry' argument lent itself readily to generalisation into an 'infant economy' argument.

The critics of import-substituting industrialisation (ISI) often accuse development economists of this school and UNCTAD of a bias in favour of ISI and against export-oriented strategy. They also maintain that too much State intervention including high levels of protective duties relied upon to encourage ISI induces inefficiency and is thus an obstacle rather than an instrument for a viable industrial development in LDCs. On the other hand, it can be argued that the critics do not take sufficiently into consideration the impact of external pressures and obstacles on development efforts of LDCs, and that they presume that export-oriented strategy is a real possibility for all LDCs, disregarding the inherent fallacy of composition as well as internal technological and capital constraints in many LDCs.

As regards the first criticism of ISI 'bias', there are two answers to this:

1. In the 1940s and 1950s the productive structure of LDCs, generally speaking, was narrow and undiversified and hence it was difficult to foresee the growth of manufactured exports from these economies. As late as 1960, in the dawning days of UNCTAD, primary commodities constituted 79 per cent of the total exports of low-income countries and 89 per cent of those of middle-income countries (Singer, 1984a, p. 16). And even in 1980, these shares had only been reduced to 55 per cent and 63 per cent respectively. In fact, export substitution would have been equally favoured by the ISI advocates – their emphasis was on the S for *substitution*, rather than on the I for *imports*. The real message or 'bias' was on the last I for *industrialisation* – get out of primary commodities – but *I*SI seemed to be more realistic than *E*SI.

2. The critics of ISI, such as Ian Little *et al.* (1970), for the OECD,

Bela Balassa *et al.* for the World Bank (Balassa, 1982) and Krueger and Bhagwati for the National Bureau of Economic Research (Bhagwati, 1978), all tended to disregard or underestimate the importance of a previous phase of IS as a necessary base for subsequent or even simultaneous export-led growth. This is confirmed by the actual experience of the two often-mentioned examples of successful exporters, the Republic of Korea and Taiwan Province of China. In both cases, an IS strategy was pursued in the 1950s; and even in the 1960s and 1970s, when substantial emphasis was laid on development of manufactured exports, a considerable degree of IS still took place in a number of industries (Park, 1981; Luedde-Neurath, 1984; Evans and Alizadeh, 1984). In the case of the Republic of Korea, it can be shown that IS and export promotion were carefully and consciously interlinked as alternating phases in shifting industrialisation between the different sectors. In the case of Brazil also, exports of manufactured goods were in those industries where large-scale IS had been successfully accomplished (Tyler, 1981; Chenery, 1980). This is not to underrate the importance of export-promotion policies which were introduced in these countries in the 1960s. Nevertheless, it is true that such export-promotion policies simply appeared as a way of exploiting the export potential which had been built up during the IS phase. The critics tend to argue that the shift from IS to export orientation was the result of enlightenment and of bad experience with IS. Yet the shift can equally be presented as a rational and natural sequential development in the progress of industrialisation (Singer, 1984a). (It can also be presented as due to a shift in the external environment in a more expansionist/optimistic direction at around 1960, as discussed in more detail in a subsequent section; this shift has been sharply reversed more recently.) Prior learning about the technology and product via production for the home market is usually considered a prerequisite for effective competition in world markets for manufactured goods; hence the emphasis by List, Hamilton and others on the 'transitional' or temporary nature of infant protection. Also IS was often needed to provide the necessary volume basis for competitive export production. Seen in this light, IS and export promotion are complementary rather than alternative strategies.

There is also a point of methodology here. If country A shows better growth and development when it moves from ISI to export oriented industrialisation (EOI) (and vice versa), the critics take this as evidence of the inferiority of ISO and the superiority of EOI. But another possible explanation is that the ISO phase is a necessary 'infrastructure investment' type of outlay which is needed to prepare the ground for the extra EOI 'push' – which then provides the 'pay-off' in terms of faster growth.

Turning to the second criticism of ISI, i.e. too much intervention and interference with the play of market forces and consequent departure from comparative cost principles, neoclassical critics of ISI have maintained that too much intervention not only has led to bureaucratic inefficiencies, corruption and delays but also that the imposition of a high level of protection duties for import-substituting industries has induced the establishment of high-cost inefficient industries; allowed overvaluation of domestic currency, and led to the neglect of agriculture and other sectors, etc.

The policy implications drawn from this analysis are that protective duties should be substantially reduced, the exchange rate should be devalued and the play of market forces should be encouraged. These policies are supposed to be a prerequisite for successful export oriented industrialisation. Of course EOI is not a crude *laissez-faire* strategy, but also requires appropriate government measures, incentives and subsidies to encourage exports, and to provide equal economic incentives to production for domestic and foreign markets (Kirkpatrick *et al.*, 1984; Krueger, 1983); also World Bank Report, 1984, 'Toward Sustained Development' (TDS Report). While the extent as well as the duration of government intervention, from this perspective, should possibly be reduced,[3] the main requirement is a change in its direction, and 'degrees' of interventionism are not easily measured or compared. But criticism of intervention and statism is not identical, although it may overlap, with criticism of ISI.

The fact that IS policies in certain instances have led to 'inefficiencies' and other undesirable side-effects should not be interpreted to imply that extensive State intervention is not of crucial importance for a rapid and viable industrial development. Excluding special cases of city States, like Hong Kong and Singapore, the industrial development of other newly industrialising countries (NICs) has been accompanied by a substantial degree of State intervention, far beyond what is often realised by the critics of ISI. But it must certainly be acknowledged that there are many other kinds of government intervention which may be more important and more constructive than 'distortion' (or correction) of market prices.

The high degree of intervention and 'statism', which has prevailed in Latin American NICs, including Brazil and Mexico, is well known.

Moreover, the detailed study of economic policy in most NICs shows that industrial development has been accompanied by a high degree of centralised planning and government regulation, with strict import, banking, credit and foreign exchange controls (Kirkpatrick, Lee and Nixson, 1984, p. 199; Luedde-Neurath, 1984; Park, 1981). The Republic of Korea 'is a country where a strong State overrides market forces without hesitation, with an effective tightly-planned economy, with strict controls, an essentially nationalised banking system, and a private sector organised in government-sponsored trade associations for easier control. It is as far removed from free market policies as it is possible to be' (Singer, 1984b, p. 86). The government's overwhelming control over the banking sector provided the most important tool in influencing the direction and distribution of investible funds by varying the interest rate charged according to the field of investment, depending on the priorities attached to the different lines of economic activity.

In this respect it is worth remembering that in both the Republic of Korea and Taiwan Province of China, although import restrictions on average were substantially lowered since the early 1960s, most import-competing industries remained highly protected during the period of rapid growth of manufactured exports in the 1960s and 1970s. A statistical division of increases in domestic output as between import substitution, additional exports and 'indigenous increases' shows a continuing high share for the first category as compared with the second. Korean planners have also been consistently concerned to reduce the import content of exports. That is to say that ISI applied to exports. The high import content of exports, e.g. compared with Japan, also makes the net export performance, and the contribution of exports to the balance of payments, less impressive than the gross figures suggest. The legal tariff rates on textile fibres, fabrics and products, leather and leather products, rubber products, and wood and furniture products (which then constituted major Korean export commodities)were in the range of 50 per cent to 200 per cent throughout the period 1964–74 (Hong, 1977, p.138). Also, quantitative restrictions on imports were quite substantial. In 1970, out of 1312 basic items, 524 were restricted and 73 were prohibited (Frank, *et al.*, 1975, p. 59).

Thus it is not surprising that Park, while summarising the relevance of the Republic of Korean experience concludes that 'one lesson is that the Korean experience hardly provides a model in which the functioning of a free trade regime, or operating close to such a regime, assure efficiency in resource allocation and reasonable growth as well' (Park, 1981, p. 115).

The Krueger/Balassa/Deepak Lak school, claiming 100 per cent virtues for outward orientation and 100 per cent damnation for import orientation, has a 'no-win' argument against its critics. If you point out that in fact countries like the Republic of Korea have had a good deal of import substitution, this is turned into an argument not in favour of emphasis on import substitution but on outward orientation. The argument runs as follows:

> apart from promoting exports, an outward-oriented policy contributes to efficient import substitution. In fact, it has been shown that during the 1973–78 period of external shocks, newly industrializing countries pursuing outward-oriented policies undertook more import substitution from [*sic*] their inward-oriented counterparts. . . . All in all, the advantages of outward orientation are to be found in the establishment of an efficient structure of production that entails exporting as well as import substitution. (Balassa, 1985, p. 209)

Where does this leave us? The import substitution achieved by 'outward oriented' countries is declared to be 'efficient', and by implication the import substitution of other developing countries would be 'inefficient'. Hence the superiority of outward orientation is tautological and cannot be disputed. Any argument that the efficient countries showing a high rate of growth have in fact placed considerable emphasis on policies promoting import substitution and have, as Balassa admits, in fact had more import substitution than the so-called inward-oriented countries, is in this way nipped in the bud and in fact turned into an argument in favour of export promotion. The logical duplicity of this reasoning should be obvious. We have also argued that export promotion, as in the Korean case, has often implied complementary import substitution; but this argument is somewhat different from the one of Balassa and hopefully does not involve the same logical duplicity or tautologicality.

It may be added that Bela Balassa, in the paper quoted, also produces a second or parallel 'no-win' argument in favour of outward orientation. In criticising Mexican industrial policy, allegedly under the influence of the Cambridge Economic Policy Group and Dr Ajit Singh in particular, he finds that while industrial output was 43 per cent higher in 1979 than in 1970, 'productivity deteriorated' as indicated by an increase in industrial employment by 77 per cent (Balassa, 1975, p. 215). One should have thought that the fact that industrial employment increased so heavily could have been taken as evidence that the growth of industrial production was of a desirable labour-intensive character – of the kind alleged to be promoted by outward orientation and obstructed by inward orientation – and helped to reduce Mexican unemployment. But no: it is a sign of deteriorating efficiency. So the Cambridge group and Ajit Singh cannot win and take the credit for the increase in industrial employment! Is there a clearer example of having it both ways?

ARGENTINA/BRAZIL VERSUS THE REPUBLIC OF KOREA

The inter-weaving of sequences of import substitution and export promotion pointed out for the Republic of Korea also applies to the two largest Latin American economies of Argentina and Brazil, even though the nature of the sequencing is rather different. The best source for this is a perceptive article by Simon Teitel and Francisco E. Thoumi on 'From import substitution to exports: the manufacturing exports experience of Argentina and Brazil' (Teitel and Thoumi, 1986, pp. 455–90). The authors, who are connected with the Inter-American Development Bank as well as academic institutions, find that the now conventional characterisation of the IS-dominated process of industrialisation in Latin America as inefficient is very questionable. They point out that the process of import substitution and development of domestic markets has served to develop technological capacity, economies of scale, linkages and infrastructure, which subsequently provided a useful basis for vigorous exports of manufactures. They state that

> IS policies followed by these countries do not seem to have resulted in permanent inefficiencies in many manufacturing industries. Rather, protection provided during the 1950s and 1960s to metalworking and metallurgical industries producing consumer durables, capital goods and transportation equipment has been later reduced, and efficiency has evolved leading – sometimes in spite of significant anti-export policy biases – to a substantial volume of exports in the 1970s. (Teitel and Thoumi, 1986, pp. 485–6)

As they describe it, IS has been a preamble to the export stage, providing the learning required before reaching out for markets abroad.

Their final conclusion is to 'cast doubts on the wisdom of urging the larger and more industrialized countries of Latin America to follow, as in South-east Asia, an export-oriented strategy largely based on unskilled labour-intensive industries' (Teitel and Thoumi, 1986, p. 486). However, as we have argued in our own analysis, even in the economies of South-east Asia, at least as far as the Republic of Korea is concerned, there has been nothing like the conventionally alleged clear-cut export-oriented strategy.

Likewise in Taiwan Province of China, rapid growth of the industrial sector in general and of manufactured exports in particular during the 1960s and 1970s was not accompanied by the adoption of a free trade regime, or anything approaching it.[4] By the late 1970s, more than a quarter of imported items were still subject to quantitative restrictions and import control (Balassa, 1981, p. 415).

The purpose here is not to provide a blanket argument for any sort of State intervention, or to dismiss the fact that extensive State intervention in a number of instances has not been particularly successful in the development of a viable industrial base. Nevertheless, it is becoming increasingly clear that it is not the extent and the duration of State intervention which determines the success or failure of ISI or EOI. It is rather the economic-political situation the State faces both internally and externally, its political commitments and its administrative capacity which matter (Kirkpatrick, Lee and Nixson, 1984, p. 194). The State is not a '*deus ex machina*', but neither is the international market. Which is the better guide, or rather which combination is best, depends on country-specific, or even sector-specific, conditions.

Effective and efficient implementation of any trade policy, whether IS or EO or a combination of both, depends on the organisational ability of the State as well as on the economic and political peculiarities of a given economy. This point has been well demonstrated by Datta-Chaudhuri in his comparative study of South Korea and the Philippines (Datta-Chaudhuri, 1981, pp. 47–79). The two countries are similar in terms of population size, and in the early 1960s they also had comparable levels of GDP per capita. Moreover, both countries, Datta-Chaudhuri argues, adopted more or less similar trade policies in the 1950s and 1960s, in the sense that in the early 1960s both countries shifted their trade policies to encourage manufactured exports. Nevertheless, the performance of the Korean economy in terms of overall growth, employment generation, rise in real wages, and particularly the expansion of manufactured exports, was far more spectacular than that of the Philippines in the 1960s and 1970s.

In explaining the differences between the two growth processes, Datta-Chaudhuri outlines certain factors which might have stronger explanatory power than trade policies, including the relationship between the State and the industrialist class, the administrative capability and political commitment of the State to formulate carefully and implement effectively an appropriate industrial strategy etc. In the case of the Republic of Korea, since the early 1960s the State devised a discretionary and selective regulatory system to guide the allocation of resources in the desired direction.[5] Also, export promotion policies were accompanied by a close collaboration between the State and a relatively well-developed industrialist class, so that the development priorities were defined in consonance with entrepreneurial interests. In the case of the Philippines, the dominant class with which the State collaborated was the agrarian hierarchy and the efficiency and planning capacity of government and administration were far inferior to that of the Republic of Korea.

WANTED: A NEW SYNTHESIS OF ISI AND EOI

The shift back in thinking 'towards favouring the domestic market', the 'avoidance of domestic inequalities', 'less emphasis on the market as sole allocator of resources', is particularly marked in Latin America which has suffered more in the recession and is more threatened by the debt crisis than Asia. All the above objections in quotation marks are taken from a publication by PREALC (the Latin American branch of the ILO World Employment Programme), which is typical of this recent shift in thinking ('Beyond the Crisis', PREALC, ILO, 1985). There is particular emphasis on the 'multiple distortions' of markets there which implies that concentration on the removal of one or two key distortions (e.g. exchange rates or subsidies) may well increase rather than diminish overall distortions and the difficulties of reaching an optimum solution.

At the same time, there is also emphasis on avoiding the errors of the past. Any new domestically-oriented industrialisation strategy must pay more attention to monetary, price and balance of trade and payments implications than the old ISI did. It must also encourage exports more. In other words, it must be a synthesis of the old ISI and the more recent EOI, both of which have been proved to be flawed, at least in the case of Latin America; more a move forward to something new than a return to the old. In this sense, also, the debate between the proposals of ISI and EOI as exclusive alternatives is dangerously misleading. We need ISIEOI, a strategy which combines the best elements of both and utilises the complementarities of the two.

Paradoxically, both the old-style ISI and the recent attempted EOI resulted in an inefficient industrial structure, with insufficient vertical integration and horizontal linkages. The future synthesis must pay more attention to the structure and quality of industrialisation as distinct from its simple volume and simple industrialisation ratios. The purely quantitative Lima target (25 per cent of global industrial production for the LDCs) was also vulnerable in this respect. The PREALC report criticises the 'disarticulated structure' of industries resulting from ISI and the low weighting of the 'modern industries'.

In fact, an ISI which results in such a 'disarticulate structure' and absence of modern industries fails in the purpose of ISI, which was put forward as a natural escape out of primary commodities with their unfavourable price trends. The terms of trade of the 'old' industrial consumer products versus the 'new' and capital goods, may be no more favourable than those of primary commodities; hence old-style ISI often proved a dead-end way out of 'unequal exchange' (Singer, 1975). The watchword of the new synthesis must be 'Integrated Industrialisation'.

The PREALC study also rightly lists neglect of domestic food production leading to increased dependence on food imports (and food aid) as one of the weaknesses of old-style ISI. But here the advocates of EOI also find themselves in a dilemma. They advocate, like everybody else, greater emphasis on domestic food production and elimination of 'urban-bias' distortions. But if IS is right for food, why not for manufactures and specifically capital goods and 'modern' products? No really convincing answer has been given (or rather, the question has not been asked); and in the absence of an answer there must be a lingering suspicion of assignment of LDCs to be hewers of wood and drawers of water. The EOI tools of exchange devaluation and removal of food subsidies may serve to reduce 'urban bias', but more in the direction of increasing exports of food and agricultural products rather than food production for domestic consumption. The priority for domestic food production, although during the EO ascendancy labelled as removal of a distortion debited to ISI policies, is in fact a part of a return to a reformed IS. But undoubtedly the present dependency on food imports is also a consequence of unenlightened ISI. It is perhaps ironic that the removal of a consequence of ISI requires now a return to import substitution – but such complexities are part of the new synthesis.

Similarly, there is an irony in the relationship between a renewed emphasis on the domestic market and the basic needs strategy. Superficially, the two go well together. The poor are part of the domestic market; their needs are for the simple goods which – except for food – are usually home-produced, sometimes in the informal sector; their frustrated buying power potential, or lack of 'entitlements', represents a powerful opportunity for a new ISI, or at least inward-oriented push. Yet the emphasis on basic consumption goods may again lead to the 'disarticulate structures' with lack of vertical integration. So what is needed is a deepening of the basic needs concepts which encompasses the activities indirectly needed and related to basic needs. In other words, basic needs must be the orientation of the whole economy, a matter of macroeconomic management, rather than a selection criterion for specific commodities to be produced. When the domestic market is the engine of growth, and when incomes or entitlements are equally distributed, we can be philosophical as between sectoral and product priorities – by all means let the market decide. That must be the objective for the new enlightened ISI. In such an economy, the production of exports also serves the same purpose since the foreign exchange earned will be used for the better satisfaction of basic needs. So again the alleged cleavage of ISI 'or' EOI vanishes, and the desired synthesis emerges as blending both – ISIEOI.

The new industrial strategy must be less dualistic than either ISI or EOI, both of which have shown themselves capable of creating pockets of modernity, with more links abroad than domestically and many of the inputs imported, while leaving the poorer section to survive with an 'informal sector' capital-starved and discouraged. The new synthesis should blend the two technologies into an intermediate technology, or blend them purposefully together in both intra-firm and inter-firm linked structures. New technological advances have created opportunities in this direction, and their exploration in the framework of the new industrial strategies now widely groped for in Latin America and elsewhere opens up a big new agenda (Boon, 1983).

What is suggested here is not so much an industrialisation strategy which is 'neutral' as between IS and EO. This is the formulation favoured, among others, by the World Bank (see, for example, the 1981 *World Development Report*). Rather, what is suggested is a systematic combination of IS and EO, with a different emphasis on IS and EO at different periods and for different sectors. In the nature of things in developing countries, the sequence from IS to EO will be more frequent than the reverse, both in time and for given sectors. But EO itself will also lead to new opportunities for IS, to reduce the import content of exports and increase linkages from the export sector to the rest of the economy, preventing dualism and a disarticulated industrial structure.

In fact, certain successful exporters, including the Republic of Korea and Taiwan Province of China relied on high and non-uniform rates of effective protection, far above 20 to 30 per cent and sometimes as high as 100 per cent effective. Westphal (1981) in explaining the difference in industrial performance between these two and those developing countries that pursued more inward-looking policies argues that it is not so much the magnitude of protectionism but rather the selectivity of infant industry protection and attention to promotion of export growth which distinguishes the former cases from the latter.

He argues that promotion of fewer infant industries at a time can be more conducive to a rapid achievement of international competitiveness than a strategy of 'wholesale import substitution' which accompanies simultaneous protection of a large number of infant industries from the start. Greater selectivity permits scarce investment resources to be concentrated in one or a few sectors at a time; it also allows the concentration of scarce entrepreneurial resources and qualified technical personnel and thus avoids spreading the high-level manpower so thinly that no industry has adequate technical personnel. Greater selectivity 'also accompanies delaying the construction of initial plants until the market has grown to an appropriate size.' In other words, it is the quality of import substitution that counts, rather than its volume.

EXTERNAL ENVIRONMENT AND EXTERNAL PRESSURES

The debate about ISI versus EOI is, in one sense, misplaced and hence partially senseless. Probably the best position in the light of available evidence is that neither ISI nor EOI is the superior strategy in any overall and absolute sense, but rather depend for their relative advantages and disadvantages on assumptions about the external situation facing LDCs. The early advocates of ISI, consciously or unconsciously, made pessimistic assumptions about global growth and trade policies of industrial countries; such pessimistic assumptions were natural around 1950 when the more recent experience of the Great Depression of the 1930s was put together with the disruption and heavy setbacks caused by the Second World War. Similarly 20 years later, by 1970, it was equally natural for critics of ISI to project the favourable external environment of the 1950s and 1960s into the future. Perhaps both schools of thought were right on their own different assumptions. Given the recent much less favourable international outlook, it is as natural that ISI should have regained a great deal more respectability. Apart from explaining some of the fluctuating fortunes and fashions in ISI versus EOI, such a position would also indicate that the optimal industrial strategy in LDCs would be something that is flexible between ISI and EOI: switching emphasis towards ISI in times of global recession and towards EOI in time of global prosperity. It would also indicate that the choice between the two strategies is much more a matter of what is ultimately a *political* judgement about the state and future of the world economy, rather than a matter of firm *economic* analysis as it has usually been debated in the past.

Fortunately, we can confirm this approach as a result of a recent careful quantitative analysis (Kavoussi, 1985). Mr Kavoussi looked at the period 1967–77. Dividing it up into a period of favourable market conditions (1967–73) and unfavourable market conditions (1973–7), he found that when a sample of some fifty developing countries was divided by certain criteria into free trade – outward oriented, or trade restrictive – inward oriented, the correlation between export orientation and growth performance in the first favourable 1967–73 period showed superior performance by the export oriented countries; but in the less favourable 1973–7 period there was no evidence of any such correlation. In his own words:

> free trade appears to enhance growth only when external demand is favourable. When foreign markets are slack, the association of the economy's growth with export-orientation tends to be quite weak. This result seems to imply that when free trade produces a moderate expansion of export earnings (when external demand is

weak), the gains from openness are likely to be cancelled by its negative effects. On the other hand, when export-orientation leads to an exceptionally rapid expansion of export earnings (when external demand is strong), the benefits of openness clearly outweigh its costs.

He concludes:

> Different phases of the cycles of global economic activity require different commercial policies. While export-oriented policies can produce substantial gains during the phase of strong international demand, they may be self-defeating if followed by a large number of developing countries when world markets are depressed. (p. 391)

It is a pity that such an analysis is not available for, say, 1979–83 when the external situation was even less favourable than 1973–7. One can only surmise that for that period there may well be a definite finding that inward-oriented LDCs did better; the cases of India and China would seem to support such a conclusion. It is hoped that the results of such a more recent analysis will soon be available.

On Mr Kavoussi's findings that there is little difference in performance between inward and outward-oriented countries during unfavourable external periods, one may also surmise that in that case the ISI strategy may well appear to national decision-makers safer and more appealing on grounds other than growth rate arguments. ISI increases a country's national control over its own destiny and holds out the prospect that the growth could well be more stable from year to year, being less dependent on external conditions. On the other hand, one can also see that to an internationalist bureaucracy such as that of the IMF, EOI may be preferable even in the absence of a superior growth performance, since international integration is treated as a good thing in itself. This difference may well explain a good deal of the controversy between the IMF and many LDC governments on the question of the right way of adjusting to debt-induced balance-of-payments pressure.

Another reason why unfavourable external conditions have led to a revival of ISI strategy is the strong emphasis, recently fortified by the African drought and famine, on the need for developing countries to reverse the heavy shift from net food exports to net food imports during the post-war period. This near unanimous emphasis on higher priority for domestic food production and restoration of food security and food sufficiency in fact amounts to a recommendation of import substitution – of IS if not of ISI. Some of the sharpest critics of ISI are also among the keenest advocates of higher priority for domestic food production. There is nothing logically inconsistent in this position: one can stress the advantages of IS in agriculture and its disadvantages in industrialisation. However, it does throw a certain onus on the critics of ISI to explain what exactly are the differences between the two sectors which account for advocacy of such different strategies for them.

The critics of ISI also often overestimate the freedom of LDCs to choose their industrialisation strategy and underestimate the significance of external pressure in influencing the pattern and direction of resource allocation. Several problems which the industrialisation process of LDCs faces may be largely a result of the pressures exerted on LDCs by the imperfect markets of the advanced industrialised world (Bienefeld, 1985). Donors and foreign investors might represent interests that could conflict with the national interest of a developing country. Donors, whether international agencies or governments, might attach tying and other types of conditionality on utilisation of aid/loans; also inappropriate (e.g. too capital-intensive) design and selection of their projects might substantially contribute to inefficiency of investible resources. Similarly, foreign investors might press the recipient government to implement policies, including prolongation of a high level of protective duties, to ensure a high level of profit. In such conditions, debates on 'optimal industrialisation strategies' may be beside the point, and strategies of coping with such external pressures may be more relevant.

The importance of external pressure is particularly pronounced in the case of those LDCs with relatively weak economies, with limited financial resources, industrial base, infrastructure and technological expertise. Such economies may lack an adequate bargaining power *vis-à-vis* donors and foreign investors and at the same time may be highly dependent on international finance and expertise for the implementation of their development plans.

In a recent World Bank report on sub-Saharan Africa, which is concerned with the failure of IS strategy there, it is acknowledged that donors must take some responsibility for the current difficulties, including the inappropriate design and selection of their projects, and the lack of co-ordination among themselves, which all contributed to the low rates of return on investment (World Bank, 'Towards sustained Development', 1984). Nevertheless the report presumes that financial agencies and expertise are primarily neutral and it fails even to consider the possibility that such agencies might represent interests that could conflict with national interests (Bienefeld, 1985).

Furthermore the imperfect markets of the industrialised world can exert a considerable degree of pressure on development efforts of all LDCs including the NICs. The severe debt-servicing problems of LDCs (including those of NICs) due to high real rates of interest which originated among other things from monetary and fiscal policies in advanced industrialised countries since the mid-1970s, is a well-known example of an external obstacle to EOI, by reducing import capacity for investment in export industries, or indeed any kind of effective industrialisation. This creates settings in which the idea of a 'choice' between various industrialisation strategies may become quite unreal.

EXPORT-ORIENTED INDUSTRIALISATION AND ITS PROSPECTS

The alternative industrial strategy which is proposed by the critics of ISI is an outward-looking strategy of EOI. There is no doubt that development and expansion of manufactured exports are of crucial importance for LDCs. Apart from the well-known 'vent for surplus' principle (i.e. the surplus part of domestic production, for which there is no domestic demand, can be exchanged for those goods and services required by the domestic economy, through exports), a country can overcome obstacles of a limited domestic market in those lines of industries which are highly susceptible to economies of scale. Also by competing in the world markets for manufactures, industries would be forced to attain a high standard of efficiency and product quality.

Nevertheless, the viability of EOI strategy for LDCs as a whole must remain subject to controversy notably in the international context of the coming decade. The question is not whether EOI is *desirable* but whether it is *possible*.

To begin with, it is a fallacy of composition to assume that what is possible for one or some of the LDCs or NICs can work for all, or the great majority, if all or most LDCs seek to pursue export-led growth at the same time. A recent analysis has indicated, on the basis of a simulation exercise, that if all LDCs in the mid-1970s had the same export intensity as the Republic of Korea, Taiwan Province of China, Hong Kong and Singapore, adjusting for differences in size and level of industrialisation, this would involve a more than 700 per cent increase in Third World manufactured exports (Cline, 1982). The analysis concludes that this would result in untenable market penetration into industrialised countries and protectionist backlash would be inevitable. Hence

> it is seriously misleading to hold up the East Asian 'Gang of Four' (i.e. Hong Kong, Taiwan Province of China, the Republic of Korea, and Singapore) as a model for development because that model almost certainly cannot be generalised without provoking protectionist response ruling out its implementation (Cline, 1982).

Even present market shares provoke protectionist response – is it conceivable to increase total trade in manufactures seven times over, to maintain present market shares? Access to the markets of OECD countries, which are the major markets for LDCs' manufactured products, is of considerable importance for the successful implementation of EOI strategy. Although there is scope for the expansion and promotion of South–South trade (to which we shall turn subsequently), entry into the markets of advanced industrialised countries will remain of crucial importance for some time. It is the continued likelihood of this market access by LDCs which requires careful assessment, notably in the coming decade.

With the drastic decline in the rate of global economic growth and global trade growth since the late 1970s the prospect for pursuing an EOI strategy in the coming decade clearly looks less promising for other LDCs which were not in 'the first wave' – even if we consider that the first wave is safely 'home'.

In contrast with the uprecedented expansion of global trade between 1950 to the mid-1970s, as the 1970s wore on the rate of global economic growth as well as the rate of growth of world trade declined. And trade seems highly sensitive to the rate of growth, with a multiplier effect (Singer, 1983b). The post-war expansion of global trade was greatly facilitated by a significant reduction in trade barriers administered by GATT. However, this situation has changed considerably since the late 1970s. In any case, the reduction in trade barriers was so considerable that it was almost by definition a 'once-for-all' rather than a continuing expansion factor.

Although there has been a general commitment to reduce tariff barriers, nevertheless 'non-tariff barriers' (NTBs) have served as the main form of protective measures in major OECD countries in recent years. Both GATT and UNCTAD have been compiling inventories of NTBs, recording both product-specific measures and general measures. Furthermore, as in the case of tariff measures, NTBs appear to be disproportionately directed at LDCs' exports, and increase as the degree of processing increases (UNCTAD, 1983). Moreover, protectionism appears to be particularly high in the labour-intensive sectors which constitute most of LDCs' manufactured exports, and are particularly important to them for employment and more equal income distribution, as emphasised by the critics of ISI.

If the economic problems now confronting the major industrial countries continue for some years, which seems a distinct possibility, the protective trade barriers are more likely to grow than decline.

In addition to protective measures, another factor which may adversely affect the export prospects of LDCs is radical technical change and diffusion of electronic-based automation technologies (Kaplinsky, 1984). With the development and diffusion of these two technologies, which are largely a phenomenon of the post-1970 period, the comparative advantage of LDCs in presently labour-intensive sectors may be considerably weakened. One of the impacts of automated technology is a general reduction in labour input which in turn undermines the advantage of low wage costs in LDCs.

SOUTH–SOUTH TRADE

At present, developing countries are highly dependent on developed countries, both for their export markets and for their imports, with trade among developing countries accounting for only a quarter of their total exports (and imports) (Adams, 1983). Nevertheless, with a growing tendency towards protectionism in the major developed countries, and also with lack of progress in North–South discussion on development of trade relations on the basis of a trading system more favourable to the South as part of a new international economic order, LDCs are now bound to look elsewhere and increasingly among themselves for markets if the growth of their trade is not to be stifled.

Intensified South–South trade can be either treated as outward-looking or EOI (from the viewpoint of the individual LDC) or as inward-looking or ISI (from the viewpoint of developed countries). That question is as insoluble – and as sensible – as debating whether a glass of water filled to the half-way mark should be described as 'half-full' or 'half-empty'. A lot will depend on whether South–South trade is developed to substitute for North–South trade (in which case it can reasonably be described as inward-looking or ISI) or to be additional or complementary (when it is reasonably considered as part of, or a stepping stone to, outward-looking EOI). As a general proposition, much of the expansion of South–South trade advocated by UNCTAD would be of the latter type and to the advantage of the North as well as the South (Singer, 1983a). But the main critics of ISI often include South–South as another manifestation of an inward-looking spirit and of a failure to accept integration into the world economy. Certainly, there is little enthusiasm for South–South among the proponents of EOI, while the proponents of ISI have seized upon this chance of adding the advantages of international trade to the case for self-reliance – as indicated by the phrase 'collective self-reliance'. So South–South has become more or less a part of ISI, by a process of self-selection, and is thus here included.

Developments during the 1970s suggest an emerging tendency towards the intensification of inter-developing countries' trade relative to their trade with developed countries. The share of developing countries' exports, excluding petroleum, going to other developing countries increased from 19.2 per cent in 1970 to 26.2 per cent in 1978. In particular, a number of developing countries including the East Asian 'Gang of Four', Brazil, Mexico, and a few other LDCs which have emerged as exporters of manufactures, have been able, to a growing extent, not only to penetrate the markets of OECD countries but also to capture an increasing share of markets in other developing countries.

Promotion of economic co-operation among developing countries (ECDC), including expansion of South–South trade, has been one of the main concerns of UNCTAD since the early 1970s, although there are a number of major obstacles for attainment of this objective. Some of these obstacles are posed by the present policies of developed countries and some by the policies of the developing countries themselves. Among the first type of obstacles are the tying of aid and the rules of origin in the generalised system of preferences (GSP) and other preferential schemes (Singer, 1983a, p. 322). The endemic balance-of-payments problems which most LDCs face, and their dependence on international financial institutions, have provided through tied aid and other forms of restrictions pressures in favour of North–South trade and against LDC sources of supply.[6]

Among the second type of obstacles are the trade policies of developing countries themselves. For instance, those products which are the most promising for the expansion of South–South trade, including light consumer goods and semi-finished manufactures, are also those which are highly protected by tariff as well as 'non-tariff barriers' in developing countries. Moreover, consumer preferences are often biased against products of other developing countries, sometimes quite irrationally.

Of course important steps have been taken already by developing countries themselves as manifested by the initiation of a number of economic co-operation and integration schemes at the regional and similar levels, which include the great majority of the developing countries as members of one or other of such schemes. In most of these schemes the principal approach to trade co-operation has been the gradual liberalisation of trade barriers to 'intra-group' trade. Nevertheless the full potential for such co-operation among LDCs may take some time to be realised, and the landscape shows many disputes and lack of implementation, with lack of finance a main reason for failure to put sufficient steam behind ECDC.

CONCLUDING REMARKS

The sluggish growth of the world economy and the rising trend towards protectionism, or what has been called the 'new protectionism', will adversely affect the export prospects of LDCs. It might be argued whether the same considerations do not also apply to protectionism on the part of LDCs. We cannot do better than reply to this in Gamani Corea's words:

> The answer has to be that there is no exact parallel between the two phenomena. The rationale for protectionism in developing countries has been well recognised in terms of the 'infant industry' argument – extended also to take into account the wider limitations in terms of infrastructure of a growing but weak economy. In the long term, such protectionism, which would still be temporary but of much longer duration, can be seen as contributing to growth and efficiency. The same cannot be said for the merits of protecting aging industries – except temporarily as a means of smoothing out

the frictions that stand in the way of adaptation to change. Protectionism in the developing countries could of course be carried too far – to the detriment of growth and efficiency in these countries, and it is right to draw attention to this danger. But here the criticism is of the incorrect use of the instrument rather than of the instrument itself. From the international point of view there is another, even more important consideration. Protectionism imposed by the industrial countries can be directly restrictive to world trade by reducing the earning capacity of developing countries and hence their capacity to import. Protectionism imposed by the developing countries does not have quite the same effect since these countries tend in any case to spend all their export earnings, and more, on imports – mostly from the developed countries. The foreign exchange saved by restrictions on some types of goods are utilized for imports of other types. Hence protectionism has more of an impact on the pattern of imports than on their total.

The entire question of market access and how to improve it is, of course, the central issue of the multilateral trade negotiations. It remains to be seen how far these negotiations will succeed in improving the access of developing countries to the markets of the industrialized countries. (1979, p. 119)

However, there is little likelihood that in the present international context multilateral trade negotiations will deal adequately and decisively with the problem of the new protectionism. Hence ISI will still have to play a significant role in the industrialisation process of LDCs, notably in the case of those developing countries which are in the very early stages of development.

The point made by Corea, that import substitution affects 'the pattern of imports more than the total' is of great importance. When thought through to its logical conclusion, it indicates that the identification of ISI with 'inward-looking' policies can be misleading. 'Inward-looking' policies are enforced upon the developing countries by the foreign exchange bottleneck, intensified in recent years by falling commodity prices, debts and by lower growth and protectionism in industrial countries. In other words, the critics of ISI would be well occupied in suggesting changes in the external environment as well as in the policies of developing countries. Some do, but others do not. EOI and the new international economic order should be natural allies. It is ironic that we find them so often on opposite sides of the fence.

One of the well-known difficulties with ISI is the difficult nature of transition from the early phase, the assembly or fabrication of consumer goods, to the production of intermediate inputs and capital goods, or expansion into export markets, or a combination of both. ISI is a highly sequential process, yet realisation of sequences beyond the easy or early phase has proved to be difficult in many instances (Kirkpatrick and Nixson, 1983, p. 12). But EOI can also meet rising protectionist resistance increasing with successful penetration. A plague on both your houses?

The 'mainstream' economists have focused on protective trade regimes as the main underlying reason for the difficulties with ISI. They have argued that restrictive trade policies give rise to the establishment of high-cost industries which are not able to compete in the world market. Moreover, these industries cannot achieve vertical integration due to the limitations set by the small size of the domestic market in the case of intermediate inputs and capital goods which are highly susceptible to economies of scale.

However, one can equally argue that the difficult nature of transition beyond the first stage reflects an inappropriate choice of industry rather than an inescapable feature of protective trade regimes *per se*. In other words, the choice of the industry the State protects and promotes is of great importance so far as the future viability of any industrial strategy is concerned. There is no doubt that basic economic principles including size of the domestic market, the level of technological development of the country in question, resource endowment, etc., require careful consideration for an appropriate choice of industries. In other words, the difficulties arising from the transition of ISI to higher stages are not inevitable provided the industries which are protected and promoted are not 'white elephants', without export prospects or possibilities to grow into vertically integrated industries, and/or develop dynamic linkages.

In this respect, the knowledge and organisational and administrative abilities of the policy-makers to make and implement the right choices both in terms of industries as well as the package of policies are of considerable importance. Also, the political commitment of the State not to surrender to pressure groups, which for their own sectoral interest are in favour of a particular industry (regardless of its appropriateness for the national economy) is another important consideration. The hotly debated level and extent of State intervention is perhaps less important than the much less debated question of quality, consistency and administrative competence (as well as political support) which State intervention can enjoy, as well as the policy tools at its disposal.

Notes

1. The empirical (statistical) basis of the thesis has continued to be debated. But the recent authoritative study by Professor J. Spraos (1983) has reaffirmed a qualified version of the thesis, shifting from net barter Terms of Trade to the 'Employment Corrected Double Factoral Terms of Trade (ECDFTT). Spraos gives the net barter Terms of Trade between primary products and manufactures since 1950. According to his data, based on United Nations statistics, this index of Terms of Trade deteriorated between 1950 and 1970 from 114 in 1950 to 85 in 1970, a deterioration of 25 per cent. Between 1970 and 1977 there was a further deterioration of 9 per cent in the net barter Terms of Trade between primary products and manufactures, excluding petroleum (Spraos, 1980, 'Statistical Debate', p. 123). However, if petroleum is included, obviously the picture changes dramatically. For the whole period 1900–1970, Spraos finds generally negative trends for the different series, but is doubtful about their statistical significance. However, Spraos agrees that a countercase for significant deterioration could be made (for further discussion on this, see also Singer, 1984c). Most recently, Spraos (1985) has conceded much of this in his response to Sapsford (1985) when Sapsford showed that when allowing for the once-for-all upward shift during the Second World War, the deterioration is valid for the whole period 1900–1970.
2. The original idea of the thesis was subsequently broadened away from concentrating on Terms of Trade, and ECLA under Prebisch's guidance, in the direction of a distinction between 'centre' and 'periphery' countries (laying foundations for 'dependency' theories), and by Singer in a 're-visit' in the direction of technological control (leading to the idea of inappropriate technologies in LDCs with harmful employment and income distribution effects and their exclusion from the most profitable dynamic new industries) (Singer, 1975).
3. The critics of ISI have more recently abandoned the extreme position developed since the late 1960s, which placed a largely unqualified faith in the market's ability to rectify the problems of LDCs. For instance, compare Little *et al.* (1970) with more recent reviews of this subject including the World Bank Report on sub-Saharan Africa 1984. However, despite such recent shifts concerning the importance of State intervention, they still maintain that the basic problem in IS strategy was/is a failure to allow market forces to exert more influence over resource allocation. For an interesting discussion on this point, see Bienefeld (1985).
4. Balassa has himself pointed out that protection of a large magnitude in

the form of tariffs, as well as quantitative restrictions, prevailed in the 1960s and 1970s although there was tariff redundancy in most cases (Balassa, 1981, pp. 402–6; 415–416).

5. The government's overwhelming control of the banking sector provided the most important tool in influencing the direction and distribution of investible funds by varying the interest rate charged according to the field of investment.
6. For instance India, in negotiating a loan agreement with the World Bank in 1981 for upgrading the Indian railway system, faced a substantial degree of pressure from the World Bank to import computer equipment from one of the major developed country suppliers. At the same time, the Indian Government felt that its own computer industry could supply the necessary equipment (cited in Adams, 1983, pp. 124–5). The World Bank in fact recognises the principle that domestic procurement should be encouraged by allowing a 15 per cent price preference to domestic suppliers before assessing the best-value offer for their projects. But one may question whether a 15 per cent preference is sufficient to allow for the dynamic comparative advantages, learning effects, employment and income effects, etc., of domestic procurement. Moreover, apparently the World Bank fails to extend the 15 per cent preference rule to other developing countries which could encourage South–South trade. (I am indebted to my colleague Adrian Wood for clarifying World Bank policy on procurement.)

References

Adams, N. A. (1983) 'Trade Among Developing Countries: Trends, Patterns and Prospects', in B. Paulic *et al.* (eds), *The Challenges to South–South Co-operation* (Westmain Press) pp. 109–127.

Balassa, B. (1975) 'Reforming the System of Incentives in Developing Countries', *World Development*, vol. 3, pp. 215.

Balassa, B. (1978) 'Export Incentives and Export Performance in Developing Countries: A Comparative Analysis', *Weltwirtschaftliches Archiv*, vol. 114, pp. 24–61.

Balassa, B. (1981) *The Newly Industrializing Countries in the World's Economy* (New York: Pergamon Press, 1981).

Balassa, B. (1982) *Development Strategies in Semi-industrialized Economies* (Baltimore: Johns Hopkins University Press), for the World Bank.

Balassa, B. (1985) 'The Cambridge Group and the Developing Countries', *World Economy*, vol. 8 (1985), no. 3, p. 209

Beryman, J. (1974) 'Commercial Policy, Allocative and x-efficiency', *Quarterly Journal of Economics*, vol. LXXXVIII pp. 409–25.

Bhagwati, J. N. (1971) 'The Generalized Theory of Distortions and Welfare', in J. N. Bhagwati, R. W. Jones *et al.*, *Trade, Balance of Payments and Growth* (Amsterdam: North–Holland) pp. 69–90.

Bhagwati, J. N. (1978) 'Anatomy and consequences of exchange control regimes', *Foreign Trade Regimes and Economic Development*, vol. XI

(Cambridge, Mass.: Ballinger, 1978), J. N. Bhagwati and A. O. Krueger (eds), for the National Bureau for Economic Research.

Bienefeld, M. (1985) 'The Lessons of Africa's Industrial "Failure"', *IDS Bulletin*, University of Sussex, vol. 16, no. 3.

Boon, Gerald K. (1983) 'Dualism and Technological Harmony for Balanced Development', *Industry and Development*, no. 9.

Chenery, H. B. (1980) 'Interaction between Industrialization and Exports?', *Proceedings of the American Economic Association, 1980*, World Bank Print Series, No. 150 (Washington, DC).

Cline, W. R. (1982) 'Can the East Asian Model of Development be Generalized?', *World Development*, vol. 10, no. 2, pp. 81–90.

Corea, G. (1979) *Need for Change: Towards the New International Economic Order*, Report to UNCTAD V – 1980 (Pergamon Press).

Datta-Chaudhuri, M. K. (1981) 'Industrialization and Foreign Trade: The Development Experience of South Korea and the Philippines', in E. Lee (ed.), *Export-led Industrialization and Development* (Geneva: International Labour Office).

Dobb, M. (1960) *An Essay on Economic Growth and Planning* (London: Routledge & Kegan Paul).

Donges, J. B. (1976) 'A Comparative Survey of Industrialization Policies in Fifteen Semi-industrial Countries', *Weltwirtschaftliches Archiv*, vol. 112.

Evans, D. and P. Alizadeh (1984) 'Trade, Industrialization and the Visible Hand', in R. Kaplinsky (ed.), *Third World Industrialization in the 1980s: Open Economies in a Closing World*.

Frank, C. R., K. S. Kim and L. Westphal (1975) *Foreign Trade Regimes and Economic Development* (Cambridge, Mass.: Ballinger).

Hirschman, A. O. (1958) *Strategy of Economic Development* (New Haven, Conn.: Yale University Press).

Hong, W. (1977) *Trade Distortions and Employment Growth in Korea* (Seoul: Korean Development Institute).

Kaplinsky, R. (1984) 'The International Context for Industrialization in the Coming Decade', in R. Kaplinsky (ed.) *Third World Industrialization in the 1980s: Open Economies in a Closing World* (Frank Cass) pp. 75–96.

Kavoussi, R. M. (1985) 'International Trade and Economic Development: The Recent Experience of Developing Countries', *The Journal of Developing Areas*, no. 19 (April) pp. 379–92.

Kirkpatrick, C. H. and F. J. Nixson (eds) (1983) *The Industrialization of Less Developed Countries* (Manchester University Press).

Kirkpatrick, C. H., N. Lee and F. J. Nixson (1984), *Industrial Structure and Policy in Less Developed Countries* (London: George Allen & Unwin, 1984).

Krueger, A. O. (1983) 'Trade Policies in Developing Countries', Institute for Economic Studies, University of Stockholm, Seminar Paper No. 249, ISS No. 347–8769.

Little, S., T. Scitovsky and M. Scott (1970) *Industry and Trade in Some Developing Countries* (London: Oxford University Press).

Luedde-Neurath, R. (1984) 'Import Controls and Export Oriented Development: A Re-examination of the South Korean Case, 1962–82', Institute of Development Studies (University of Sussex), mimeo.

Maizels, A. (1984) 'A Clash of Ideologies', *IDS Bulletin*, vol. 15 (University of Sussex) no. 3.
Park, Y. C. (1981) 'Export-led Development: the Korean Experience, 1960–78', *Export-led Industrialization and Development* (Geneva: ILO).
Rosenstein-Rodan P. N. (1970) 'The Theory of Big Push', *Leading Series in Economic Development*, G. Meier (ed.) (Oxford: Oxford University Press).
Sapsford, D. (1985) 'The Statistical Debate on the Net Barter Terms of Trade between Primary Commodities and Manufactures: Comment and some Additional Evidence', *Economic Journal*, vol. 95 pp. 781–8.
Singer, H. W. (1975) 'The Distribution of Gains Revisited', *The Strategy of International Development* (London: Macmillan, 1975).
Singer, H. W. (1977) and J. Ansari, *Rich and Poor Countries* (Baltimore: Johns Hopkins University Press).
Singer, H. W. (1979) Policy Implications of the Lima Target', *Industry and Development* (UNIDO, 1979), No. 3, Special issue for the Third General Conference of UNIDO.
Singer, H. W. (1983a) 'North–South and South–South: The North and the ECDC', *The Challenges of South–South Co-operation*, B. Paulic *et al.* (eds), pp. 317–29.
Singer, H. W. (1983b) 'North–South Multipliers', *World Development*, vol. 11, no. 5 pp. 452–4.
Singer, H. W. (1984a) 'Ideas and Policy: Sources of UNCTAD', *IDS Bulletin*, vol. 15, no. 3 (University of Sussex, 1984) p. 16.
Singer, H. W. (1984b) 'Industrialization: Where do we Stand? Where are we Going?', *Industry and Development*, no. 12 (Vienna: UNIDO) pp. 79–87.
Singer, H. W. (1984c) 'The Terms of Trade Controversy and the Evolution of Soft Financing', *Pioneers in Development*, G. M. Meier and D. Seers (eds), (Published for the World Bank by the Oxford University Press).
Spraos, J. (1980) 'The Statistical Debate on the Net Barter Terms of Trade between Primary Commodities and Manufactures', *Economic Journal*, vol. 90, pp. 107–128.
Spraos, J. (1983) *Inequalising Trade*? (Oxford: Clarendon Press).
Spraos, J. (1985) 'The Statistical Debate on the Net Barter Terms of Trade: a Response', *Economic Journal*, vol. 9, pp. 121–30.
Teitel, S. and F. Thoumi (1986) 'From Import Substitution to Exports: the Manufacturing Exports Experience of Argentina and Brazil', *Economic Development and Cultural Change*, vol. 34, no. 3.
UNCTAD (1983) 'Protectionism, Trade Relations and Structural Adjustment', in *Proceedings of the United Nations Conference on Trade and Development*, Sixth Session, Volume III, pp. 95–131, United Nations.
Tyler, W. G. (1981) 'Growth and Export Expansion in Developing Countries', *Journal of Development Economics*, vol. 9, pp. 121–30.
Westphal, L. E. (1981) 'Empirical Justification for Infant Industry Protection', World Bank Staff working paper, no. 445.

5 Developing Country Debts in the Mid-1980s: Facts, Theory and Policy

Dragoslav Avramovic*

SUMMARY

The decline in interest rates in 1985–6 and the weakening of the US dollar have been favourable features of recent debt developments. The continuing pressure on commodity prices has taken a major toll on incomes of the debtors, however, with the interest rates in real terms remaining prohibitively high; while private capital market lending has continued to stagnate. Domestic investments have been slashed in most debt-affected countries, thus threatening the future capacity to produce. External debts have continued to increase in both money and real terms, despite large outward resource transfers, as interest payments have still been very large and a part of them had to be *de facto* capitalised, while the decline in debtor country export prices has raised the value of debts in real terms. For six major debtors – Argentina, Brazil, Chile, Mexico, Nigeria and the Republic of Korea – the increase in debt in real terms was 35 per cent from 1982 to 1985. A change in debt strategy is indicated.

The past international debt policy has focused predominantly on the need for adjustment in debtor countries. Commercial banks have adjusted by postponing principal repayments (amortisation) of most debtors in difficulty, at a fee and mostly over the short term. Almost the whole burden of interest payments has fallen on the debtor countries, in an international environment marked by falling prices and growing obstacles to trade. In order to alleviate the debt burden and help resume economic growth, it is necessary to supplement 'the case-by-case approach' with across-the-board measures focused on the international framework: reduction in the international rate of interest, standstill on obstacles to trade and then their roll-back, and improvement in commodity prices. The experience has shown that domestic adjustment efforts, while essential for financial viability, can be frustrated unless accompanied by such concerted measures.

The latter would not be necessary if market interest rates were to continue to fall towards 3–4 per cent per annum, commodity prices were to stabilise at a satisfactory level, and most obstacles to trade were alleviated by individual action of major importing countries. It is unlikely that such a combination of circumstances will occur in the foreseeable future.

A concerted approach, even if it were agreed, would take time to develop. In the meantime, it is essential that quickly disbursing lending to debtor countries be resumed or that their interest payments be reduced, in order to avoid further deflationary pressures on them. The implementation of the 'Baker Plan', which involves lending to middle-income major debtor countries by commercial banks and development finance institutions, would make a contribution over the three years 1986–8. A substantial gap in resources would still remain, however; in addition, lending commitments have been very slow to develop. The Group of 24 has proposed that consideration be given to maintaining new credit flows together with a reduction of interest rates below the market on past debt. This proposal needs to be worked out in detail. With respect to low-income countries in Africa, the World Bank has estimated an uncovered financial gap of $US2.5 billion per year, which would have to be met on concessional terms, including highly concessional debt reorganisation in a number of countries.

The quickest, most efficient, and probably the only way of providing the resources now missing, while preserving creditworthiness of debtor countries, would be through special issues for the benefit of the developing countries of Special Drawing Rights (SDRs) over the next two years. This time should be used for organising a concerted approach to the debt problem and to improvement of conditions in Africa. No significant inflationary effects of such SDR allocation should be feared, in view of the existing surplus capacity in major sectors of the world economy and present deflationary pressures in the international market for most products. While the IMF Interim Committee at its April 1986 meeting declined to agree to an SDR allocation, the SDR issue will be coming back at its next meeting.

CONTINUING GROWTH OF DEBT

External debt of developing countries continued to increase through 1985, despite a suspension since 1982 of new bank lending to most

Table 5.1 External debt of developing countries 1980–85

	1980	*1981*	*1982*	*1983*	*1984*[a]	*1985*[b]
(1) Billions of $US	632	729	809	871	908	950
(2) Export unit value index of developing countries	100.0	106.4	102.1	91.8	90.9	87.4
(3) Billions of constant 1980 $US	632	685	792	949	999	1 087

[a] Preliminary.
[b] Estimate.
Sources Debt series from World Bank, *Development and Debt Service* (Washington, DC, 1986); export unit value index from International Monetary Fund, *International Financial Statistics*, April 1986.

countries suffering from acute debt servicing difficulties in Latin America, Africa and elsewhere. Debt growth occurred in both money and real terms.

Two reasons account for debt growth in money terms (row 1 in Table 5.1):

(a) A number of countries, mostly in Asia, continued to borrow on a considerable scale in order to supplement their domestic resources. Considered creditworthy by the capital market, these countries have now emerged as major 'new' debtors. This group includes: Indonesia (external debt of $US36 billion at the end of 1985); India ($US35 billion); Egypt ($US28–35 billion); Malaysia ($US20 billion); Thailand ($US18 billion). Two of these major 'new' debtors, Egypt and Greece (debt of $US15–20 billion), have recently experienced balance-of-payments problems.

(b) Debts of countries with large existing debts ('old' debtors) also continued to grow, even though most of them were making massive foreign debt service payments during the last four years. The combined debt of six 'old' debtors, Argentina, Brazil, Chile, Mexico, Nigeria, and the Republic of Korea, rose from $US291 billion in 1982 to $US337 billion in 1985, or 16 per cent.[1] Debt growth resulted from a *de facto* partial capitalisation of interest.

As export prices of most developing countries were falling during the last four years (row 2 in Table 5.1), their debts in real terms rose faster than in money terms. For the six-country group of 'old' debtors, the increase in debt in real terms was about 35 per cent from

1982 to 1985. This increase is reversible if export prices of developing countries were to recover. As the matters now stand, however, the situation resembles earlier debt crises:

> When credits are no longer extended to the same degree as before, cash-hungry debtors begin to liquidate inventories. Prices of many commodities begin to fall, a phenomenon long described by economists. The fall in prices makes life much harder for the debtors, because the value of the dollars owed, in terms of those commodities they are producing, is rising. It may even happen, as Irving Fischer so magnificently put it in an article published in *Econometrica*, 1933, first quarter, that 'the liquidation of debts cannot keep up with the fall of prices which it causes. In that case, the liquidation defeats itself. While it diminishes the number of dollars owed, it may not do so as fast as it increases the value of each dollar owed. . . . Then we have the great paradox which, I submit, is the chief secret of most, if not all, great depressions: *The more debtors pay, the more they owe*' (Fischer's italics).[2]

It is the combination of high interest rates and of falling export prices which has made the debt crisis of the 1980s so intractable. The extraordinarily large efforts at adjustment which many debtors have made in order to generate resource (trade) surpluses have not sufficed to reduce the monetary amount of the debt, as the surpluses have been all absorbed in interest payments. The same adjustment efforts, consisting in a number of cases of excessive expansion of exports of primary products in the face of frequently stagnant world demand, have led to falling export prices and thus to an increase in the real value of the rising monetary amount of the debt.

It follows that the international debt policy pursued during the last four years had strategic flaws. Debts of major debtors continued to increase, despite major efforts at adjustment.

INSUFFICIENCY OF THE CASE-BY-CASE APPROACH

Concentration on debtor country measures of adjustment was the dominant feature of the past international debt policy, known as the case-by-case approach. The strong points of such an approach are first, that without a focus on domestic efforts to raise savings and improve the balance of payments, no financial viability is feasible, almost whatever the external circumstances; and secondly, the case-by-case approach permits remedies to be tailored to individual country circumstances, which almost inevitably differ.[3] The weak points of the approach are first, that it does not provide for any changes in the international rate of interest and world commodity prices, even though it is recognised that these factors played a substantial role in causing and perpetuating the present international debt crisis;[4] secondly, by pressing excessively for debtor country export expansion, it can contribute to commodity price falls; and thirdly, case-by-case approach can do nothing to remove or alleviate trade obstacles which affect the transfer of debt service.

In one respect, the case-by-case approach was broadened: commercial banks were willing to postpone principal repayments (amortisation) of most debtor countries in difficulty. This normally involved a fee, which in effect meant an increase in the rate of interest. In most cases, postponement was short-term, thus providing only a temporary relief, and this has called for a continuing renegotiation.

If disturbances in the international economy are moderate, debtor countries can overcome them through extra efforts at adjustment. If they are serious, these extra efforts may entail prohibitive social costs. This is the case under present circumstances in world commodity markets. They can frustrate domestic adjustment efforts of commodity-dependent countries. The insufficiency of the case-by-case approach in these conditions was clearly stated by the Prime Minister of Jamaica at the Annual Meeting of the International Monetary Fund and the World Bank in Seoul, South Korea, in early October 1985:

> 'A balance must be struck so that what we gain in improved financial health is not lost in reduced growth'. Mr. Seaga added that his country had done everything that supply-siders or free-enterprisers could possibly desire: it had devalued its currency to make its exports more competitive; it had diverted government programmes to the private sector, even including garbage collection and hospitals; it had got rid of burdensome regulations, rebuilt tourism, increased agricultural output and exports, and reached record levels of investment. Yet all this had not solved the nation's debt problems. For Jamaica had added $US270 million in new foreign earnings, but had lost more than $US500 million in the mining sector, as world commodity prices dropped and market for Jamaica's exports, especially bauxite and aluminum, fell. 'We must earn our way out of this,' he said, 'but we cannot do it unless world markets strengthen.' His is the common problem of the developing

world. And throughout that world the threat of protectionism is adding to anxieties about its future.[5]

The situation is similar with respect to international interest rates. Despite their decline recently, they remain 'higher than at any time since Jesus Christ', in the eloquent phrase of the former German Chancellor, Helmut Schmidt. As argued by a prominent financial daily last year:

> It has been clear for years rather than months that real interest rates near the 10 per cent level are simply unsustainable in the long run. Only consumers, who may have to tighten their belts, and governments, who can impose the same pain through taxation, can meet such demands in reality. Only the most successful industrial projects can earn such returns. More exposed borrowers, be they developing countries or American public utilities, cannot pay such rates. If the demands are too long sustained some debtors are likely to collapse, taking some of their bank creditors with them. This familiar nightmare explains why the markets so obstinately hope that interest rates are on a long-run falling trend . . .[6].

Table 5.2 shows the real interest rates experienced by six large debtor countries in 1982–5:

Table 5.2 Real interest rates paid by selected major debtors, 1980–85[a]

	1982	*1983*	*1984*	*1985*[b]	*Average*
Argentina	26.3	23.8	11.3	11.6	18.25
Brazil	22.2	19.6	12.6	12.0	16.00
Chile	33.8	8.9	21.6	8.4	18.20
Mexico	27.4	16.9	9.9	15.0	17.30
Nigeria	25.9	25.4	11.5	18.2	20.25
Republic of Korea	14.0	12.5	5.8	7.1	9.90
Average	24.9	17.8	12.3	12.3[c]	16.73

[a] Real rates are nominal (money) rates adjusted by the country's export price index.
[b] Estimate.
[c] For all debtor countries, the World Bank estimates the 1985 real rates at 10 per cent (oil-importing countries) and 12.5 per cent (oil exporters), respectively (The World Bank,) *Development and Debt Service* (Washington DC, 1986).
Source Annex A.

These rates compare with the long-run historical average real rate of about 2 per cent.

It follows that the case-by-case approach now consisting mostly of supply–demand adjustments within debtor countries, ought to be supplemented by an across-the-board approach covering interest rates, commodity prices, and trade restrictions. Attempts to modify these last two variables with respect to specific debtor countries only, such as by paying only some of them higher prices for their exports, or by eliminating obstacles only to their exports, may work over the short run, but would encounter difficulties over the medium term and would eventually become inoperative.

An across-the-board approach would not be necessary if money interest rates were to continue to fall towards a 3–4 per cent level, commodity prices were to stabilise, and most obstacles to trade were to be removed.

RESOURCE FLOWS[7]

World Aggregates: DAC Resource Flows Measurements

In 1984, total resource flows to developing countries, public and private, from all sources, grants, debt-generating and equity, in cash and in kind, as measured by the Development Assistance Committee of OECD, amounted to $US92 billion (at 1983 prices and exchange rates). This was some $US26 billion below the preceding year and also lower than in any year since 1980. The 1984 decline occurred in private flows ($US28 billion), and was only marginally compensated by an expansion in official flows ($US2 billion). In 1984, the latter consisted of official development assistance (ODA), provided on concessional terms, of $US36 billion, and non-concessional official and officially-supported flows of $US20 billion, making for a total of $US56 billion. This total was under the level of 1980: the decline and stagnation of private lending and investment in the 1980s have not been offset by an increase in official flows.[8] DAC figures, covering the period 1950–84, are shown in Annex B.

DAC data do not indicate net transfers. To arrive at the latter, it would be necessary to deduct return flows on debts and investments, i.e. payments of interests and profits, from DAC resource flow figures.

World Aggregates: World Bank Net Transfer Estimates

The World Bank has provided estimates of net transfer, focused on long-term debt flows. In 1984, service on long-term debt (amortisation and interest) paid by 107 developing countries, exceeded their receipts (disbursements) of long-term loans by $US13.7 billion, and in 1985, by an estimated $US22 billion. This negative 'net resource flow associated with long-term lending', or reverse transfer, compared with a peak positive transfer of $US34.4 billion in 1981, which has been falling steadily since.[9] World Bank data covering the period 1974–84 are shown in Annex C.

It is possible to broaden the Bank's coverage somewhat, by including data on short-term debts and the use of IMF credit. The result is an increase in the negative (reverse) transfer to $US33 billion in 1984 and an estimated $US38 billion in 1985, and a shift from a small positive transfer to a negative one, of the order of $US23 billion, in 1983. The reason is high interest charges on, and net repayment of, short-term debts in these three years. They were offset only in part by the use of IMF credit. Details of the computation are shown in Annex D.

A complete statement of net transfer would further call for the inclusion of grants on the positive and profit remittances on the negative side of the account.

Latin America: Reverse Transfers

In 1984, payments of debt service and profit remittances of the Latin American countries are estimated to have exceeded capital inflow by $US28.3 billion, only marginally lower than the $US30.7 billion in 1983 (Table 5.3). The estimate for 1985 is back to $US30 billion, as the gain from a reduction in interest rates was swamped by an almost complete drying out of net private capital inflow. In contrast, the region was a net recipient of resources of about $US15 billion annually during 1978–80. The swing in resource availability has thus amounted to a staggering sum of $US45 billion per year, or more than 6 per cent of aggregate Latin American GNP. To appreciate this magnitude, it should be recalled that the increased oil bill for the industrialised countries in 1974 was equivalent to about 2.5 per cent of their GNP. The rate of investment in Latin America in 1984 was 30 per cent below the average in the 1970s.[10] It is probable that the decline in investment continued in 1985. As stated in the Declaration

Table 5.3 External financial flows in Latin America ($US billions)

Year	*Net capital inflow* (1)	*Net payment of profits and interest* (2)	*Net financial transfer* (3) = (1) – (2)
1975	14.2	5.5	8.7
1976	18.2	6.8	11.4
1977	17.0	8.2	8.8
1978	26.1	10.2	15.9
1979	28.6	13.6	15.0
1980	30.0	18.0	12.0
1981	37.7	27.7	10.0
1982	19.3	38.4	–19.1
1983	4.2	34.9	–30.7
1984	9.3[b]	37.6	–28.3
1985[a]	n.a.	35.3	–30.0

[a] Preliminary estimates.
[b] Includes both 'voluntary' and 'involuntary' lending.
Source United Nations Economic Commission for Latin America (CEPAL), *Balance Preliminar de la Economia Latinoamericana Durante 1984*, Table 12; *Panorama Economico de America Latina 1985*, Table 2; Consensus of Cartagena, Meeting of Ministers, 16–17 December 1985, for Net Financial Transfer in 1985.

of Montevideo of the Cartagena Consensus Group, this was the fourth year in succession that financial resources were transferred out in net terms, 'making a grand total in excess of $US100 billion, equivalent to one year's gross investment in the region'.[11]

Sub-Saharan Africa: Declining Positive Transfers

It is reported that net financial transfers to sub-Saharan Africa, another debt-affected region, declined dramatically in 1984, as a result of a rapid rise in debt service liabilities, disappearance of private credits and reduction of IMF credit. The effects of the switch in the allocation of official development assistance in the direction of Africa, which occurred in the 1970s, have now been overwhelmed by these later developments.

It is possible that the data in Table 5.4 exaggerate the decline in net transfers. This would happen if some debt service payments recorded to have been made were in fact postponed. This would then result in payments arrears which would affect adversely future transfers by

Table 5.4 Sub-Saharan Africa: net financial transfers[a] ($US millions)

Source of funds	*1978*	*1980*	*1982*	*1983*	*1984*
IMF	51	463	579	1 137	126
World Bank Group	436	473	887	816	1 006
Other multilateral groups	599	881	714	545	333
Bilateral grants and loans	4 161	6 776	5 885	6 419	5 157
Commercial lenders	3 306	2 660	3 181	1 675	–3 071
Total	8 553	11 253	11 246	10 591	–3 551
Of which 24 countries with per capita incomes under $400 per head	4 527	7 070	5 901	5 584	3 683
Other 15 countries	4 026	4 183	5 344	5 008	– 132

[a] Net transfers are based on official grants, medium- and long-term public and publicly-generated loans, and on medium- and long-term private non-guaranteed loans.
Source Robert S. McNamara, *The Challenges for Sub-Saharan Africa*, Sir John Crawford Memorial Lecture, Washington, DC, 1 November 1985, based on the work of World Bank staff.

either causing a reduction of new credits or raising future debt service as payments arrears are liquidated. Out of 43 countries which had payments arrears at the end of 1984, 20 were from sub-Saharan Africa.

In some cases, reverse resource transfer seems to have already occurred, following the Latin American pattern:

> The rise in private capital and donor inflows which Zaire was led to expect as a reward for three years of impeccable financial behaviour have been tortuously slow to materialize. In 1984, Zaire repaid some $US191.5 million *more* to medium- and long-term creditors than it received in new funds. And despite praise for its programme from Western bilateral donors, new aid disbursements from these sources have lagged well behind Zaire's repayments to them of principal and interest.[12]

An increase in resource flow to Africa of more than $US1 billion occurred in 1985 as a result of a generous response of the outside world to the famine.[13] This is now falling back, however, as the emergency recedes.

Investment has declined. In 29 low-income countries in sub-

Table 5.5 Manufactured goods exports: unit value indices in US dollars

	1980	*1981*	*1982*	*1983*	*1984*
Developing market economy countries	100	99	91	87	n.a.
Developed market economy countries	100	94	92	88	85

Source United Nations, *Monthly Bulletin of Statistics*, December 1985.

Saharan Africa, the investment rate was estimated at 14.3 per cent of GNP in 1984, compared with 19 per cent in 1980,[14] and it probably continued depressed in 1985 and 1986.

Transfer Cost

The mechanism through which resource outflows have been extracted has frequently included devaluations of debtor country currencies significantly in excess of domestic inflation. The resulting greater profitability of export industries has led to export volume expansion and to a declining tendency for (dollar) export prices. Countries exporting manufactures, particularly those at a more advanced stage, have been in a better position than those exporting primary products, as a rule: demand for manufactures is normally more price-elastic, and therefore the degree of the required price reduction to increase volume is smaller, while the capacity of countries exporting manufactures to shift to other lines of production is substantially greater than that of primary exporters. This generalisation needs to be confirmed by specific exporting country analyses: there have been reports of severe price cutting in many instances and terms of trade deterioration in particular developing countries exporting manufactures. The general picture as now known from the United Nations statistical work indicates that the dollar export prices of manufactures of developing countries have been falling since 1980, but so have the prices of developed countries, and roughly to the same degree; although one would have expected a sharper fall for developing country exporters (Table 5.5).

It is with respect to primary product exports where the price experience of the last five years has been almost catastrophic. Export commodity prices of developing countries, other than oil, fell some 35 per cent during the 1980–82 recession. A part of this decline,

Table 5.6 Dollar export commodity prices of developing countries, UNCTAD Index, 39 products excluding oil, 1979–81 = 100

1980–82	Recession		
	Peak	October 1980	119
	Trough	October 1982	75
1983–5	Recovery		
	Peak	March 1984	90
	Trough	September 1985	72
1985–6	Mini-recovery		
	Peak	January 1986	86
	Last month available	February 1986	84

Source UNCTAD Secretariat.

about one-third, was recouped during 1983, mainly in response to the US economic recovery. Prices started to weaken again already in early 1984, however, to the surprise of many observers. By the fall of 1985, they had fallen below the bottom of the 1980–82 recession. A mini-recovery ensued in late 1985, led by a coffee price upswing under the influence of a short crop in Brazil. By February 1986, the cycle turned downward again. The story of the rise and fall of oil is well known: in April 1986, its price was one-third of the level two years previously.

Annex E presents the World Bank's commodity dollar price series in real terms for the last 38 years. The 1985 average prices of non-oil commodities were lower, in real terms, than at any time since the Second World War, including each of its recessions.

No comprehensive investigation has yet been undertaken of the relative weight of different causes of the current price decline. Those quoted include: the weakness of the 1983–5 industrial recovery, its skewness in favour of services and high technology industries which do not consume much raw materials, technological change resulting in savings of materials, adverse effects on demand for inventories of improvements in inventory control and high rates of interest, the emergence of new producers because of high prices in some cases. There has been one factor, however, which has operated across all commodity markets and in all subperiods: the pressure to expand exports irrespective of market conditions, in order to acquire foreign exchange needed to meet rising debt service payments and critical import requirements. Export sales are maintained in the face of heavy competition, insufficient foreign demand, and frequent trade obstacles; a large number of primary producing countries are devaluing one after another in order to be able to compete at present low world prices; as demand is frequently depressed and does not respond to price cuts, the main result of devaluations in these cases is to reduce real wages all around and further depress world prices.

During the great debate concerning payment of German reparations in the inter-war period, Keynes was of the view that debtors face the double burden: paying the debt service (budget burden) and experiencing a deterioration in their terms of trade.[15] This view was vindicated in the present debt crisis: the inelastic demand of the debtors for foreign exchange confronted an inelastic foreign demand for the debtors' export products, and their terms of trade gave in. The present dominant theory of adjustment has forgotten the lesson from the earlier debate. This theory advocates relentlessly 'export-led' growth in virtually all debtor countries. It frequently disregards the composition of such export growth. Under present conditions of weak world demand for most primary products, this theory cuts the roots on which adjustment rests by helping to drive down export prices and thus to depress the export revenue of developing countries as a group. The effect is a massive transfer of income by primary producers, which is additional to that reflected in the monetary amounts of debt service payments which they are making.

Another aspect of the transfer problem is restrictions on trade and trade subsidies. In some goods they set an absolute ceiling on exports; in others, they have the effect of driving down export prices and pushing the producing countries into lower-value-added production:

> Farm products make up 80 per cent of Argentina's exports, and in the first half of this year, Mr. Campero, the Argentine secretary of Commerce, says Europe's tactics have cost Argentina $US650 million in beef and wheat sales. . . . In the past year, world wheat prices have dropped from $US130 a metric ton to $US93, and beef prices have dropped to below $US1,000 a ton – well under Argentine's production cost, the world lowest. 'We have had to sell beef in Egypt at $US950 for half carcass of boneless meat, 25 per cent below our costs', says Mr. Vazquez Platero, Agriculture Minister of Uruguay, 'because the European Communities give their farmers a 100 per cent subsidy. We can't continue to meet these prices'. . . Argentine beef exports, which totaled 740,000 metric

tons in 1979 are not expected to reach 200,000 tons this year. 'I don't see how either Argentina or Uruguay can continue to be a factor in meat exports in these conditions', says a diplomat stationed in Buenos Aires. Uruguay's land is only good for pasture, so it hasn't any crop it can substitute for cattle. But the Argentines are farming more and more of their rich pampas to grain and oilseeds. 'With meat we are losing markets, but with grain we are mainly losing income meeting the low prices', says Argentine agriculture Secretary Reca. 'We are now using more agrochemicals and fertilizers to increase our grain production even more. Just to compensate for the decrease in world prices this year, we should produce and sell 30 per cent more grain.'

'We are pushed out of the market', says Vazquez Platero, and it then becomes 'absolutely impossible to pay the interest' on Uruguay's $US4.5 billion debt. . . . Campero warns that Argentina's loss of markets 'has an intimate relation to the ability to pay our foreign debt. All the efforts that we make to increase our exports and meet our international obligations are neutralized by [adverse international trade] policies.'[16]

NEED FOR A CONCERTED APPROACH

A concerted attack on the debt problem would consist of:

A. A sustained effort of debtor countries to expand production, savings and investment, and improve their balances of payments, paying particular attention to:

(a) fiscal balance;
(b) resumption of investment activity;
(c) price incentives; and
(d) an appropriate exchange rate.

B. Complementary measures by the international community to alleviate the debt burden and improve the possibilities of transfer, in particular through:

(a) a substantial reduction of the international rate of interest; this would automatically reduce the charges on the floating-rate-debt and enable renegotiation of much of the fixed-interest debt; reduction of the international interest rate would call for improvements in the 'real' economy through a reduction of wasteful expenditures and in the financial-monetary sector through stabilization of exchange rates of key currencies and probably control of capital movements;

(b) support for export commodity prices of developing countries at a sustainable level and for domestic food prices in Africa;

(c) standstill on new trade restrictions and then a roll-back of the existing restrictions;

(d) a change in the conditionality rules aimed at economic expansion *pari passu* with short-run balance-of-payments improvements;

(e) a substantial and rapid expansion of quickly disbursing lending by official development finance agencies;

(f) an agreement of major commercial banks to resume lending;

(g) an insurance facility for foreign investment; and

(h) conversion of a part of the debt of the least developed countries, owed to official agencies, into IDA-type credits or grants.

Of all international measures listed above, one clearly in prospect is insurance of foreign investment. The establishment of a Multilateral Investment Guarantee Agency (MIGA) as an affiliate of the World Bank was approved at the 1985 Annual Meeting of the Bank. It will take some time before the agency becomes operational, and it is not clear at present how broad will be its membership. There are doubts as to how much can be done for stimulating foreign private investment in developing countries until their fundamental economic position improves. Direct private investment fell from $US17 billion in 1981 to $US12 billion in 1982 and $US8 billion in 1983.[17] It is probably at that level today, if not lower, despite the incentives provided by a number of developing countries in recent years. In time, however, MIGA should prove helpful.

It would not be realistic to expect quickly an agreed international action to stabilise commodity prices. The World Bank could be the agency playing a major role, in view of its actual and potential influence on investment and production, including diversification into alternative lines of activity, in support of the Common Fund when ratified and directly before ratification. For World Bank commodity action to become a realistic prospect, a change is needed in the attitude of some major developed country members and in the present theory of economic policy of some of its senior staff.[18] Regional development banks could also play a major role, and at least in some of them the theory of economic policy should not present a major obstacle. The alternative to a North–South action is an initiative only by developing countries, including OPEC and non-OPEC, in defence of their interests covering a broad range of commodities. This was one of the thoughts underlying the concept of the Bank of Developing Countries (South Bank). No agreement could be reached so far on this concept, although the matter continues under consideration in the Group of 77. While the difficulties of undertaking joint commodity action of developing countries are substantial, as experience has shown, this is a field where such action appears indispensable. Commodity stabilisation would have to have modest price objectives, at least in the initial period.[19]

An agreed reduction of the international rate of interest would call for a high degree of international political and economic co-operation. It would require readiness to shift resources from military and related uses into civil occupations and thus contribute to world financial equilibrium; it would call for action to sustain a high level of economic activity and full employment in the transition, through expansion of productive investment, other development and social expenditures including foreign aid, and personal consumption, aimed at a smooth conversion from military to non-military economy;[20] it would require restoration of exchange rate stability and thus lead to a reduction of financial risks which now impart an upward bias to the rates of interest; and it would call for readiness to control international capital movements. All this is possible and perhaps inevitable, but it will take imagination, statesmanship, patience and time.

Standstill on trade restrictions and their subsequent roll-back are closely linked with re-introduction of order in international exchange markets. After ten years of checkered experience, with a growing amplitude of fluctuations, it is increasingly recognised that the present chaos in money values is not sustainable. As none of the reserve currencies is linked to anything else but only floats in a constantly moving relationship with each other, the world economy operates without a fixed point of reference. As Professor Mundell said:

> Today, in 1983, the U.S. does not have a gold standard, or a Keynesian commodity standard, or a Friedman paper standard. It has a Volcker standard. But who can predict the future value of the pound, the dollar or the yen on the basis of a Thatcher standard, a Volcker standard or a Nakasone standard?[21]

It is not only the disorder in exchange rates which causes trouble, however. In 1983, industrial countries imposed non-tariff barriers on about one-fifth of the goods they imported from developing countries. Only one-tenth of the goods imported from other industrial countries faced such barriers.[22]

To a substantial degree, a reduction of the international rate of interest, commodity stabilisation, and action on trade restrictions are interchangeable with respect to their effect on the debt problem. The greater the difficulties encountered in commodity stabilisation and market access, the larger the required cut in the rate of interest if the debts are to be serviced and if future debt growth is not to exceed the growth in stock of productive capital. This is the application of the general principle that depressed selling prices and obstacles to sales make for a low return to investment and therefore require a low rate of interest on borrowed funds. Ultimately, all the key actors – governments of debtor countries, governments of creditor countries, banks and international organisations concerned – will have to work out a consistent approach to these three areas – interest rates, commodity prices and access to markets – which make the international framework for solution of the debt problem.

CURRENT INITIATIVES AND VIEWS

Baker Plan for Middle-Income Countries

Expansion of borrowing is an immediate measure which relieves the situation in the sense that it enables the debtors to reduce or eliminate the cash drain on their economies resulting from debt service and thus may permit resumption of investment and economic growth, provided new borrowing is sufficiently large. At the same time it adds to the stock of debt, which will continue to grow at a compound rate of interest; the higher this rate, the faster the growth of debt; if loans carry an interest rate of 10 per cent and interest payments have to be financed by additional borrowing, the size of the debt will double every seven years. None the less, expansion of lending may help complete investment projects under way and remove critical bottlenecks to production, and thus may yield high returns, and it provides for time in which a concerted approach to debt reorganisation can be undertaken. There is also a possibility that international interest rates

Table 5.7 Outstanding debt of 15 countries, 1984 ($US billions)

Country	*Outstanding debt*	*Average interest rate*
Argentina	47.8	11.6
Bolivia	4.1	10.7
Brazil	102.0	11.2
Chile	20.4	10.6
Colombia	12.6	9.0
Ecuador	7.6	11.1
Ivory Coast	6.2	n.a
Mexico	96.6	12.0
Morocco	13.2	4.7
Nigeria	19.2	8.7
Peru	13.4	10.0
Philippines	26.2	8.9
Uruguay	4.7	9.3
Venezuela	34.8	12.1
Yugoslavia	18.5	9.7
Total	427.5	10.3%

Source *Financial Times*, Institute of International Finance (Washington, DC: 28 October 1985).

may fall sharply and commodity prices rise sharply, thus automatically relieving the debt burden from both old and new borrowing, even though this does not seem probable as now seen.

In early October 1985, the US Secretary of the Treasury proposed a three-year programme of expansion of lending to major debt-affected countries by commercial banks, aggregating $US20 billion, and an increase of lending by the World Bank and the Inter-American Development Bank of 50 per cent, or $US9 billion. This works out at about $US10 billion per year. There are fifteen reported candidate borrowers, ten of which are in Latin America.

The special significance of the US Baker Plan is that it shows the readiness of the government of a key developed country to get involved directly in debt matters. The initiative also indicates the awareness that new measures are needed to handle the debt problem. The Baker Plan contains some features of the 'General Agreement to Lend' proposed by the InterAction Council of the former heads of state and government.[23]

The objective of the Baker Plan is to help resume economic growth in debtor countries through injection of additional resources, badly

Table 5.8 Fifteen debtor countries: external financial flows (estimated, $US billions)

A.	*Ongoing flows*			
	(1) Direct investment	2.8 (1985)		
	(2) Multilateral lending, ongoing programmes, net (other than IMF)	3.7 (1985)		
	(3) Other official flows, net	4.4 (1985)		
	(4) Official transfers	1.0 (1985)	11.9 (1985)	
B.	*Baker Plan, per year, 1986–8, net*			
	(1) Participating commercial banks	6.7		
	(2) World Bank and IADB	3.0	9.7	
C.	*Repayment to private creditors, net*			
	(1) Commercial banks	–2.3 (1985)		
	(2) Non-bank creditors	–1.3 (1985)	–3.7 (1985)	
D.	Total financing (A + B + C)		17.9	

Source *IIF Overview*, vol. 1, no. 3, Institute of International Finance (November 1985), for 1985 estimates.

needed after four years of austerity. One of the difficulties is that the funds envisaged are not sufficient for the job at hand. This was recognised, it appears: it is understood that in the initial phase of the Plan formulation, the amounts envisaged were substantially larger, but were then scaled back on the grounds of feasibility.

The outstanding debt of the prospective fifteen borrowers was $US428 billion at the end of 1984, at an average-actual interest rate slightly above 10 per cent per annum. The aggregate interest cost was therefore around $US44 billion, equivalent to 31 per cent of exports of goods and services of the fifteen countries. The interest rate has gone down since 1984, but the absolute debt has gone up, so that the aggregate interest cost now perhaps runs at $US38 billion. The Baker Plan, if implemented fully, would provide new lending equivalent to slightly more than one-quarter of the aggregate interest cost of the fifteen prospective borrowers. In addition, there will be net lending by development finance agencies under their ongoing programmes, as well as some net suppliers' credits guaranteed by developed country governments, and some direct foreign investment. The total of these ongoing flows was running at an estimated $US12 billion in 1985. Against these flows there may be some repayments to private creditors, bank and non-bank, which do not participate in the Baker Plan: they were running at almost $US4 billion in 1985. No net transactions with the IMF are assumed: large repayments are owed to the Fund over the next several years, but they will hopefully be rolled over. If the ongoing flows in the future remain the same as in 1985 the total of Baker and non-Baker funds would be about $US18 billion per year, compared with interest payments of $US38 billion. It follows that the major fifteen debtor countries would still be experiencing a financial outflow of about $US20 billion per year; this remains the difference, on present indication, between the new capital they will be receiving and the interest payments they will be making. It is, of course, possible that interest rates will fall further and there may be less capital repayments in the future than in 1985; these factors would reduce the financial outflow, but a very large gap would still remain. It is equally possible that the situation may deteriorate.

Whatever the precise figure of needs – and Mr Baker recently stated that the original estimates were not set in concrete[24] – meeting them has proven a slow affair. Private banks have continued to be reluctant to undertake new lending.[25]

World Bank Programme for Africa

The World Bank has prepared its fourth report on Africa,[26] which is more optimistic concerning the future of the African economies than its predecessors, on two grounds:

(a) improved economic performance in some African countries and particularly new decisions made in a number of them to provide incentives to production, especially in agriculture, and streamline government administration;
(b) improved foreign exchange position over the short-run due to an increase in coffee prices and, in a number of them, by the decline in the price of imported petroleum. (This latter benefit is offset in some other countries – notably Nigeria, Gabon – by expected large losses.)

Despite this improvement, the World Bank continues to be deeply concerned with the future of economic development in Africa, and appeals for an increase in external assistance. After allowing for the foreseen increases in bilateral and multilateral flows of assistance, it finds that a further $US2.5 billion per year on concessional flows and debt relief is required in 1986–90 to restore African import capacity per capita to its 1980–82 level, even assuming a significant increase in exports. The increased flows for multilateral agencies, including an

Table 5.9 African IDA-eligible countries with prolonged debt problems[a]

Benin	Niger
Gambia	Somalia
Liberia	Sudan
Madagascar	Tanzania
Mali	Togo
Mauritania	Zambia

[a] The officials of the World Bank's Eastern African Region added Zaire and Mozambique to this group, with Uganda and Ethiopia as borderline cases. (E. V. K. Jaycox, Ravi Gulhati, Sanjaya Lall, Satya Yalamanchili, 'The Debt Problem in Eastern and Southern Africa: Genesis and Solutions', paper prepared for the Conference on African Debt and Financing, Institute for International Economics and Georgetown University: February 1986.)

Source The World Bank.

enlarged IDA–8, IMF Trust Fund reflows, and an enhanced replenishment of the African Development Fund, when due, might provide, the World Bank hopes, up to $US1 billion per year of these additional funds. For the remainder of $US1.5 billion, a major effort is required in bilateral assistance – whether through new money or more liberal debt relief.

The Bank considers the debt situation particularly critical in the twelve countries shown in Table 5.9, for which debt relief on highly concessionary terms is implied.

The details of possible concessional debt relief operations have not been provided. As examples, the following are quoted: donors could retroactively convert existing official loans into grants – as proposed in the UNCTAD declaration of 1977; enable their export credit agencies to refinance scheduled debt service payments on concessional terms; widen the group of creditors that participate in rescheduling of principal and interest; and increase their aid budgets, particularly in the form of balance-of-payments support for adjustment programmes. Sweden is quoted as an example of the latter approach: the Swedish government recently added to its aid budget a special supplement for use by recipients to repay commercial credits.

The World Bank's estimate of uncovered capital requirements of $US2.5 billion per year is lower than other recent estimates. The US Committee on African Development Strategies suggested that new finance of $US5–6 billion per year was needed during the next few years, and the only possibility to meet this need was through a combination of debt refinancing and new aid.[27] Mr McNamara, former President of the World Bank, suggested that minimum financial requirements of the 24 lowest income African countries were of the order of $US6.5 billion per year in 1985–90, and that no more than 40 per cent were likely to be forthcoming, implying an uncovered gap of around $US4 billion per year.[28] UNCTAD has estimated net capital requirements of 36 least developed countries, a wider group than low-income Africa and including Bangladesh as the largest country, at $US14.6 billion in 1990 (base projection), compared with an estimated level of $US6.3 billion in 1985 – an increase of $US8.3 billion.[29] With respect to debt reorganisation, the Executive Secretary of the UN Economic Commission for Africa has proposed a debt moratorium of ten years.[30] The country coverage has not been reported.

Further work is needed to review these different estimates and their underlying assumptions. The existence of uncovered needs and the case for highly concessional debt reorganisation in a large number of countries seem universally agreed, however, despite the differences.

Position of Developing Countries

At the Buenos Aires meeting of Ministers of the Group of Twenty-Four on 6 March 1986, the following position was taken on the debt issue:

> Ministers expressed their conviction that in view of the deterioration of the debt situation, the continuous utilization of present market interest rates, plus other fees, can only threaten the adjustment efforts of many countries by worsening their already heavy debt servicing problems. The repayment capacities of debtors could be strengthened if mechanisms and strategies could be found to maintain the flow of credit together with a reduction of interest rates below the market level on past debt. Unless this is undertaken, all efforts at refinancing the debt will be neutralized and new debt will accumulate at an unsustainable pace. In this respect, and in order to provide incentives for new flows of funds to debtor countries, Ministers recommended that, for countries heavily indebted to the international banking system, the possibility of differentiating existing debt from new credit flows should be explored for the purpose of determining interest payments.

Ministers stressed that the debt problems of the low-income countries – especially in Sub-Saharan Africa – have not received enough attention, although the debt burden of these countries relative to their income has contributed to a decline in their living standards that is almost disastrous. The Ministers therefore expressed the wish that the international community consider more innovative solutions, including conversion of part of their debt into grants and long-term rescheduling on less onerous terms. These solutions should not in any way reduce concessional flows to other low-income countries, including those which are in the process of implementing adjustment programmes involving structural changes.[31]

The idea of distinguishing the 'old' debt from the newly incurred debt was first put forward, it seems, by Professor Assar Lindbeck two years ago.[32] A similar proposal was made by Mr Peter Chadder, from the Bank of Credit and Commerce International.[33] These proposals have the purpose of safeguarding the current level of economic activity and trade from the constraining effects of financial liabilities incurred in the past, by placing the latter on an interest rate regime lower than the current market rate. Further work is needed to elaborate the Buenos Aires position and put forward a specific proposal.

Also in early March, the President of Mexico, in response to a foreign exchange and domestic resource squeeze, resulting mainly from the double blow of the earthquake and the collapse of oil prices, proposed that the creditor banks share in the burden, through a reduction of interest rates on existing debt.

Part-payment of Interest in Local Currency

Dr Victor Urquidi, a distinguished Mexican economist, has recently proposed that interest payments be split in two parts. One part, corresponding to the LIBOR rate less current rate of inflation, would continue to be paid in cash foreign exchange; the second part, corresponding to the difference to the market interest rate, would be payable in local currency, to be used by foreign creditor banks for local lending and investment for purposes agreed to by the debtor country government; the return on such investment would be transferable in a given, perhaps considerable, proportion into foreign currency in which the older loans were expressed.[34]

A somewhat similar idea of splitting interest payments into the foreign exchange and the local currency components was suggested in August 1984, with the additional proposal that the latter be reduced and the foreign exchange component be *pro tanto* increased as obstacles to exports of the debtor countries are alleviated or Special Drawing Rights (SDRs) allocations are increased; and that the overall level of interest rates payable on existing debt be negotiated down through a collective proposal of the major debtors.[35]

These ideas can be combined.

NEED FOR EMERGENCY FINANCE

Even with the best will in the world, it would take time to translate into action the initiatives and proposals discussed above. The quickest, most efficient and probably the only way in which the urgent financing needs can be met while preserving creditworthiness of debtor countries in full is through special issues of SDRs over the next two years. This two-year period should be used for organising a concerted long-term approach to the debt problem and a recovery programme in Africa. The alternative to SDR issues is a further deflationary pressure on many debtor countries, already weakened by the developments in 1982–5, whose ultimate outcome is uncertain.[36] What is called for is a monetisation of a part of debt service, in order to gain time in which more permanent arrangements can be made.[37]

There should be no concern about the inflationary effect of an SDR allocation of, say, $US50 billion to developing countries over the next two years. No conflict exists between satisfying these countries' needs and the requirements for growth of global monetary reserves. The value of the latter, after a sharp fall in 1981 caused by the collapse of the price of gold, continued to erode in the following years.

Stability of producer prices in the domestic markets of such key developed countries as the US, Federal Republic of Germany, and Japan, and the ongoing fall of world market prices of both commodities and manufactures started in 1980, suggest that additional liquidity can be absorbed without inflation. Economic writers are virtually unanimous in arguing that there is an imminent danger of world deflation, in the absence of an expansionary policy:

> By every estimate, enormous output gaps prevail today in the major industrial countries. . . . They will not be closed – indeed

Table 5.10 Global world reserves (billions of $US, end of year)

	1980	*1981*	*1982*	*1983*	*1984*
Gold, at market prices (1)	560.2	379.9	424.2	360.8	290.5
Foreign exchange	315.4	302.6	283.1	279.5	300.0
IMF reserve positions	21.5	24.8	28.1	41.0	40.7
SDRs	15.1	19.1	19.6	15.1	16.1
ECUs	63.6	49.8	41.4	45.0	37.7
Non-gold, total (2)	415.6	396.3	372.2	380.6	394.5
Grand total (1+2)	975.8	776.2	796.4	741.4	685.1

Source *Annual Reports*, Bank for International Settlements (1981/2–1984/5).

they may not even shrink – during the next several years if policy makers persist with their present objectives for moderate growth. The inflationary pressures of excess demand impinging on limited capacity are simply not a reality today in most sectors of the world economy.[38]

In London, an eerie silence hangs over the tin trading ring at the Metal Exchange; trading has been halted because there are simply not enough buyers for the vast quantities of tin that producers in far-away Malaysia keep turning out. In America's farm belt, more than a million bushels of this year's record corn crop went directly into storage, piling up on top of last year's surplus. In corporate America, such blue chips as General Motors, Warner-Lambert and Standard Oil of Ohio are reeling from lackluster demand for their products. They have been forced to cut prices, lay off thousands of workers and write off billions of dollars in redundant production capacity.

All over the globe, in developed and developing nations alike, producers in a broad spectrum of industries are turning out more than consumers can buy, creating a new world economy – a glut economy.[39]

The world economy differs from that of five years ago in two important respects. First, there is a surfeit of agricultural, energy and other industrial commodities. Second, the strong dollar promoted the development of substantial manufacturing capacity in the Far East, particularly among the newly industrialized countries of Hong Kong, Singapore, South Korea and Taiwan. As a result, these exporters have an excess supply of commodities and, thus,

text cont. p. 117

ANNEX A

Debt growth of selected major 'old' debtors
(Millions of $US)

	1980	1981	1982	1983	1984[a]	1985[b]
Argentina						
(1) External debt	27 162	35 671	43 634	46 005	47 821	50 770
(2) Resource balance[c]	–2 596	– 843	2 582	2 988	3 042	3 104
(3) Interest payments	–2 178	–3 869	–4 925	–5 424	–5 537	–5 114
(4) Current account (2)+(3)	–4 774	–4 712	–2 353	–2 436	–2 495	–2 010
(5) Average interest rate (%)	8.0	10.8	11.3	11.8	11.6	10.1
(6) Average real interest rate (%)[d]	– 8.1	13.6	26.3	23.8	11.3	11.6
Brazil						
(1) External debt	63 470	74 072	85 310	93 556	102 039	103 526
(2) Resource balance[c]	–4 980	– 688	– 2 208	4 125	11 966	10 383
(3) Interest payments	–7 457	–10 305	–12 551	–10 263	–11 449	–10 727
(4) Current account (2)+(3)	–12 437	–10 993	–14 759	– 6 138	517	– 344
(5) Average interest rate (%)	11.7	13.9	14.7	11.0	11.2	10.4
(6) Average real interest rate (%)[d]	5.5	21.1	22.2	19.6	12.6	12.0
Chile						
(1) External debt	12 301	16 894	17 780	18 331	20 422	21 919
(2) Resource balance[c]	– 868	–2 861	– 73	694	58	438
(3) Interest payments	–1 152	–1 943	–2 300	–1 813	–2 158	–2 113
(4) Current account (2)+(3)	–2 020	–4 804	–2 373	–1 119	–2 100	–1 675
(5) Average interest rate (%)	9.4	11.5	12.9	9.9	10.6	9.6
(6) Average real interest rate (%)[d]	– 6.0	30.9	33.8	8.9	21.6	8.4

Mexico						
(1) External debt	58 493	77 287	92 286	92 431	95 489	96 352
(2) Resource balance[c]	–1 889	–4 336	6 211	15 183	15 392	10 644
(3) Interest payments	–5 477	–8 383	–11 264	–9 861	–11 493	–10 034
(4) Current account (2)+(3)	–7 366	–12 719	– 5 053	5 322	3 899	610
(5) Average interest rate (%)	9.4	10.8	12.2	10.7	12.0	10.4
(6) Average real interest rate (%)[d]	– 20.8	10.3	27.4	16.9	9.9	15.0
Nigeria						
(1) External debt	6 870	8 761	14 948	19 530	19 210	17 970
(2) Resource balance[c]	5 597	–5 432	–6 955	–4 027	1 450	2 560
(3) Interest payments	– 643	– 850	–1 178	–1 548	–1 650	–1 700
(4) Current account (2)+(3)	4 954	–6 282	–8 133	–5 575	– 200	800
(5) Average interest rate (%)	9.4	9.8	9.1	10.0	87	9.9
(6) Average real interest rate (%)[d]	–38.9	1.0	25.9	25.4	11.5	18.2
South Korea						
(1) External debt	27 974	32 516	37 120	40 448	43 140	46 698
(2) Resource balance[c]	–2 778	–1 142	1 037	1 720	2 627	2 309
(3) Interest payments	–2 597	–3 585	–3 769	–3 327	–3 995	–3 593
(4) Current account (2)+(3)	–5 375	–4 727	–2 732	–1 607	–1 368	1 284
(5) Average interest rate (%)	9.3	11.0	10.2	8.2	9.3	7.7
(6) Average real interest rate (%)[d]	4.7	7.6	14.0	12.5	5.8	7.1

[a] Estimate.
[b] Forecast.
[c] Balance on trade and services account, less interest payments abroad.
[d] Adjusted by changes in the export price index.

Source International financial organisations, Washington, DC, October 1985.

ANNEX B

Total resource flows to developing countries by major types of flow, 1950–84
($US billion at 1983 prices and exchange rates)

	1950–55	*1960–61*	*1970*	*1971*	*1972*	*1973*
I. Official development assistance	(8.35)	19.54	22.18	23.37	22.13	23.93
1. Flows from bilateral sources	8.35	18.60	19.38	20.22	19.12	20.24
(a) DAC countries	8.35	15.87	14.82	15.32	14.40	13.34
(b) OPEC countries	—	—	1.02	1.07	1.44	3.82
(c) CMEA countries	. . .	1.80	2.60	2.53	2.24	2.19
(d) Non-DAC/OECD	. . .	0.02	0.01	0.02	0.02	0.02
(e) LDC donors	. . .	0.91	0.93	1.28	1.02	0.87
2. Flows from multilateral agencies	. . .	0.94	2.80	3.15	3.01	3.69
II. Grants by private voluntary agencies	. . .	. . .	2.25	2.21	2.27	2.58
III. Non-concessional flows	7.54	15.29	28.66	28.72	28.98	37.41
1. Official or officially supported	. . .	6.57	10.36	11.94	8.17	9.15
(a) Private export credits (DAC)	. . .	2.03	5.47	6.58	3.14	2.18
(b) Official export credits (DAC)	. . .	2.80	1.54	1.75	1.61	2.13
(c) Multilateral	. . .	0.80	1.86	2.23	2.20	2.47
(d) Other off. and private flows (DAC)	0.94	0.65	0.68	0.98	1.92	1.43
(e) Other donors	. . .	. . .	0.84	0.70	0.24	0.45
2. Private	. . .	8.72	18.30	16.78	20.81	28.25
(a) Direct investment	. . .	6.54	9.66	8.04	9.22	8.89
(b) Bank sector[a]	. . .	2.18	7.85	8.01	10.46	18.27
(c) Bond lending	. . .	. . .	0.79	0.73	1.13	1.09
Menra: Official development finance[b]	8.35	20.34	24.04	25.60	24.33	26.40
Total resource flows (I+II+III)	(15.89)	34.83	53.09	54.30	53.38	63.92
For information:						
ODA to developing countries and multilateral agencies, total	. . .	20.80	22.86	23.30	24.93	24.29
DAC countries	8.8	18.02	18.19	18.33	20.05	17.14
OPEC countries	—	—	1.05	1.09	1.54	4.02
CMEA countries	. . .	1.85	2.62	2.55	2.26	2.20
Non-DAC/OECD	. . .	0.02	0.03	0.02	0.02	0.03
LDC donors	. . .	0.91	0.97	1.31	1.06	0.90
Total bank lending	. . .	. . .	. . .	. . .	. . .	. . .
of which:						
Short-term	. . .	. . .	. . .	. . .	. . .	. . .
IMF purchases, net	. . .	. . .	0.89	0.12	0.65	0.68

[a] Bank sector includes, for 1983 and 1984, significant amounts of rescheduled short-term debt. The real evolution of bank lending is best reflected in the line showing 'Total bank lending' at the bottom of the table above. The evolution of total resources flows needs to be adjusted accordingly.

1974	*1975*	*1976*	*1977*	*1978*	*1979*	*1980*	*1981*	*1982*	*1983*	*1984*
28.62	31.59	29.50	27.98	32.06	32.93	36.05	36.23	33.69	33.80	35.75
23.77	25.88	23.92	21.59	25.25	26.53	28.75	28.52	26.21	26.23	27.35
14.15	14.56	13.70	13.34	14.87	16.74	16.99	17.71	18.35	18.53	20.10
7.13	8.44	7.46	5.66	7.82	7.13	8.19	7.46	4.56	4.33	3.79
1.69	2.23	2.07	2.01	1.87	2.20	2.48	2.88	2.86	2.94	2.95
0.01	0.02	0.05	0.11	0.16	0.14	0.81	0.21	0.18	0.07	0.10
0.79	0.63	0.64	0.47	0.53	0.32	0.28	0.26	0.26	0.26	0.41
4.85	5.71	5.58	6.39	6.81	6.40	7.30	7.71	7.48	7.57	8.40
2.10	1.99	1.94	1.97	1.87	2.00	2.17	1.97	2.30	2.34	2.50
34.06	51.01	54.59	58.53	64.79	53.45	55.66	68.56	60.10	82.12	54.00
13.14	15.66	19.21	20.79	21.29	18.84	22.91	21.55	21.90	19.82	20.00
4.13	6.57	9.72	11.70	11.00	9.07	10.43	10.99	7.06	5.50	5.00
1.38	1.78	2.00	1.91	2.52	1.77	2.31	1.95	2.65	2.10	2.50
3.11	3.76	3.66	3.56	3.50	4.26	4.55	5.57	6.58	7.22	7.50
1.12	1.15	0.83	1.54	1.17	2.10	1.91	2.62	3.00	3.00	
3.09	2.42	2.67	2.79	2.73	2.57	3.52	1.13	2.99	2.00	2.00
20.92	35.35	35.38	37.74	43.50	34.61	32.75	47.01	38.21	62.30	34.00
3.25	16.89	11.98	12.99	13.14	13.75	9.89	16.77	11.81	7.80	9.50
17.19	17.84	21.63	20.51	25.93	20.16	21.57	29.19	25.89	54.00[a]	24.00[a]
0.48	0.62	1.76	4.23	4.43	0.70	1.29	1.05	0.51	0.50	0.50
31.73	35.35	33.16	31.54	35.56	37.19	40.60	41.80	40.27	40.92	43.25
64.78	84.59	86.03	88.48	98.72	88.38	93.88	106.76	96.09	118.26	92.25
30.31	32.81	31.75	31.54	34.53	33.88	37.60	36.37	36.88	36.39	37.40
19.96	20.59	20.12	20.82	22.66	23.38	25.57	24.85	27.61	27.54	29.30
7.87	9.82	8.80	8.03	9.23	7.84	9.06	8.14	5.80	5.43	4.60
1.71	2.25	2.08	2.03	1.88	2.22	2.50	2.84	2.92	3.04	3.00
0.03	0.04	0.10	0.17	0.21	0.20	0.19	0.27	0.27	0.12	0.20
0.74	0.65	0.65	0.49	0.55	0.24	0.28	0.27	0.28	0.26	0.30
. . .	. . .	. . .	41.68	45.20	36.56	45.96	50.59	40.83	35.00	18.00
. . .	. . .	. . .	21.17	19.27	16.40	24.39	21.40	14.94	–19.00	–6.00
2.99	4.82	4.30	–0.57	–0.96	0.53	2.45	6.01	6.38	12.48	5.50

[b] Bilateral and multilateral ODA plus multilateral non-concessional flows.
Source OECD, *DAC 1985 Report*, Paris, November 1985, p. 162.

ANNEX C

Public and private long-term debt and financial flows, 1975 and 1980–85 ($US billions)

Long-term debt and financial flows	*1975*[a]	*1980*	*1981*	*1982*	*1983*	*1984*[b]	*1985*[c]
All developing countries[d]							
Debt disbursed and outstanding[e]	162.2	427.1	490.0	546.9	622.1	665.4	708
Disbursements (from	43.8	102.2	121.1	112.2	92.4	86.4	80
private creditors)	28.9	74.0	90.2	80.7	61.9	54.0	45
Debt service	23.1	74.0	86.7	96.2	88.8	100.1	102
Principal repayments	14.8	42.0	46.2	48.2	42.6	46.3	50
Interest	8.3	32.1	40.5	48.0	46.2	53.8	52
Net transfers[f]	20.7	28.2	34.4	16.0	3.6	−13.7	−22
Major borrowers[g]							
Debt disbursed and outstanding[e]	101.4	250.0	290.9	322.9	372.3	404.9	430
Disbursements	26.8	57.9	74.1	60.6	45.3	45.0	40
(From private creditors)	18.6	46.3	60.9	46.1	33.2	29.5	25
Debt service	15.4	47.4	54.9	60.4	53.3	60.5	62
Principal repayments	9.7	26.6	28.1	27.7	22.4	23.2	26
Interest	5.7	20.8	26.8	32.6	30.9	37.3	36
Net transfers[f]	11.4	10.5	19.1	0.2	−8.0	−15.5	−22
Low-income Africa[h]							
Debt disbursed and outstanding	8.8	22.9	25.3	26.9	28.8	28.7	30.2
Disbursements	2.0	4.4	4.2	3.4	3.2	2.6	2.7
(From private creditors)	0.8	1.6	1.3	1.0	0.6	0.3	0.2
Debt service	0.7	1.6	1.6	1.5	1.5	1.9	1.9
Principal repayments	0.4	0.9	0.9	0.9	0.9	1.1	1.1
Interest	0.2	0.7	0.7	0.6	0.6	0.8	0.8
Net transfers[f]	1.4	2.8	2.6	1.9	1.7	0.7	0.8
Memorandum items: all developing countries							
The share of long-term debt (%)							
Public credits from financial markets	25	39	40	41	44	45	..

Public credits at floating interest rates	16	26	29	32	35	37	..
On concessional terms	32	23	22	21	19	18	..
From private sources	56	62	64	64	65	65	54

. . Not available.
[a] Excludes data for Hungary and Romania.
[b] Data for 1984 are preliminary.
[c] Data for 1985 are estimates. For each group of countries, debt-service payments are estimates of actual amounts paid, rather than projections of amounts due as in the tables beginning on page 2.
[d] From 1980, data are for 107 countries reporting under the Debtor Reporting System (DRS). For countries that do not report it, private non-guaranteed debt has been estimated.
[e] Data reflect the rescheduling of short-term debt into longer maturities in 1983–5.
[f] Net transfers are defined as disbursements less debt service.
[g] Major borrowers are Argentina, Brazil, Chile, Egypt, India, Indonesia, Israel, Republic of Korea, Mexico, Turkey, Venezuela, and Yugoslavia. Each of these countries owed at least $16 billion of long-term debt to external creditors at the end of 1984.
[h] Lending, mainly on concessional terms, is an important source of finance for African countries, but official grants are even more important for some countries, and these are not tracked in the DRS. To the extent that grants are substituted for official loans, countries would benefit from a reduction in lending.

Source to Annex C The World Bank, *Development and Debt Service: Dilemma of the 1980s*, Abridged version of 1985–6 World Debt Tables, Washington, DC. 1986. p. xii.

---

are not likely to risk losing their market share in the United States by raising prices.
This world-wide picture of excess manufacturing capacity and raw material abundance means this year's decline in the value of the dollar is unlikely to add much if anything to the inflation rate next year.[40]

Mr de Larosière, Managing Director of the IMF, in his address to the Annual Meeting in Seoul on 7 October 1985, after stating that the Fund had a role in providing liquidity to the system through the SDR mechanisms, referred to the recent contraction of financial markets, which had affected especially the developing countries, and indicated

ANNEX D

Net transfer to developing countries on debt account (billions of US dollars)

	1983	*1984*	*1985*[a]
(1) Net transfer on long-term debt, World Bank compilation	3.6	−13.7	−22.0
(2) Interest on short-term debt	−20.5	−18.8	(−12.0)
(3) Short-term lending, DAC Report	−19.0	− 6.0	−4.0
(4) IMF purchases, net DAC Report	12.5	5.5	
Total	−23.4	−33.0	−38.0

[a] Preliminary

Sources (1) The World Bank, *Development and Debt Service*, 1986 p. xii. (2) OECD, *External Debt of Developing Countries in 1984*, Paris, December 1985, p. 21, for 1983 and 1984; estimate for 1985. (3) and (4) OECD, *DAC 1985 Report*, Paris, November 1985, p. 162, for 1983 and 1984; for 1985, derived from World Bank data on changes in external liabilities, which lump together short-term debt and debt to the IMF (World Bank, *Development and Debt Service*, 1986, p. xi).

---

that this is an 'important additional consideration to be taken into account when assessing the case for an allocation of SDRs at this time'.[41]

Despite these facts and arguments, the Interim Committee of the IMF, at its April 1986 meeting,

> again discussed the question of SDR allocations and determined that, although most members favoured an allocation, the broad support needed for an allocation was lacking at this time. The Committee urged the Executive Board of the IMF to continue its discussions on the role of the SDR in the present international monetary system and . . . to report to the Committee at its next meeting on the progress in these discussions.[42]

The SDR route remains closed for the time being, reportedly due to the attitude of three major powers,[43] 'but we will come back to the SDR at our next meeting', according to the Chairman of the Committee.[44]

ANNEX E

World Bank index of commodity prices in constant 1979–81 dollars

Year	*33 Commodities (excluding energy*	*Petroleum*	*Year*	*33 Commodities (excluding energy*	*Petroleum*
1948	112.4	30.0	1968	111.8	14.6
1949	113.2	25.9	1969	112.5	13.9
1950	149.3	26.2	1970	111.0	13.0
1951	155.9	22.7	1971	97.6	16.1
1952	137.7	21.8	1972	93.9	16.6
1953	131.7	23.6	1973	124.1	20.4
1954	144.6	25.5	1974	134.3	69.3
1955	146.0	25.0	1975	101.1	60.7
1956	138.2	24.2	1976	112.1	64.3
1957	128.4	23.7	1977	122.8	63.9
1958	117.6	22.1	1978	101.5	56.0
1959	117.6	19.9	1979	104.9	71.3
1960	115.9	18.3	1980	105.0	106.6
1961	109.8	18.0	1981	90.5	119.3
1962	106.6	16.5	1982	81.9	109.3
1963	110.5	16.8	1983	88.8	101.8
1964	116.6	15.2	1984	91.6	101.5
1965	119.2	15.1	1985	80.5	97.2
1966	119.1	14.6			
1967	110.6	14.5			

Notes

1. See Annex A for country breakdown and balance of payments detail.
2. Paul Fabra, 'It's Profits – not interest rates – that count', *The Wall Street Journal* (15 December 1983).
3. In practice so far, the remedies proposed by the lenders have been remarkably similar for most debtor countries. See Sidney Dell, *The World Debt Problem: A Diagnosis*, Report to the Group of 24 (January 1986), p. 22 (mimeo).
4. See William R. Cline, 'International Debt and Stability of the World Economy', in *Analyses in International Economics*, no. 4 (September 1983), Institute of International Economics, Washington, DC; Thomas O. Enders and Richard R. Matione, 'Latin America: the Crisis of Debt and Growth', in *Studies in International Economics* (1984), The Brookings Institution, Washington, DC.

5. Leonard Silk, 'The new ideas at Seoul Talks', *The New York Times* (11 October 1985).
6. 'Return of the Poltergeist', *Financial Times* (12 May 1984).
7. This section is partly an updated version of a part of the author's paper 'Transfer of Resources to Developing Countries', Report to the Group of 24 (29 January 1986), pp. 1–4 (mimeo).
8. OECD, *DAC 1985 Report*, Paris (November 1985), p. 162.
9. The World Bank, *Development and Debt Service*, 1986, pp. x–xii.
10. World Bank, *Annual Report 1985*, p. 174.
11. Consensus of Cartagena, Meeting of Ministers, 16–17 December 1985, p. 3.
12. *Financial Times* (6 November 1985).
13. OECD, *DAC 1985 Report*, Paris (November 1985), p. 103.
14. The World Bank, *Financing Adjustment with Growth in Sub-Saharan Africa, 1986–90* (February 1986), p. 8.
15. For the debate, see J. M. Keynes, 'The German Transfer Problem; the Reparations Problem; Views on the Transfer Problem', in *Economic Journal* (March 1929, June 1929 and September 1929); Bertil Ohlin, 'The Reparations Problem', *Index*, Svenska Handelsbanken (April 1928); Bertil Ohlin, 'Transfer Difficulties, Real and Imagined', *Economic Journal* (June 1929); Bertil Ohlin, *Interregional and International Trade*, Cambridge, Massachusetts (1935).
16. *The Wall Street Journal* (18 October 1985).
17. World Bank, *Report of the Executive Directors on the Convention Establishing the Multilateral Investment Guarantee Agency* (12 September 1985).
18. A change is possible, however unlikely it may now seem. For example, the Bank's affiliate, the International Finance Corporation, recently made a loan to Oil Corporation Development Ltd of Kenya to enable it to contract annually with farmers to purchase their oilseed harvest at prices agreed on ahead of time. In Chile, the Bank is supporting 'an innovative copper stabilization fund which will ensure that severe copper price fluctuations do not derail its adjustment programme'. These measures are on a country level, however, and it is a large step to move to international commodity stabilisation. A. David Knox, Vice-President, Latin America and the Caribbean Regional Office, The World Bank, *Address at the Bankers Club* (Tokyo, 20 February 1986), p. 15.
19. For further analysis of the possibilities and problems of commodity stabilisation, see Dragoslav Avramovic, 'Depression of Export Commodity Prices of Developing Countries: What Can be Done?', *Third World Quarterly* (July 1986).
20. For an analysis of the opportunities offered by reduction in armament spending and the problems of conversion see 'In Pursuit of Disarmament: Conversion from Military to Civil Production in Sweden', *Report of the Special Expert Inga Thorsson*, Government of Sweden (Stockholm, 1984).
21. Robert Mundell, 'The Debt Crisis: Causes and Solutions', *The Wall Street Journal* (31 January 1983).
22. *The Economist* (30 November 1985), p. 67, quoting World Bank findings.

23. InterAction Council, *Final Statement Adopted at the Second Session* (Brioni, Yugoslavia, 24–26 May 1984). The InterAction proposal further included the restriction of annual debt service payments to an agreed maximum and capitalisation of interest, on a country-by-country basis. The proposal was based on a report of a meeting of experts in Wolfsburg, Federal Republic of Germany, on 5–6 May 1984, chaired by Chancellor Schmidt, a member (and now Chairman) of the InterAction Council.
24. Statement before the Meetings of the Interim Committee of the IMF and Development Committee of the World Bank and the IMF (Washington, DC, 9–11 April 1986), p. 4.
25. Statement by Mr de Larosière, Managing Director of the IMF, as reported in *Financial Times* (23 April 1986).
26. The World Bank, *Financing Adjustment with Growth in Sub-Saharan Africa, 1986–90* (February 1986). The earlier reports were prepared in 1981, 1983 and 1984 respectively. Financial requirements refer to 29 low-income (IDA-eligible) countries. This may explain the differences from other estimates (p. 20).
27. Compact for African Development, *Report of the Committee on African Development Strategies*, a Joint Project of the Council on Foreign Relations and the Overseas Development Council (New York–Washington, DC, December 1985), p. 15.
28. Ibid., pp. 27–8;
29. UNCTAD, *Capital requirements for the development of the least developed countries in the second half of the 1980s*, TD/B/AC.17/25/Add. 2(C) (31 July 1985), p. 8.
30. As reported in *Journal de Genève* (14 April 1986).
31. Intergovernmental Group of Twenty-Four on International Monetary Affairs, *Press Communiqué*, paras 14 and 15.
32. *Consequences for the Developing Countries of the International Economic Turmoil* (Stockholm), a lecture delivered at the Royal Institute for International Affairs (London: 23 January 1984).
33. 'The LDC Debt Crisis: Origin and Solutions', *BCC Economic Review* (June 1984).
34. Proposal of February 1986.
35. Dragoslav Avramovic, 'Foreign Debt and the Financial System', paper presented at the First International Congress on Economic Policies: 'The Alternative for International Crisis' (Rio de Janeiro, 12–17 August 1984), and later published in *Development and South–South Cooperation*, vol. I, no. 1 (Belgrade, Yugoslavia, December 1985).
36. Since it would take time to effect the amendments to the Fund's Articles of Agreement required to modify the present rules of distribution of SDRs, it would be necessary for the industrial countries to agree to forego the allocations to which they are entitled. This proposal was made by Sidney Dell on a recent occasion in: 'The Case for World Economic Recovery', UN *Journal of Development Planning*, no. 14 (1984), p. 23. The distribution among the developing countries could be modified as required by using an analogous procedure.
37. A similar proposal, apparently referring to monetisation of the principal of the debt, has been made by Alain Lipietz, 'Mirages et miracles,

problèmes de l'industrialisation dans le tiers monde' (Editions La Découverte, Paris, 1985), as reported in Philippe Amez-Droz 'Plan Marshall pour le tiers monde?', *Journal de Genève* (18 November 1985).
38. 'Countering World Deflation', Morgan Guaranty Trust Company of New York, *World Financial Markets* (December 1985), pp. 1 and 3.
39. 'Waking up to the Glut Economy', *The New York Times* (8 December 1985).
40. Joel Popkin, 'Why the Lid is on Prices, at Last', *The New York Times* (1 December 1985).
41. *Press Release No. 3* (8 October 1985), pp. 5–6 and 10–11.
42. *Communiqué of the Interim Committee* (10 April 1986), para. 8.
43. *Financial Times* (7 April 1986).
44. Statement by Mr H. Onno Ruding (Netherlands) at the Press Conference, IMF (10 April 1986).

6 Direct Foreign Investment and Manufacturing for Export in Developing Countries: A Review of the Issues*

Gerald K. Helleiner

1 INTRODUCTION

The precarious condition of the global financial system has generated a wide range of suggestions for reform, and continuing advocacy of 'adjustment' for the developing countries. Among the most consistent instruments suggested for achieving the twin objectives of more stable development finance and structural adjustment in production is a quite traditional one: direct foreign investment. Too much reliance was placed upon debt finance in the 1970s, particularly short-term debt, the argument runs, a form that has proven highly unpredictable both in its servicing obligations and in its gross flow to the developing countries; its future is now very much in doubt, except for those few creditworthy countries who 'underborrowed' in the past (e.g. India, Malaysia), as commercial banks attempt to restructure their portfolios in response to the adverse experience of the post-1981 period. At the same time, the urgent need for key inputs of management and marketing skills, technology, and know-how in 'nontraditional' tradeable goods and services sectors – into which the balance of payments pressures of recent years are driving the developing countries – seem most readily available in the familiar and traditional 'packaged' form of direct foreign investment, however desirable it might be to 'shop' for individual components thereof in less desperate

*This chapter was originally prepared for the Economic Affairs Division of the Commonwealth Secretariat as an input to its research project on direct foreign investment policies. A shorter version appears in Vincent Cable and Bishnodat Persand (eds), *Developing with Foreign Investment* (Croom Helm and the Commonwealth Secretariat, 1987) pp. 67–83. I am most grateful to Vincent Cable, Sidney Dell and Louis Wells for their comments on an earlier draft.

and more leisurely times. Efficiency considerations have led most analysts to place greater emphasis upon 'nontraditional' exporting – notably from the manufacturing sector – than upon new areas of import substitution.

To the longstanding advice to improve incentives for export-oriented manufacturing has now been added widespread calls for the relaxation of screening procedures, and the provision of fresh incentives for foreign investors in developing countries. At the Western Economic Summit Conference in London, for instance, this new conventional wisdom was vigorously expressed again, as the leaders spoke of

> encouraging the flow of long-term direct investment: just as there is need for industrial countries to make their markets more open for the exports of developing countries, so these countries can help themselves by encouraging investment from the industrial countries.

The more internationalist of recent commentators recommend strengthened efforts to complete the UN's code of conduct for transnational corporations to ensure a more stable and balanced policy regime within which investors and governments can confidently encourage increased investment flows. According to the latest UN survey of transnationals and world development there has already been some relaxation in host country policies on direct foreign investment (UNCTC, 1983, pp. 9–11).

Questions must nevertheless be asked about the efficacy of the suggested new reliance upon direct foreign investment. By now there has been enough experience with this form of international economic interaction that it may be possible to anticipate some of the problems that will arise if there is to be a significant policy shift back to it. Particularly relevant, when every developing country is at the same time being urged to expand its exports, is the experience with export-oriented direct foreign investment.

A major initial constraint upon the use of foreign direct investment, analogous to that for other commercial sources of finance, is the geographic concentration that has always characterised it. Eleven NICs were the destination for more than half of total OECD direct investment flows to developing countries in recent years. Low-income countries (as defined by the OECD) received only 4 per cent of the 1981 flow of OECD direct investment to developing countries and accounted for 7 per cent of the end-1981 stock (see Appendix tables). (Foreign investment may nevertheless account for a significant share of a small or poor country's total external resource inflow.) According to the OECD its direct investment has gone primarily to countries 'with a dynamic and outward looking economic stance, sustained by appropriate financial and economic policies, a disciplined labour force and, at the time of transaction, a good international credit standing' (OECD, 1983, p. 8).

The links between investment and trade flows should, in any case, be a matter for more detailed investigation. The debt crisis of the early 1980s dramatically underscored the global interaction between finance and trade. If exports cannot be expanded – or imports cut still further – there is no way in which developing countries can service their debt. Continuing protectionist pressure can contribute to financial disaster. Conversely, easier terms for credit and increased liquidity and longer-term capital flows to debtor nations can ease pressures upon the trading system and assist liberal approaches to international trade to survive.

Similarly, US monetary and fiscal policy is inextricably intertwined today with its trading policies. The story is well known – large budget deficits (amounting to about 10 per cent of the world's total supply of savings) generating, with current monetary policies, high interest rates; high interest rates and the prospect of low inflation generating capital inflow to the US and an appreciated dollar; dollar appreciation generating record US trade deficits and pressure for protectionism – especially against countries with relatively undervalued currencies like Japan's has been. The US dollar was for a long time severely overvalued – misaligned – in terms of the competitiveness of its producers internationally, relative to 'normal' circumstances. How can the protectionist pressure that resulted be fought off until 'normalcy' returns? (Needless to say, the US interest rate also has a significant bearing on the debt-servicing problems mentioned before.) Joint consideration of macro/financial issues and what are generally thought of as the more micro-issues of trade policy are now essential.

The traditional approaches to international trade – buttressed by 200 years of economic theorising – have probably taken us just about as far as we can go with them. Rather than thinking of the micro-level problems of world trade in terms of *international* trade, i.e., as trade between nations, it is time – in the global village – to begin to think of them in terms of *global industrial organisation*.

What is at issue, industry by industry, is the location of new investment, and the incentives to *locate* in different places, not just policies relating to trade – after production begins. Tomorrow's trade is the product of today's investment decisions. When one talks of 'fair trade' and export subsidies, there is no logical reason not to worry equally about 'fair investment' and investment incentives. The big actors in global industrial organisation – in investment and in trade – are governments and transnational firms. Governments now regularly take over, or bail out, large firms; offer a variety of incentives (and dis-incentives) to both investment and trade; and develop industrial policies and adjustment policies with varying degrees of success.

Transnationals have internalised and, to some degree, cartelised large proportions of their global trading activity. In the automobile industry, General Motors, Ford and Chrysler each team up with Japanese auto firms and each US firm seeks to influence the inter-firm disposition of quotas for the entry of 'their' Japanese products to the US market. Much of international trade is consequently already 'managed' – by governments and firms.

It seems likely – it may even be desirable – that future international consultations in steel, automobiles, wheat flour, textiles, etc. will take place between governments and transnational firms in sectorally specialised 'committees' that are, in effect, negotiating global industrial policy.

Where there are scale economies, learning effects, other countries' trade barriers, investment incentives and trade-related performance requirements, and where oligopolistic multinational firms are key decision-makers, it would be foolhardy for a developing country to proceed with policy on the basis of traditional models of pure competition, perfect markets, and comparative advantage. On the other hand, the state of the policy art in these real world circumstances is still distressingly weak. What is clear is that investment and trade policies must be considered together as 'codeterminants of the location of production and pattern of trade' (McCulloch and Owen, 1983, p. 353; see also Helleiner, 1982).

This chapter will review, within this broader context, the issues and research requirements concerning the role of direct foreign investment in manufacturing for export in developing countries. In Section 2, the two principal approaches to the analysis of direct foreign investment – financial and organisational – are presented and compared with one another. Section 3 considers the evidence regarding the supply elasticity of direct foreign investment. In Section 4 the direct foreign investment form is compared with alternative forms of economic organisation for export-oriented manufacturing. Section 5 analyses the role of government policies – in both developing and developed countries – in the encouragement of direct foreign investment and manufacturing for export. A brief summary of the main areas for further research may be found in Section 6.

2 ALTERNATIVE APPROACHES TO ANALYSIS OF DIRECT FOREIGN INVESTMENT POLICIES

Consideration of the merits and demerits of direct foreign investment for the expansion of manufactured exports (or any other productive activity) requires a norm against which comparisons are to be made. Different analyses of these issues frequently employ quite different standards of comparison.

Much of the new international emphasis upon direct foreign investment flows from disaffection with and gloomy forecasts of commercial bank lending as a source of external capital for developing countries. Direct foreign investment is thus seen primarily, although usually not exclusively, in terms of its role as a source of international capital. But is this new foreign investment to provide additional capital? It could be extremely helpful if more of the current debt obligations could be converted to equity, and the IFC and others have some innovative proposals in this regard. The discussion is usually, however, focused upon the prospect of *new* inflows of capital to the developing countries. It is not always clear how the expansion of transnational corporate investments that is so widely recommended is to be financed.

Some may be financed from the firms' own earnings, although significant expansion would seem to be predicated upon substantially increased earnings (above previous 'normal', non-recession, rates) which do not at present seem to be in prospect. The bulk of any expansion would presumably have to be financed through new issues of equity or debt. An OECD-sponsored survey of 68 projects in which new capital was raised by direct foreign investors in the pre-banking-boom period found that almost half of the new capital was made up of debt rather than equity issues. Over half of the debt capital (54 per cent) and 40 per cent of the equity was raised in the developing countries themselves (Reuber, 1973, p. 67). By no means all of any expansion in direct foreign investment would therefore constitute net additions to local savings. Some governments inhibit and others encourage resort to local finance on the part of foreign enterprises; local equity is usually favoured relative to local debt.

Transnational corporations have nevertheless traditionally played an important intermediation role in international capital markets. Earlier analysts have noted that,

> Measures that prevent private foreign corporations from doing business at all or that restrict their activities, either preclude or restrict access to international capital markets in developed countries via the most important international financial intermediaries functioning today and the intermediaries that are largely responsible for the large increase in international capital flows that have occurred during the past decade. (Reuber, 1973, p. 67)

Is it contemplated that transnational corporations (and their subsidiaries) are now again to intermediate between cautious Northern investors, including commercial banks, and developing country borrowers?

As far as debt issues are concerned, such intermediation should be seen, above all, as a device to keep commercial bank lending to developing countries a little higher and perhaps a little cheaper than it would otherwise be by assigning more of the risks in particular sectors and cases to direct investors and less to banks. There might be a somewhat wider spread of borrowing countries, a somewhat narrower range of activities and, conceivably, sometimes longer terms, notably when bond finance is involved, in such financing than was the norm for commercial bank finance in the developing countries in the 1970s. But otherwise little would be changed by redirecting bank flows through transnational corporate intermediaries. A relevant norm for comparison, if short- to medium-term debt finance is seen as a major source of expanded direct foreign investment in developing countries, is the cost, country-mix, sector-mix, and maturity of the financial flows that would follow from expanded World Bank or other official intermediation or co-financing activity instead.

New equity and bond issues, to the extent they are taken up in developed countries, rather than in the developing host countries, are a highly desirable means of acquiring expanded external flows to developing countries. Such flows seem to be what most financial commentators who speak of the need for expanded direct foreign investment in developing countries in the 1980s and 1990s actually have in mind. (See, for instance, Helleiner, 1983.) But how great are the prospects of significantly expanded flows? Are they significantly responsive to governmental policies towards foreign investment in the developing countries? Are direct foreign investment and commercial bank borrowing substitutes for one another? What other means may be found for mobilising development capital and/or sharing risks in more acceptable ways than in current commercial bank lending arrangements? What about, for instance, developing the proposals for insuring bank lending to developing countries? (An excellent summary of the issues surrounding such insurance schemes can be found in Wallich, 1984.) What are the relative merits of co-financing of various kinds and direct foreign investment? What can be done to ensure that any new gross inflows of foreign equity or bond finance will not be offset, as so much bank credit to Latin America was in the 1970s, by private speculative outflows?

A quite different strand of the literature relates not to the alternative forms or means of acquiring external finance but, rather, to alternative forms of economic organisation. In this approach, direct foreign investment represents an internalised or hierarchical form of trade in goods and services, a form with certain advantages and disadvantages relative to the market alternative (e.g. Dunning, 1981; Casson, 1979). In the relevant literature a variety of non-equity forms (or 'new forms', in some sources, e.g., Oman, 1983) of interaction are considered, e.g. licensing; subcontracting; franchising; management contracts; marketing contracts; technical assistance contracts; joint ventures; turnkey plant sales; co-production or production-sharing agreements and so on.

Although the data are imperfect there seems to have been an overall shift away from traditional majority-owned foreign investment towards 'new forms' of investment in developing countries, notably joint ventures and licensing agreements, during the 1960s and 1970s. Most dramatic in the petroleum and metals industries it was also found in manufacturing, and particularly in manufacturing for host country markets (import substituting activities) and in those with mature technologies, although there was considerable inter-country variation in manufacturing sector experience (Oman, 1983, pp. 201–4, 227–8; UNCTC, 1983, pp. 40–46). There is also evidence of similar organisational restructuring in export-oriented agriculture (Glover, 1983).

This trend has been less noticeable in manufacturing for export than in other traditional areas of foreign direct investment activity. That direct investment is by no means necessary for successful export-oriented manufacturing is illustrated by the Korean case where the bulk of the exporting has been done by local firms (Westphal *et al.*, 1979). The UNCTC has noted that transnational corporate involvement has been unnecessary and relatively limited in the export of standardised labour-intensive goods; it has been much more important in the export of differentiated products and inputs to industries making them, and, in the Japanese case, in capital-intensive raw material processing (UNCTC, pp. 182–3; see also Keesing, 1983). In large part the changes towards non-equity forms of foreign investment or involvement were a response to governmental policies in the host countries. To the extent that government policies generated the alternative forms, their 'liberalization' could be expected to induce some return to the original direct investment mode. To some degree, however, the new forms involved an independent evolution of investment and international business practices relating to risk-sharing, management and financing, and the appearance of smaller internationally oriented firms, the product of business evolution and decision-making rather than government policies.

A careful consideration of the benefits and costs of alternative forms of interaction with foreign firms, including direct foreign investment of the traditional kind, is desirable, whatever the prospects for expanded finance of one kind or another. Some of the advocates of expanded direct foreign investment (particularly those in chambers of commerce and business) clearly feel that the direct foreign investment form is a superior one, whether for their own self-interested purposes or in the broader interests of social efficiency. More particularly, what they frequently mean to advocate is less governmental restriction of the range of business choice. What they are typically interested in is a favourable 'investment climate' that provides firms with maximum predictability and freedom. As the OECD has put it, 'Stability of investment conditions, non-discrimination ("national treatment"), freedom of capital movements, and satisfactory arrangements for the settlement of investment disputes are features of investment security to which foreign investors attach particular importance'. (OECD, 1983, p. 8).

By confusing the discussion of finance (everyone is for more of it) with that of economic organisation, they seek to alter previous governmental policies with respect to the latter. They imply that easing policies towards direct foreign investment – an improved 'investment climate' – will, in fact, increase the flow of external capital. But this link is by no means self-evident. Only when previous prohibitions are removed can there be a reasonable presumption of increased foreign investment, and even that may not involve flows from abroad. Prohibitions have not typically been found in manufacturing activities likely to be competitive in world markets; indeed, in general, restrictions on foreign investors have typically been at their least in manufacturing for export.

Direct investment flows are, in any case, overwhelmingly the product of more fundamental determinants of profitability – the overall state of the host country and the world economy.

3 THE SUPPLY OF DIRECT FOREIGN INVESTMENT

The most fundamental issue concerning the proposed new policy orientation towards direct foreign investment (DFI) is its supply elasticity. How much expansion can one sensibly anticipate in response to altered policies, either at the national level or at the global level? There has long been controversy about the nature of the supply schedule for foreign investment, always assuming that one can analyse the market for the foreign investment 'package' rather than breaking it down into its constituent markets for capital, technology, management, etc.

No doubt each global industry possesses its own peculiar characteristics, and the supply schedule for DFI can be expected to look different from industry to industry. One recent study hypothesises that the 'market' for DFI in manufacturing oriented to worldwide export markets is separable from 'markets' for DFI geared to national or regional product markets (Guisinger, 1985. For more details see below). Equally, individual country characteristics vary greatly with the result that 'price' variations are likely to influence the supply of foreign investment differently from country to country as well. No less important is the stage at which the foreign investor is in his relations with the host country. Responsiveness can be much greater at the point when an investor is still contemplating putting resources into a 'green field' investment than after he has already made a commitment and is, in some respects, 'trapped' in his elected environment. (In some instances, however, the build-up of local political allies can increase firms' resistance to governmental pressures as time goes on (Newfarmer, 1983, pp. 86–7). Thus the supply elasticity of direct foreign investment is most usefully considered in terms of the specifics of a particular industry in a particular country at a particular point in time.

Generally, investment incentives have been considered to play a minimal role in foreign investment decision-making. For instance, a recent OECD survey notes that

> Experience has shown that measures undertaken by home and host governments to improve the flow of foreign direct investment or to direct it to specific sectors and locations influence investment decisions only marginally. Such incentives can never substitute for the 'fundamentals': the investment climate, political security and profit opportunities (OECD, 1983, p. 8).

Profit prospects typically dominate foreign firms' decisions to locate in particular countries – as determined by such needs as resource availability, access to or defence of significant markets, together with the necessary security and political stability. A survey of 52 major international corporations based in twelve countries, undertaken by the Group of Thirty, confirmed that the dominant influences on their foreign direct investment decisions were, overwhelmingly, the need to gain access to local or regional markets and to avoid trade barriers. This was as true of investment in developing countries as elsewhere although 'In the case of LDCs, higher risk and lower-than-expected growth rates were beginning to offset the desire to gain access to new markets.' (Group of Thirty, 1984, p. 31.)

Most striking in this survey, from the standpoint of current concerns (and the concerns of this chapter), were its findings with respect to (a) government policies and (b) export prospects. Tax and other inducements offered by host countries were regarded as 'unimportant influences on investment decisions, though some companies stressed that specific inducements could, on occasion, tip the balance of a decision in favour of investment in a particular country if all other conditions were satisfactory – which was, however, rare' (p. 32). Not a single respondent listed tax advantages in the top three influences upon investments in developing countries. As far as DFI for exporting was concerned, comparative labour costs were mentioned by relatively few firms in the survey (though twice as high a proportion with respect to investments in developing countries as elsewhere) – not at all by firms in high-technology industries, chemicals, food and drink, electrical or pharmaceutical industries, or even some labour-intensive industries – and 'The idea of using LDCs as exporting bases was not attractive to most companies' (p. 32).

This survey did not include within its definition of direct foreign investment, however, any international sub-contracting to independent companies or what the report itself calls 'direct investment without investment' (p. 12), in which frequently 'the local company has in effect been brought into existence and is kept in being by the international company' (p. 12); and 'the economic and balance of payments effects are almost identical to those of FDI' (p. 13). Foreign firms engaging in international sub-contracting achieve these results 'without going through the motions of conventional foreign direct investment or incurring the same kind of risks as those attaching to conventional DFI' (p. 12). Growing resort to such non-DFI forms may seriously distort interpretations of foreign firms' interest in exporting that are based on questions relating purely to conventional ownership modalities.

Against the substantial body of survey and theoretical evidence of the limited impact of governmental inducements to foreign investors, a recent World Bank study (Guisinger, 1985) appears to argue quite differently – at least with respect to the industries and countries studied: automobiles, computers, food products and petrochemicals, in ten countries of which seven were developing (Brazil, India, Indonesia, Kenya, Mexico, Philippines, and Singapore). While the impact is certainly uneven across industries and countries, and it is recognised that incentives may not be the most important influences upon foreign investment in particular locations, this study purports to find that incentives do matter to foreign investment decisions and that countries compete in (differentiated) markets for foreign investment. In two-thirds of the 74 cases studied, host country government policy influenced the choice of country by investors. The enormous variety of possible policy instruments (far beyond the tax issues that typically dominate debate) makes it extremely difficult to ascertain what exactly the overall net impact of any individual government's policies is; it also permits a high degree of 'product differentiation' on the part of governments seeking to attract investors and a low degree of transparency regarding their policies. Governments are also found to be offering firm-specific incentives and thereby effectively practising price discrimination. Since tariff protection is included among this study's 'incentive policies', it is not obvious on closer inspection, that its results are inconsistent with earlier ones. Indeed, where investment flows are stimulated by protectionist policies they may even reduce national income in the host country (Brecher and Diaz-Alejandro, 1977).

The study argues that there are three separate markets for foreign investment – one for investments directed at the market of individual host countries, one for those relating to common markets, and one for investments geared to production for export; and there is competition in each. In the competition for foreign investment, the effectiveness of any individual countries' policies clearly depends upon other countries' reactions, and these may themselves depend upon the direction of change. Increases in incentives are more likely to be followed by competitors than are decreases. The existence of competition among countries such that all offer more or less the same incentives could explain why firms so frequently say that investment incentives do not influence their location decisions; yet if one country were to abandon its incentives in the absence of others' doing similarly there would indeed be effects upon the geographic pattern of investments. These results accord with casual empirical observations of intergovernmental bidding for foreign investment projects, and with the views of those who have predicted 'investment wars' for the future (Bergsten, 1974).

None of this evidence of competition among countries for foreign investors offers any guidance as to whether increased incentives will increase the aggregate flow of direct foreign investment to developing countries. Since there was very little direct competition for investments observed between developing and developed countries – although there was some indirectly, via the erection of trade barriers – there is still no presumption that improved incentives will increase the flow of direct investment to the developing countries. Increased incentives on the part of developing countries, inevitably matched by others in the competitive struggle for foreign investment, may simply reduce their earnings from it without significantly increasing its flow. It may still be true that, 'With better general economic policies and a better entry system, the same amount of investment could be attracted at a lower cost.' (OECD, 1983, p. 14.) There would also seem to be scope for joint, or at least co-ordinated, approaches to the provision of incentives to foreign investors. Such approaches need not require total uniformity of policies – probably an impossible attainment anyway. They could provide explicitly for differential incentives, for instance, to offset the disadvantages of the poorest countries.

Radetzki has shown that one can be seriously misled about the response of foreign firms to changing investment regimes and Third World overall market shares if one relies purely upon traditional data sources. What at first blush looks like supply response and deteriorating market shares may in fact merely be altered forms of involvement (1982). He wrote with reference to minerals development but the point is a general one. The great variety of institutional forms of foreign firms' involvement in developing countries' manufacturing for export has always made the interpretation of data on the degree of transnationals' involvement and the role of direct foreign investment in this activity very difficult (e.g. Nayyar, 1978). Alternative forms of foreign involvement are considered in the following section.

There must, in any case, continue to be doubt as to *how much* and *what kind* of incentive is necessary to induce the desired expansion in *net* foreign investment at the national level. It would certainly be wrong to consider that all of the investment that benefits from incentive programmes is additional to the investment that would otherwise have occurred. There is bound to be some 'redundancy' in incentive programmes, i.e., investors receive subsidies they do not require in order to invest; the selectivity and discrimination observed in actual programmes undoubtedly reflects governmental attempts to reduce such 'redundancy'. Even so, some of the additional foreign investment apparently successfully induced by selective incentives may simply displace investment by others, both foreign and local. (See Usher, 1977.) There are also differential effects created by different kinds of incentives: product-oriented incentives, factor-oriented incentives, tax incentives of various types, etc. While such incentive arrangements may, in some sense, be aggregated in firms' calculations as to the desirability of alternative locations, they do not all generate the same structure of investments, the same product-mix, or the same technologies, in the incentive-granting country. These issues deserve more careful theoretical and empirical investigation.

4 DIRECT FOREIGN INVESTMENT AND ALTERNATIVE FORMS OF ORGANISATION

According to conventional industrial organisation theory, vertical integration (internalisation) is more efficient than market exchange when the relationship is on-going, but complex and subject to frequent change. Internalisation improves the flow of information between transactors, reducing the possibilities for the provision of untruthful and misleading data, and reduces the prospect of small numbers bargaining problems. The purchasing firm, in addition to such savings in transactions costs, may also benefit from reduced supply uncertainties, protect itself from foreclosure by vertically integrated rivals, and derive increased scale economies via increased intra-firm specialisation (Williamson, 1975). Internalisation and its capital requirements may also generate significant barriers to others' entry to particular industries.

Foreign ownership thus carries certain potential advantages in entering world markets. Apart from foreign firms' ownership of particular technology and management not readily available to local firms they can bring information about foreign markets, experience and expertise in the many complex facets of international marketing, and influence upon commercial policymakers and customs authorities in home markets (de la Torre, 1974). They may also benefit from scale economies associated with their worldwide operations. (In some instances, foreign firms may restrict exports so as to protect the established markets of the parent firm or other subsidiaries; but this is unlikely to be important in cases where 'fresh' DFI is brought specifically to expand exports.)

The advantages of foreign firms over local ones are obviously most marked in industries where technology is least standardised, scale economies are prevalent, and marketing is most difficult. In other industries they may not possess significant advantages over local firms. Aggregative data comparing foreign firms' export performance with that of local firms may therefore be quite misleading with respect to the potentially important role direct foreign investment and foreign firm participation may play. At the industry level, foreign firms have frequently been found to be relatively effective exporters (e.g. Lall and Mohammad, 1983; see also references in Newfarmer, 1983).

Foreign direct investment of the traditional type, by linking control over investment with a measure of control over international markets, provides some protection to the prospective exporting country against gross miscalculation. Where foreign firms are not directly involved in the profitability of new enterprises they may happily sell equipment or technology, especially if the sales are backed and insured by governments, to more competitors than can eventually be accommodated in world markets. The dispersed and unco-ordinated investment activities of a variety of national firms in developing countries, all competing with one another, may generate excess capacity, worsened terms of trade, and eventually some losers (Cline, 1982).

Oman has pointed out (1983, p. 202) that 'the long-term global investment planning perspective which multinational firms are relinquishing may be assumed by multinational banks and international financial organisations, at least to the extent that host countries require foreign loans to undertake their investment projects'; but there are limits to their capacities in this regard. Besides, from the standpoint of individual national interest the object of 'non-traditional' approaches ('new forms') is presumably to get loose from external control over domestic investment decisions, marketing policies, and the like, The substitution of external bankers for external producing firms, as controlling institutions, would seem to constitute rather limited progress towards the goal of greater independence.

The moves towards global industrial organisation and cartelisation outside the transnationals clearly involve major risks for the developing countries. At their worst they may lead to more MFAs, explicitly and unashamedly discriminating against 'low-cost' producers. Still, there is undoubtedly considerable room for further experimentation and development of non-DFI manufacturing for export.

Some firms, notably some Japanese trading companies and recently others based in Hong Kong, already specialise in the assembly of efficient 'packages' of equipment, know-how, management and marketing skills from a variety of sources. As far as DFI is concerned, Third World multinationals may play an expanding role in manufacturing for export not only within the South but also to the North. Some Third World multinationals have developed considerable specialised knowledge of small-scale and labour-intensive production procedures in the manufacture of standardised products (Wells, 1983; Lall, 1983).

The specifics of relationships between separate contracting firms or between parents and subsidiaries are governed by traditions that vary from country to country. International trading and investment relationships may be formally constrained by international laws, codes and guidelines; but these do not begin to tell the complete story as to how these relationships were built or the conventions by which they are maintained. A complex web of law, economics and custom operates to determine the details of particular relationships and contracts.

In the US it is traditional to deploy batteries of lawyers to work out voluminous contracts specifying in enormous detail how hypothetical circumstances may in future be handled. Changing or unexpected circumstances require altered contracts – and more lawyers. In East and South-East Asia where litigation does not play so prominent a role, there is typically greater care taken in the early stages to investigate the overall circumstances, rather than the strict legalities, of a possible agreement. Once made, there is implicit agreement that the relationship must be flexible, that risks must be shared, and that the details can be worked out when required, provided that there is mutual trust and genuine commitment; if trust is breached, it is understood that the relationship will be terminated.

> Many Overseas Chinese firms have no truck with written contracts, feeling that if you need a contract to hold a man to his obligations you ought not to be doing business with him at all. . . . A company places a small order with a new supplier or sub-contractor as a test of reliability and integrity. Ample opportunity is often deliberately left for cheating. Trust, and the size of the orders, builds up gradually over many years. . . . Lacking enforceable contracts, Overseas Chinese businessmen cannot afford to be aggressive competitors who seek to screw the best deal they can out of their suppliers and customers. They need instead to negotiate deals where both parties benefit, if possible equally. This, above all, is why western and Overseas Chinese businessmen find themselves talking a different language. The idea that everybody can be a winner is strange to western firms – and western business schools. (*The Economist*, 28 April 1984, pp. 82–3)

Other things being equal, trust is probably maximised through internalised transactions, i.e. through relationships of ownership or family ties. In large and more Western oriented firms, where family or traditional modes of interaction are of limited relevance, ownership ties are a prime means of reducing risk and uncertainty, lowering transactions costs, and frequently also deriving economies of scale in information, marketing, sourcing and production systems. As information and management systems become more sophisticated – and computerised – there is likely to be an ever higher efficiency premium upon reliability. Tight control systems seeking to reduce the capital tied up inefficiently in inventories, while necessarily incorporating back-up procedures, build upon absolute reliability of delivery and quality. Modern management and information technology may therefore generate increased tendencies for more centralised control and, quite possibly, internalisation and direct investment.

In principle, the exporting country that is host to a subsidiary engaged in exporting may gain both from the increased stability and from the increased income created by the foreign firm via such internalised organisational arrangements. But there is no guarantee that it will. Moreover, other exporting firms and countries may suffer from lower income and increased uncertainty and instability in consequence of one country's 'success' with such approaches: as they are relatively 'residualised' in what are often fairly thin and sometimes oligopolistically organised markets.

It is striking that there has not been more independent study of the relative advantages of different forms of investment, different governmental policies and performance requirements, and different general relationships between host countries and foreign firms in particular industries, both for firms of varying characteristics and for various actors in different kinds of host countries. Business schools have addressed some of the issues in terms of firms' interests, but little research has been done on others' interests.

5 GOVERNMENT POLICIES

Developing (Host) Countries

Far more important to the prospects for successful manufacturing for export than whether or how foreign firms participate is the overall profit potential from export activities in particular countries and industries. To a substantial degree the short-run determinants of profitability are the product of nature, factor endowment, location, history and other uncontrollables. Governmental policies with respect to exchange rates, tax systems, subsidies, infrastructure provision, licensing and other bureaucratic requirements are usually none the less an important element in the determination of such profitability; and they, of course, are likely to impact upon both foreign and local firms. If exports are to be expanded, government policies must be directed at the provision of the required incentives.

If the desired future trade balance is to materialise from expanded investment activities, whatever their nature, the structure of incentives must encourage import-substituting and exporting activities. There is a vast literature on incentive structures in developing countries, the bulk of which concludes that they have typically been characterised by an anti-export bias and frequently also an anti-tradeables bias (from overvalued currencies). Appropriate exchange rates and a fairly uniform tariff structure is the conventionally recommended recipe for maintaining efficiency and external balance, although due account is also to be taken of the possibility of terms of trade gains through targeted restrictions upon trade, learning effects and infant industry encouragement, and irrational consumer preferences for imported goods and services, all of which are justifications for departures from unified exchange rate systems (Balassa, 1982, pp. 66–71). There remains some disagreement concerning the significance and the potential for 'learning', and therefore about the appropriate degree and character of infant industry policies (e.g. Westphal, 1981; Stewart, 1982; Streeten, 1981). Analogous arguments about learning can be deployed in support of the encouragement of infant national firms, presumably at the expense of foreign firms some of which may be investors or potential investors in the protecting country.

Another set of policy instruments that has been deployed in support of trade objectives is that of performance requirements, either with respect to raising exports or lowering imports. They may, of course, offset the effects of some of the investment incentives. United States data suggest that whereas US affiliates overseas benefit from investment incentives with about the same frequency in developed and developing countries, they are subject to performance requirements (of various kinds, not all trade-related) four times as frequently in the latter countries as in the former. Fully 25 per cent of US affiliates in developing countries were affected by them in 1977; and there was wide intercountry variation (McCulloch and Owen, 1983, p. 342; Safarian, 1983, p. 614). A GATT panel has recently ruled that those relating to domestic procurement and the consequent limitation of imports contravene the GATT whereas those requiring a certain level of export performance do not. This legal distinction, whether or not it is eventually upheld in other cases, seems to have no justification in economics. Performance requirements, unless they are redundant, deflect trade from the channels in which it would otherwise flow and are therefore equally 'distorting' of the market, regardless of their nature. Whether the 'free' market flows generated by imperfect markets are themselves socially efficient is a much larger question (that the GATT has never addressed). It can be argued that some performance requirements move the trading outcome back towards the equivalent of the competitive equilibrium solution that is theoretically optimal, serving to offset restrictive business practices and other real-world distortions that get in the way of efficient overall outcomes.

In some circumstances it may be possible to induce or require direct foreign investors who originally entered production in a developing country location to meet local markets to shift to exporting, but this is typically more difficult than the encouragement of 'fresh' export-oriented investors since it requires alteration of the firms' global production and marketing strategies (Bennett and Sharpe, 1979). It may also involve inefficiencies and large government subsidies to overcome them. The widespread existence of export restrictions – explicit or implicit – in technology contracts and subsidiary operations relating to import-substituting production is evidence that transnational corporate involvement can impede, as well as assist, the expansion of exports.

Project-specific performance requirements, in the form of 'buy-back' agreements, may also be deployed to ensure desired trade effects from new direct foreign investments. With the growth in countertrade and state trading this non-market means of overcoming early marketing problems seems likely to increase in importance.

The deployment of trade-related performance requirements for foreign firms is a matter of growing international concern. If the developing countries that have been most active in their use are to take informed positions in their defence, and if others are to benefit from their experience, it is essential that there be careful assessments of the degree to which they have worked. Have domestic sourcing, minimum export requirements and the like achieved the results that they were intended to achieve? What costs and difficulties have been experienced in their use? How do the costs and benefits of such performance requirements compare with those of alternative policies that could be directed to the attainment of the same objectives? In what circumstances (industries, countries, firms) are these policy instruments likely to be most effective or least effective?

There are many other possible objectives besides balance of payments improvements that might influence the nature of bargains struck with foreign investors, e.g. employment creation, training, local R and D, etc. If development is seen in terms of technical change, productivity improvement and learning-by-doing, these elements of performance are far more important than those relating to relatively short-term trade effects. There have been very few empirical analyses of 'learning', total factor productivity change and their correlates in export-oriented manufacturing as compared with other activities, foreign-owned firms compared with local firms, or combinations thereof. (Some work has been undertaken by Dudley, 1972; Krueger and Tuncer, 1982; among others.)

If capital, management, marketing skills and the like are required in particular export industries, government policy must be directed at their acquisition. But there is no *necessary* connection between these two sets of objectives (exporting and the acquisition of scarce inputs) and therefore no necessity for linking them through the use of only one policy instrument. Some countries nevertheless seek particularly to steer foreign investment into export activities.

One much-discussed means for so linking them are the so-called 'export processing zones' (EPZs). These zones typically provide strong incentives for export activity at the same time that they particularly encourage the participation of foreign-owned firms. They have proven highly controversial because of their enclave character and their obvious reliance upon an inflammable mixture of foreign capital and local low-wage (frequently teenage and female) labour. Their relative importance in manufactured exports from those developing countries that have created them is highly variable but is typically still quite small: e.g. 4 per cent in Korea, 12 per cent in the Philippines, 26 per cent in Sri Lanka, 41 per cent in Malaysia (Maex, 1983, p. 63). If there exists a conventional wisdom on the utility of EPZs in developing countries it is probably summarised in the UNCTC's latest survey as follows:

> Because the viability of the export-processing zones rests to such a considerable extent on the strategies and interests of transnational corporations and on technological developments and because the possibilities for domestic firms to expand operations in the zones are limited, an industrial development strategy relying on export-processing zones alone would not be prudent. In those developing countries for which the availability of unskilled labour is the main, and perhaps the only, economic resource, the export-processing zones may be of value in the initial phase of industrialization. In other developing countries they can be an important supplement to other industrialization efforts. In both cases, the export-processing

zones can create employment opportunities and yield export earnings. In the long run, attempts should be made to further the integration of the zones into the overall industrial development process, for example by the establishment of forward linkages between semi-conductor production and the manufacture of certain consumer electronic products such as calculators, digital watches, and electronic games. The use of export-processing zones in conjunction with import-substitution oriented activities and export-oriented activities of a more general kind, would provide diversified and viable industrial capacity and capability in the developing countries. (UNCTC, 1983, pp. 184–5)

Despite considerable controversy over their role in development, there is a striking dearth of careful empirical economic analysis of their overall costs and benefits. Studies to date are either highly theoretical or purely descriptive – neither very helpful for policymakers trying to decide whether to create EPZs or, if they do, how they should be structured. (A benefit-cost analysis of some EPZs has recently been undertaken in a PhD dissertation by Kai-Y Tsui at the University of Toronto (1987); predictably, the results suggest considerable sensitivity to assumptions with respect to the opportunity cost of labour.) (See also Basile and Germidis, 1984).

Developed (Home) Countries

Governments of the home countries of direct foreign investors have been concerned to encourage their firms with promotional activities, favourable tax treatment and the provision of protection against otherwise uninsurable risks, particularly political ones. These insurance and related arrangements typically cover loans, suppliers' credits, service sales and even some earnings remissions, as well as equity. (For more details on individual home governments' programmes, see OECD, 1983.)

But the importance of these home government policies can easily be exaggerated. The total share of the direct foreign investment stock in developing countries that is covered by governmental insurance arrangements is only about 9 per cent (OECD, 1983, pp. 30–33). No doubt the percentage coverage of new direct investment flows is somewhat larger but most direct foreign investors do not seem to be heavily dependent upon such governmental insurance and guarantee schemes. It is said that such insurance as is desired by direct investors is increasingly being obtained on private markets (UNCTC, 1983, p. 96; OECD, 1983, pp. 117–18). Many elements of uncertainty concerning host country policies and circumstances are not readily covered by insurance contracts. Re-interpretations of the details of contractual arrangements, for example, are far more complex and difficult to consider or protect oneself against in advance than such obvious measures as expropriation, exchange controls, or civil disturbances. There has consequently not been great enthusiasm, even within parts of the originating institution, for the World Bank's complementary Multilateral Investment Insurance Agency. But knowledge as to which types of firms seek which types of insurance in which industries and which countries is scarce.

Home governments providing insurance for their investing firms prefer to do so only for investments in countries with which they have intergovernmental agreements on foreign investment. Bilateral treaties providing for the protection of foreign investments are usually asymmetric in the obligations imposed upon the relevant parties. Foreign owners of capital benefit from 'national' treatment or most favoured nation provisions, assured convertibility of earnings and capital repatriation, fair and prompt compensation upon nationalisation, and the like; the only return to the host country signatory is the increased likelihood that foreign investors will be insured by their home governments against the very events (plus wars and insurrections) which the treaties ostensibly forbid. Vernon has described these treaties as 'patently unbalanced . . . too unbalanced to provide the basis for a durable regime' (1982, pp. 10–11).

Home governments are also subject to other pressures regarding the nature of their promotional, insurance and overseas assistance programmes. The US government, for instance, is mandated not to extend favourable export credit terms to projects that are likely to compete with American products in home markets, and has exerted pressure upon the World Bank similarly to constrain its lending. 'Industrial co-operation' agreements and programmes, such as those run by the EEC through the Lomé Convention, routinely incorporate protectionist biases in their advice, technical assistance and other supports.

The long-standing efforts to construct a code of conduct for transnational corporations under UN auspices continue. Less comprehensive codes and guidelines have been negotiated or are under discussion in the ILO, UNCTAD, and OECD; and there have long been proposals for a 'GATT for investment'. An overall legislative and regulatory framework that seeks to minimise conflict and encourage accommodation in the general global interest remains a worthy aspiration. But what can be agreed in such a way as to cover all sectors and circumstances in a multilateral forum inevitably will be too general to carry many specific teeth. Few expect any of the new codes significantly to affect the flow of new direct investment to developing countries. (More information on their contents may be found in OECD, 1983, and UNCTC, 1983, pp. 95–6 and 107–21.)

The commercial policies of the industrialised countries to which most Third World manufactured exports at present are directed, are obviously of crucial importance to the export prospects of the developing countries. As South–South trade in manufactures expands, the commercial policies of other developing countries will also become increasingly important.

In the former case there is reason to believe that commercial policy may be responsive to domestic political pressures in such a way as relatively to favour imports from subsidiaries or affiliates of home firms; much of this relatively favoured trade is likely to be intra-firm. On the other hand, developing countries' governments can be expected to exert disproportionate bargaining effort on behalf of their own home firms, those that are *not* owned by foreign investors. Other things being equal, the influence of domestic political interests within the industrialised countries is likely to prevail over those of developing country governments, whose weak overall bargaining strength is indicated by the relatively poor results that they have achieved for their exports in developed country markets in successive GATT tariff bargaining rounds. Although econometric investigation of the US tariff is unable to confirm the hypothesis that imports from US-owned firms are particularly well treated in international tariff bargaining (Lavergne and Helleiner, 1984), it seems roughly to accord with observed practice with respect to US non-tariff barriers. Even 'neutral' reductions in trade barriers may disproportionately benefit international firms relative to national ones, particularly in the short term, since they are better able quickly to serve established markets via known external sources and to capture the potential efficiency gains from liberalisation (McCulloch and Owen, 1983, p. 346).

Selective barriers to developing country exports, such as voluntary export restraints, apart from their direct effects upon current trade, can also influence the geographic pattern of further investments in the affected industries, as investors and buyers seek new 'uncontrolled' exporting bases and sources in which to expand the activities that are constrained in their original locations. These incentives for export-oriented direct foreign investment and sourcing in new locations are severely damped, of course, when the trade managing authorities show signs of imposing restraints upon newcomers as soon as they begin to succeed. In Canada, for instance, imports of cotton tailored shirts from Sri Lanka were described as 'disruptive' and restrained when they achieved a level of only 0.02 per cent of total Canadian imports of this product in 1979 (Biggs, 1980, p. 85).

A particularly significant commercial policy inducement for transnational and other firms to locate export-oriented production in developing countries is the value-added tariff, offering customs duty relief on manufactured imports when inputs into the product in question originate in the country that imports the final product. Imports under these provisions reached 7.5 per cent of total US imports in 1982 (USITC, 1984, p. 15). In 1982, 42.7 per cent of the value of these US imports under tariff item 807 (the major relevant item) came from developing countries; since imported US inputs made up a much higher proportion of the total value of the exports in developing countries, their share of dutiable value was only 28.9 per cent. The EEC's scheme, unlike that of the US, requires that the 'outward processing' be undertaken by a firm resident in the EEC in order to qualify for favourable customs treatment. An analogous commercial policy innovation is the special provision made for 'outward processed' textile products in the MFA. Outside the US, there has been very little information or research on the uses and effects of this important set of policies.

Also relevant are the GSP, although it is subject to unilateral withdrawal without compensation and such regional preferential arrangements as the Lomé Convention and the Caribbean Basin initiative. In all of these programmes the rules of origin are crucially important to the determination of their value to the affected developing countries.

The direct effects of home government trade barriers have received quite a lot of research attention. So, in recent years, has the structure of these trade barriers and its political determinants. Interactions between investment and restricted trade flows have not, however, been fully explored. Nor have available data permitted a full investigation of the role of direct foreign investment in the determination of the structure of trade barriers. The distribution of the 'rent' from non-tariff trade barriers and preferential schemes is also relatively unexplored research territory.

6 FURTHER RESEARCH REQUIREMENTS

Despite the new conventional wisdom that export-oriented manufacturing and direct foreign investment deserve significant new encouragement in the developing countries there is still distressingly little known about optimal policies relating to them. In a world of varied market imperfections and a myriad of governmental interventions, advice based on traditional models of pure competition is not persuasive. There is a need for simultaneous analyses of policies towards trade and policies towards investment since together they co-determine the location of global production and the pattern of future trade.

Analysis of direct foreign investment can proceed either in the context of concern with adequate levels and appropriate forms of development finance, or in that of consideration of alternative institutional arrangements for transacting with foreign firms. The research questions asked relate very much to which approach is being pursued. An investigation of financial issues will enquire as to the possibilities of sharing risks and tapping new sources of capital in ways other than through direct foreign investment, and ask whether new flows of direct foreign investment are likely, in fact, to be additional. Research focusing upon forms of economic organisation will consider the benefits and costs of conducting whatever activities are favoured through a variety of 'new forms' of investment and contracting, relative to those done through direct investment packages.

The evidence on the supply elasticity of direct foreign investment is still fairly scanty and inconclusive. More detailed investigation of the 'markets' for different kinds of direct foreign investment – by industry, by market orientation, by types of incentive-offering countries – could improve on recent World Bank research on investment incentives and performance requirements. Investigation of the effects of different types of incentives (or performance requirements) upon firm behaviour and the attainment of broader social objectives is also potentially productive. Particular attention should be paid to the possibility of developing countries' overdoing their incentive programmes through unco-ordinated competition for a relatively inelastic supply of investment.

The analysis of advantages and disadvantages, benefits and costs, of alternative forms of interaction between transnational corporations and host governments has received far more attention from those concerned with business decision-making than it has from those interested in social objectives in the host countries. Not only in the sphere of manufacturing for export but in other industries and activities as well, there should by now be enough developing country experience to permit a systematic empirical investigation of these issues.

There is room for further research on many other aspects of government policies towards foreign direct investment and towards export-oriented manufacturing both in developing countries and in industrialised ones. The effects of 'infant industry' and other 'learning'-oriented policies towards industries and firms in developing countries have not been adequately documented. (Indeed, the correlates of productivity growth have generally received much less research attention than questions of inter-sectoral and inter-industry allocation.) Neither have those of various kinds of trade-related performance requirement. Despite the burst of interest in export processing zones, and the by now considerable experience with them, there have not been enough careful empirical analyses of their costs and benefits either. As far as home country policies are concerned, there is a need for research on the detailed impact of foreign investment insurance and related programmes, exploring the types of firms, industries and countries that are affected by them. Little is known about the effects of value-added tariff and outward processing arrangements in countries other than the US. Nor has there been much research on the role of direct foreign investment in influencing the overall structure of trade barriers and other incentives and disincentives in the international arena, and in earning policy-created rents.

APPENDIX

Table A.1 Share of developing country groups in allocated DAC foreign direct investment flows (net) 1977–81 (percentages)

	1977	*1979*	*1981*
Low-income countries (LICs)	8	5	4
Middle-income countries (MICs)	19	31	27
(of which off-shore centres)	(7)	(19)	(15)
Newly industrialising countries (NICs) (11)	51	61	44
OPEC countries (13)	22	3	25
Total	100	100	100

Source OECD (1983), *Investing in Developing Countries*, p. 21.

Table A.2 Net receipts of geographically allocable DAC foreign direct investment, 1978–81, by developing country groups and selected recipients ($US million)

Group/Recipient	*1978*	*1979*	*1980*	*1981*
LICs	418	434	319	540
of which: Egypt	22	38	27	120
India	18	49	55	72
Niger	20	9	−5	−1
Zaire	98	144	111	67
MICs	1 666	2 796	2 768	3 680
of which: Colombia	79	96	113	193
Peru	66	326	98	231
Philippines	144	330	125	110
Thailand	38	38	217	218
Off-shore banking centres*	1 317	1 703	1 799	1 996
NICs	3 799	5 447	5 125	5 990
of which: Argentina	310	667	880	638
Brazil	1 738	1 533	788	1 256
Hong Kong	252	342	363	964
Korea	184	1	−208	260
Mexico	495	1 048	2 001	1 154
Spain	527	1 233	486	415
OPEC	1 905	257	1 005	3 330
of which: Gabon	9	20	25	27
Indonesia	418	−383	280	2 580
Iran	909	164	81	24
Nigeria	164	−49	92	406
Saudi Arabia	54	73	27	42
Venezuela	184	131	99	296
Total allocated	7 788	8 934	9 217	13 540

Source OECD (1983), *Investing in Developing Countries*, p. 23.
*Bahamas, Bermuda, Cayman Islands, Liberia, Netherlands Antilles, Panama.

Table A.3 Estimated stock* of DAC direct investment in developing countries at end-1981, by country groups and selected host countries (with stock – book value – exceeding $US 1 billion)

Group/Country		*$US Billion*	*Percentage share*
LICs		10.2	7
of which:	India	2.7	
	Zaire	1.6	
MICs		49.1	36
of which:	Bermuda†	5.5	
	Panama†	4.9	
	Bahamas†	3.8	
	Netherlands Antilles†	3.7	
	Malaysia	3.5	
	Peru	3.0	
	Philippines	2.5	
	Colombia	2.0	
	Chile	2.0	
	Liberia†	1.7	
	Trinidad & Tobago	1.3	
	Israel	1.2	
NICs		55.6	41
of which:	Brazil	17.2	
	Mexico	10.3	
	Spain	6.9	
	Argentina	5.6	
	Singapore	3.9	
	Hong Kong	3.8	
	Taiwan	2.3	
	Korea (South)	1.6	
	Greece	1.0	
OPEC		22.3	16
of which:	Indonesia	8.6	
	Venezuela	4.3	
	Nigeria	1.2	
	Libya	1.5	
Europe		11.5	9
Africa		15.5	11
Latin America		71.8	52
Asia		38.4	28
Total		137.2	100

* Including unallocated amounts and Japanese official support for private investment.
† Off-shore Banking Centre.
Source OECD (1983), *Investing in Developing Countries*, p. 25.

References

Balassa, Bela *et al.* (1982) *Development Strategies in Semi-Industrial Economies* (World Bank, Johns Hopkins, Baltimore).

Basile, Antoine and Dimitri Germides, (1984) *Industry in Free Export-processing Zones* (OECD, Paris).

Bennett, Douglas and Kenneth E. Sharpe (1979) 'Transnational Corporations and the Political Economy of Export Promotion: The Case of the Mexican Automobile Industry', *International Organization*, vol. 33, no. 2, Spring, pp. 177–201.

Bergsten, C. Fred (1974) 'Coming Investment Wars?', *Foreign Affairs* (October), pp. 135–52.

Biggs, Margaret A. (1980) *The Challenge: Adjust or Protect?* North–South Institute, Ottawa.

Brecher, Richard A. and Carlos F. Diaz-Alejandro (1977) 'Tariffs, Foreign Capital and Immiserizing Growth', *Journal of International Economics*, vol. 7, no. 4 (November).

Casson, Mark (1979) *Alternatives to the Multinational Enterprise* (London: Macmillan).

Cline, William R. (1982) 'Can the East Asian Export Model of Development be Generalized?', *World Development*, vol. 10, no. 2 (February).

De la Torre, J. (1974) 'Foreign Investment and Export Dependency', *Economic Development and Cultural Change*, vol. 23, no. 1 (October) pp. 133–50.

Dudley, Leonard (1972) 'Learning and Productivity Change in Metal Products', *American Economic Review*, vol. 62, no. 4 (September) pp. 662–9.

Dunning, John H. (1981) *International Production and the Multinational Enterprise* (George Allen & Unwin).

Germides, D., forthcoming, *Policies to Attract Export-Oriented Investment: The Role of Free Export-Processing Zones* (OECD, Paris).

Glover, David (1983) *Contract Farming and the Transnationals*, PhD dissertation, University of Toronto.

Group of Thirty (1984) *Foreign Direct Investment, 1973–1987* (New York).

Guisinger, Stephen (1985) *Investment Incentives and Performance Requirements* (New York: Praeger).

Helleiner, Gerald K. (1982) 'International Trade Theory and Northern Protectionism Against Southern Manufactures', in Gerald K. Helleiner (ed.), *For Good or Evil, Economic Theory and North–South Negotiations* (University of Toronto Press) pp. 47–61.

Helleiner, Gerald K. (1983) 'Direct Foreign Investment and Alternative Forms of External Non-Concessinal Finance for Developing Countries', Seventh World Congress of the International Economic Association (Madrid), mimeo.

Keesing, Donald B. (1983) 'Linking up to Distant Markets: South to North Exports of Manufactured Consumer Goods', *American Economic Review*, vol. 73, no. 2 (May) pp. 338–42.

Krueger, Anne O. and Baran Tuncer (1982) 'An Empirical Test of the Infant

Industry Argument', *American Economic Review*, vol. 72, no. 5, (December) pp. 1142–52.

Lall, Sanjaya and Mohammad Sharif (1983) 'Foreign Ownership and Export Performance in the Large Corporate Sector of India', *Journal of Development Studies*, vol. 20, no. 1 (October) pp. 56–67.

Lall, Sanjaya (1983) *et al.* The New Multinationals, *The Spread of Third World Enterprises* (John Wiley).

Lavergne, Real P. and G. K. Helleiner (1985) 'U.S. Transnational Corporations and the Structure of U.S. Trade Barriers: An Empirical Investigation', in UNCTC, *Transnational Corporations and International Trade: Selected Issues* (New York) ST/CTC/54.

Maex, Rudy (1983) 'Employment and Multinationals in Asian Export Processing Zones', Working Paper No. 26, Multinational Enterprises Programme (Geneva: International Labour Office).

McCulloch, Rachel and Robert F. Owen (1983) 'Linking Negotiations on Trade and Foreign Direct Investment', pp. 334–58, in C. P. Kindleberger and D. Audretsch (eds). *The Multinational Corporation in the 1980s* (Cambridge: The MIT Press).

Nayyar, Deepak (1978) 'Transnational Corporations and Manufactured Exports from Poor Countries', *Economic Journal*, vol. 88, no. 1 (March) pp. 59–84.

Newfarmer, Richard (1983) 'Multinationals and Marketplace Magic in the 1980s', in C. P. Kindleberger and D. Audretsch (eds), *The Multinational Corporation in the 1980s* (Cambridge: The MIT Press) pp. 162–97.

Oman, Charles (1983) *New Forms of International Investment in Developing Countries* (Paris: OECD, Development Centre).

OECD (1983) *Investing in Developing Countries* (Paris).

Radetzki, Marian (1982) 'Has Political Risk Scared Mineral Investment Away from the Deposits in Developing Countries?', *World Development*, vol. 10, no. 1 (January) pp. 39–48.

Reuber, Grant L. *et al.* (1973) *Private Foreign Investment in Development* (Oxford: Clarendon Press, for OECD Paris).

Safarian, A. E. (1983) 'Trade-Related Investment Issues', in William R. Cline (ed.), *Trade Policy in the 1980s* (Washington: Institute for International Economics) pp. 611–37.

Stewart, Frances (1982) 'Industrialization, Technical Change and the International Division of Labour', in Gerald K. Helleiner, (ed.), *For Good or Evil, Economic Theory and North–South Negotiations* (Universitetsforlaget and University of Toronto Press).

Streeten, Paul (1981) 'Outward-Looking Industrialization and Trade Strategies', Paper presented to the North–South Roundtable, Fourth Annual Session, Tokyo/Oiso.

Tsui, Kai-Y. (1987), 'A Social Cost–Benefit Analysis of Export Processing Zones in Some Asian Countries', PhD dissertation, University of Toronto.

United Nations Centre on Transnational Corporations (UNCTC) (1983) *Transnational Corporations in World Development, Third Survey* (New York).

United States International Trade Commission (USITC) (1984) *Imports*

Under Items 806.30 and 807.00 of the Tariff Schedules of the United States, 1979–82 USITC publication 1467 (Washington).
Usher, Dan (1977) 'The Economics of Tax Incentives to Encourage Investment in Less Developed Countries', *Journal of Development Economics*, vol. 4, no. 2 (June) pp. 119–48.
Vernon, Raymond (1982) 'Codes on Transnationals: Ingredients for an Effective International Regime', Harvard Business School, mimeo.
Wallich, Henry C. (1984) 'Insurance of Bank Lending to Developing Countries', *Group of Thirty, Occasional Papers*, No. 15 (New York).
Wells, L. T. (1983) *Third World Multinationals* (MIT Press).
Westphal, L. (1981) 'Empirical Justification for Infant Industry Protection', *World Bank Staff Working Paper*, No. 445 (March).
Westphal, L., Y. W. Rhee and G. Pursell (1979) 'Foreign Influences on Korean Industrial Development', *Oxford Bulletin of Economics and Statistics*, vol. 41, no. 4 (November) pp. 359–88.
Williamson, Oliver E. (1975) *Markets and Hierarchies, Analysis and Antitrust Implications: A Study in the Economics of Internal Organization* (New York: The Free Press).

7 Do Third World Countries Benefit from Countertrade?

Frances Stewart and Harsha V. Singh*

1 INTRODUCTION

In recent years there has been a rapid expansion of unorthodox methods of arranging and financing trade, especially in trade with or between Third World countries. The phenomenon is known as *countertrade* and includes all exchanges of goods and services between nations, which do not consist of a straightforward sale of goods for internationally convertible money, but involve an exchange of goods for goods, or goods for a combination of goods and money, or other unorthodox methods of payment. Traditionally, of course, the socialist countries have accounted for a major share of bilateral deals in world trade. The new phenomenon is the extension of countertrade to the rest of the world. During the late 1970s and early 1980s, for example, it became pervasive in the oil market, as well as in arms deals. In recent years, a number of developing countries – including Nigeria, Malaysia, Pakistan and Indonesia – have explicitly adopted countertrade as an important element in their trading strategies.

The aim of this chapter is to analyse major costs and benefits of countertrade, as a Third World trading strategy. To do so we first provide a brief description of the phenomenon (Section 2) considering the type of deals included (the 'modalities'), a review of the quantitative debate, and of the direction of flows and the nature of goods and services involved in recent deals. Identification of the phenomenon at a rather detailed and concrete level is important because some of the arguments about benefits and costs at a general level miss important elements necessary for any assessment. In Section 3 we consider dominating major motives which have led to

* Frances Stewart is a Fellow of Somerville College, Oxford; Harsha V. Singh is a member of the GATT secretariat. This chapter contains our personal views and does not necessarily represent those of these institutions or of Richard Blackhurst to whom we are grateful for comments on an earlier draft.

the growth of countertrade in deals concerning Third World countries. With this essential background we discuss costs and benefits in Section 4. Section 5 presents our conclusions.

2 A DESCRIPTION

'Modalities'

Countertrade covers a considerable range of deals – a range which is rapidly evolving. There is no general definition of countertrade except that there is an element of reciprocity. The reciprocal component may consist of an immediate transaction or exchange over a protracted period of time, may involve two or more partners, may cover only a small proportion of the transaction as countertrade or may require this component to exceed the value of the initial trade deal. Countertrade is not synonymous with pure barter and usually involves some cash financing (see Jones, 1984).

Countertrade deals have been categorised in a variety of (not always consistent) ways.[1] Sometimes it is difficult to decide when a deal qualifies as countertrade. For example, sometimes there is no contractual agreement involving countertrade, but there may be an understanding that one of the partners will make 'best efforts' to sell the products manufactured by the other partner.

The countertrade categories described here are those that have been commonly distinguished in the literature. A single countertrade deal may span more than one of these categories.

(1) *Barter* is exchange of goods and services for goods and services. Though third parties can be involved, they do not sign the barter agreement. Barter deals are not very common because of their limited flexibility (see, for example, Jones (1984), p. 20). 'In practice, supply of principal exports is often held up until sufficient revenue has been earned from selling the bartered goods.'[2]
(2) *Counterpurchase* appears to be the 'most common form of countertrade'.[3] Two separate contracts are signed for this and each contract has its own financial arrangement. The agreement may vary from a declaration of intent for 'best efforts' to binding commitment which involves a penalty if unfulfilled. These deals usually have a short time frame, i.e. up to three to five years.
(3) *Advance purchase* eliminates risk of non- payment. In this

situation, the receipts from the sales of one of the partners are placed in an escrow or evidence account, to be used later for counterpurchase.

(4) *Offsets* involve the condition that the exporter incorporate inputs from the importing country into its final products. This form of countertrade has been long established in trade in defence systems and aircraft. Now it is becoming a component of deals in other sectors also. Offset deals may or may not involve direct use of the products linked to the initial transaction. Direct offset includes co-production, licensed production, sub-contractor production, overseas investment or technology transfer. Indirect offsets are like counterpurchase and may be part of a wider 'offset package'.

(5) In *buyback*, the supplier of capital plant or equipment agrees to take the future product as part or full payment. These deals involve a much longer time period (e.g. five to fifteen years) compared with counterpurchase. A looser form of this type of an agreement is encompassed in *framework agreements* or long-term protocols or agreements (see OECD, 1981).

(6) *Bilateral agreements*, which use clearing accounts, bind all or some part of the trade between two countries. Normally, the goods must be from a pre-specified list. The value of goods is denominated in artificial accounting units, such as clearing dollars or rupees. Though trade is supposed to balance in a given time period, usually a maximum trade imbalance is specified. Large imbalances in these accounts could lead to *switch trading*, which involves swapping documents and destination of goods and may involve complex deals amongst several buyers, sellers and brokers across different markets.

The Extent of Countertrade

There are very wide variations in estimates of the extent of countertrade in world trading, ranging from less than 5 per cent to 40 per cent.[4] While some official estimates suggest that countertrade constitutes only 8 per cent of world trade, the US Department of Commerce has suggested that one-quarter of all world trade involves some form of barter. These variations derive from differences in definition, differential access to statistics on countertrade, which are in any case dubious because of the secrecy involved in many deals, the fact that some deals represent only a portion of a larger deal and guesstimates are therefore needed, and the inclusion of deals in process of negotiation in some estimates, while a number of deals are initiated but break down before completion.

The very low estimates certainly understate the true extent (for example, the IMF put forward an estimate of 1 per cent of world trade in 1983) but figures of 30 per cent or 40 per cent certainly exaggerate its current significance. The true figure is probably between 10 per cent and 20 per cent of world trade, with the proportion depending on the definition adopted. This can be seen by estimating countertrade separately by region.[5] Table 7.1 shows estimates of countertrade based on two assumptions about the significance of countertrade in the trade of different regions with different parts of the world. The upper estimates (A) are, we believe, unrealistically high. They indicate that, at most, countertrade amounts to 25 per cent of world trade. The lower estimates (B) represent a more realistic figure. This suggests that countertrade may account for around 15 per cent of world trade.

Despite disagreement about absolute quantities, there is general agreement that countertrade has been growing rapidly in the 1980s, especially in the trade of developing countries. According to one estimate, the number of deals increased by 50 per cent in 1981, over 60 per cent in 1982 and over 100 per cent in 1983.[6] In the early 1980s, 88 countries either had formal countertrade regulations or had initiated deals, compared with about 12 countries in the early 1970s, according to a survey of US industrial companies conducted by the National Foreign Trade Council. The increase has been especially marked in deals involving Third World countries as at least one of the partners. A number of countries now include countertrade as an acknowledged and important element in their trade strategy; this extends beyond the socialist countries and the major oil exporters to such countries as Brazil, Pakistan, Malaysia, Colombia, Argentina and Turkey.

The fall in the oil price in 1986, together with the collapse of several major companies involved in countertrade, is likely to have led to a slowdown in the growth of countertrade, but the phenomenon will remain a persistent element in trading options of Third World countries.

Table 7.2 lists countries[7] reported to have conducted countertrade deals with other non-ETA countries since 1983 and shows the broad

Table 7.1 Total trade (exports plus imports) and countertrade amongst regions as a share of global trade under different hypothetical assumptions

Trading regions	*Share of world trade in 1984 (%)*	*Two sets of assumptions about share of countertrade in total trade**		*Share of countertrade in total trade under the two assumptions*	
		A	*B*	*A*	*B*
1. Amongst Eastern Trading Area†	6	90	90	5.4	5.4
2. Eastern Trading Area and industrial countries	6	20	15	1.2	1
3. Developing Countries and Eastern Trading Area	3	100	50	3	1.5
4. South and Central America and world (ex-ETA)	9	50	20	4.5	1.8
5. South and East Asia and world (ex-ETA)	15	10	3	1.5	0.45
6. Other Developing Countries and World (ex-ETA)	12	50	20	6	2.4
7. Rest (mainly between industrialised market economies)	49	6	2	3	1.5
Total	100			24.6	14.1

* Estimates based on Barovick (1986) for US; OECD (1985) for developing countries; OECD (1981), Eastern Europe; Agarwala (1984), Indonesia; Sherwell (1985), Philippines; Dodwell (1986), China and Eastern Europe; Richter (1982), Eastern Europe.

† Eastern Trading Area (non-market economies): Albania, Bulgaria, Czechoslovakia, German Democratic Republic, Hungary, Poland, Romania, USSR, China, Mongolia, N. Korea and Viet Nam.

Source UNSO COMTRADE Data Base.

products countertraded. This shows that a large number of countries, both developed and developing, have resorted to countertrade in the recent past. The list includes all the large debtors except Morocco, all the major members of OPEC except Kuwait and Dubai, and seventeen members of OECD. It is also clear that countries using countertrade included developing countries which do not suffer from immediate foreign exchange problems. It should be noted that the list is not exhaustive.

Countries with a large number of countertrade partners are to be found among both developed and developing countries in the deals reported in Table 7.2. Countries in both categories exported primary commodities as well as manufactured products, although oil was exported in countertrade deals only by developing countries.[8] Most developing countries and five developed countries exported primary products. The trading pattern associated with countertrade broadly follows overall trading patterns. Of the 52 developing countries listed in Table 7.2 for which there is information on commodities exchanged, over 90 per cent of the countries included primary products (including oil) in their countertrade exports, while just over half the countries exported only primary products.

Manufactures, technology, etc. formed the exclusive export of just five countries (Somalia, Singapore, Taiwan, Syria and South Korea) and a part of the countertrade exports in another twenty countries. The import composition was balanced between primary commodities and manufactures, with about one-fifth of the developing countries importing only primary products, one-fifth only manufactures and three-fifths both. The manufactured exports of developing countries were in relatively less sophisticated products.

Among developing countries, two countries out of the sixteen for which there is information exported only primary products (New Zealand and Australia); nine only manufactures, civil engineering, etc. and five both. 87 per cent of developed countries' imports included some primary products (44 per cent were only primary products), and two out of sixteen countries imported only manufactures (including defence).

Defence products were exported by three developed countries – France, UK and the USA – via countertrade. But these countries accounted for 45 per cent of the developed–developing country trading partners. In the case of the USA, it has been reported that defence-related offsets accounted for $US5.8 billion out of $US7.1 billion worth of US countertrade in 1984.[9] Defence products were also exported by the Republic of Korea, Taiwan Province and Brazil but it must be noted that defence deals are probably under-reported as they generally are surrounded by secrecy.

Table 7.2 Reported recent countertrade by different market-economy countries (period covered: 1982–85)

Country	*Number of countertrading partners*		*Type of commodity countertraded*	
	Developed	*Developing*	*Exports*	*Imports*
Developing countries				
Algeria	1	1	OM	PM
Angola		1	O	PMC
Egypt	2	2	PM	MC
Ethiopia		1	P	M
Ghana	1	1	P	P
Kenya	1	1	P	P
Mozambique		1	N	N
Nigeria	3	3	OPM	OPM
Sierra Leone		1	P	N
Somalia		1	M	M
Sudan		1	P	N
Tanzania		4	PM	MC
Togo	1		O	C
Tunisia	1		N	N
Burkina Faso		1	P	P
Zambia		1	N	N
Zimbabwe		2	P	N
Bangladesh		3	PM	P
Burma		2	P	PM
India	4	6	PMC	OPM
Indonesia	6	4	PM	PMC
South Korea	2	9	DMC	OPM
Malaysia	4	10	OPC	PDMC
Nepal		1	N	N
Pakistan	2	3	PM	OPM
Philippines		4	PM	PM
Singapore		1	M	C
Sri Lanka		2	P	OP
Taiwan		1	DMC	O
Thailand		8	P	OPMC
Abu Dhabi	1		O	M
Libya	3	2	O	PC
Iran	6	8	O	PDMC
Iraq	5	8	OP	PDMC
Jordan	2	4	PMC	OPMC
Qatar	3	2	O	PMC
Saudi Arabia	2		O	DMC
Syria		1	C	O
Argentina	1	1	OP	OC
Brazil	1	14	OPDMC	OPMC
Chile	1		N	N

Colombia	3	1	P	MN
Costa Rica	1	3	PM	PM
Dominican Republic	1	1	P	M
Ecuador	1	4	PMC	OPM
El Salvador		1	N	N
Guatemala	2	1	P	O
Guyana		2	P	OP
Jamaica	1	1	P	PM
Mexico	3	5	OPM	OPMC
Nicaragua		4	PM	OM
Panama		1	P	P
Paraguay	1		P	M
Peru	1	1	OPM	PMC
Trinidad and Tobago		2	OM	PM
Uruguay	1	3	P	OMC
Venezuela	2	3	OM	OPMC
China	4	14	OPMC	PMC
Developed countries				
Australia	1	2	P	M
Austria	1	1	N	O
Belgium	1	1	M	N
Canada	2	3	MC	OPM
Finland		1	M	PM
France		11	DMC	OPM
West Germany		3	MC	O
Greece		2	PC	O
Israel	1	5	M	OF
Italy		4	M	OF
Japan	1	9	PMC	OFM
New Zealand	1	1	P	OM
Turkey	1	2	C	O
Spain	1	1	N	N
Sweden		2	M	P
Switzerland	1	2	C	D
UK	1	4	DM	OPN
USA	7	18	OPDM	OPMC

O = Oil and oil products
P = Other primary products
D = Defence equipment
M = Other manufactures
C = Other: includes civil engineering and construction, services, technology transfer and miscellaneous
N = Not known

Source Helmut Ferenz, *Special Transactions in Third World Trade*, August 1984 reported in Avramovic (1985), 'Commodity Problem: What Next?', OECD (1985), *Counter-trade: Developing Country Practices* and several newspapers and periodicals for the period 1984 onwards.

The Reality of Countertrade

The following examples of recent deals give a more concrete idea of the phenomenon of countertrade:

Brazil–Nigeria came to a $US1 billion agreement, with Nigeria exporting crude oil in exchange for raw materials, spare parts and manufactures;
Brazil–Iran: Iran exported oil in exchange for chickens from Brazil;
Brazil–West Germany: iron ore for submarines;
Israel–Guatemala: arms for Guatemalan goods using an escrow account;
Turkey–USA: purchase of F-16 fighters from General Dynamics for investment in agro-business in Turkey;
Malaysia–South Korea: oil, rubber and timber products for electrical goods and patrol boats;
France–Middle Eastern countries: Mirages for oil;
USA–Saudi Arabia: oil for 747s from Boeing worth $US1 billion;
Soviet Union–Peru: Peru supplied gold, silver and manufactures to the Soviet Union as an offset to debt obligations;
Soviet Union–Finland: 25 per cent of Finland's trade is tied up on countertrade deals with the Soviet Union;
Greece has plans to acquire military construction equipment from Japan, Czechoslovakia and the Soviet Union in exchange for Greek goods.

The examples show that countertrade can be used for various kinds of trade. A large amount is among socialist countries and between socialist and other countries. This is not a new phenomenon but has always been the socialist countries' dominant method of trade. The new phenomenon is the North–South and South–South trade financed in this way. In the deals reported in Table 7.2, about one-half are between developing countries, 45 per cent between North and South, and only 5 per cent among developed countries.[10] Not all countertrade is government to government. In the case of Boeing and General Dynamics, large private firms used countertrade methods. For the most part, Northern partners consist of large companies, while in the South governments predominate in organising deals. For the purpose of analysis, the deals may be divided into the following types:

Type 1: Military goods exchanged for other goods (mainly raw materials). These deals, though large in amount, have so far been concentrated in the exports of three developed and three developing countries.

Type 2: Raw materials exchanged for (non-military) manufactures, technology, construction, etc. This is a typical pattern for exchange between more industrialised and less industrialised countries and occurs both in North–South and South–South deals.

Type 3: Manufactures exchanged for non-manufactures: this has occurred on a small scale in some South–South deals.

Type 4: Primary products for primary products. This is a common feature of many South–South deals.

Hybrid deals also occur with some primary products and some manufactures being exported by one or both partners.

Table 7.3 shows an analysis of all South–South deals in 1982–3.

Table 7.3 Number of South–South deals, 1982–3

Type 1:	Military for other	2
Type 2:	Raw materials for manufactures, etc.	28
Type 3:	Manufactures, etc. for manufactures, etc.	4
Type 4:	Primary for primary	18

Source Helmut Ferenz, *Special Transactions in Third World Trade*, August 1984, quoted in Avramovic (1985), 'Commodity Problem: What Next?'

3 MOTIVES FOR COUNTERTRADE

The motives for countertrade are numerous and varied. To complete a deal both parties must consider that there is some advantage to be gained as compared with normal trade. Since transaction costs are usually greater for countertrade, the perceived advantage must be significant. The perceived advantage may consist of improved access to markets, improved terms of trade, reduced hard currency requirements, improved payment prospects or increased certainty with respect to market access or payments.

Northern Motives

(i) For companies in the North, the prime motivation is to secure *sales*. Unless they enter countertrade deals, companies may not be able to sell their products at all to countries with limited hard currency, strict import restrictions and a policy of countertrade deals. It is likely, then, that countertrade will be pushed more, when markets are depressed (i.e. during recession). But, even in the absence of recession, large companies are always seeking to protect and increase their share of the world market, and countertrade represents one way of achieving this. However, companies will accept higher costs (lower effective prices) for countertrade deals when markets are scarce because of recession. Countertrade offers companies the possibility of hidden and discriminatory price-cutting.

(ii) A second motivation of companies in the North is to ensure some *payment* for their sales, or some form of repatriation of profits from countries in payment difficulties. Therefore countertrade is likely to be more prevalent, the greater the financial problems of Third World countries.

(iii) *Political* motivation may support some countertrade deals; for example, an industrialised country may want to secure especially good terms of trade for a country for political reasons (e.g. Cuba), or may want to promote military sales for political reasons, and countertrade may be the preferred way of doing so (this might underly some US military countertrade deals with, for example, Turkey). The use of economic power to support political aims is also facilitated by countertrade since countertrade deals involve specific decisions, which may be used as a political instrument more readily than normal market transactions.

Southern Motives

(i) Primary producers may use countertrade as a means of *circumventing agreements* on price and quality. This was a prime motive of many of the oil deals in the early 1980s. Countertrade permitted avoidance of OPEC regulations, and may indeed have contributed to the near collapse of the OPEC arrangement in 1986. There may have been a similar motive behind some of the deals involving tin. All the primary commodities which have price setting agreements or collusive agreements among sellers have been countertraded.

(ii) *Improved terms of trade* (and/or increased certainty) has been a motive in other deals involving primary products, such as Cuban sugar exports to the USSR and some bauxite deals between Caribbean countries and the USA and the USSR. The absence of a free market in some major primary commodities – including sugar and bauxite – has meant that countries may only get market access at all or on good terms if they negotiate deals (for which the recipients may have political as well as economic motivation).

(iii) The *financial crisis* for many Third World countries has meant, paradoxically, that they may prefer to receive goods rather than hard currency for their exports, because hard currency receipts are likely to be pre-empted for payment of arrears and would not be available for imports. This seems to have been an important motive in countries trying to bypass the IMF, including Nigeria, Brazil and Tanzania, for example.[11] In some cases, countertrade lessens dependence on trade credit and thus may strengthen bargaining power in debt negotiations.[12]

(iv) For deals involving exports of manufactured or semi-manufactured products from developing countries, a prime motive for Third World countries has been to secure *greater and more certain market access* for their exports in circumstances where there are restrictions on imports of manufactures. There is also a motive for companies in advanced countries seeking sales in Third World or ETA markets. For trade with advanced countries, this possibility is more remote, but may arise because of the restrictions on imports of manufactures from developing countries in Northern countries, which may be avoided by countertrade. This is especially likely to apply to trade subject to non-tariff barriers, although gains made by one developing country may be at the expense of another. For trade with other developing countries also in financial difficulties, countertrade may be the only way of securing market access, given the lack of convertible currencies to finance imports. Brazil has extended its export markets in Third World countries by use of countertrade deals.

(v) Countertrade in manufactures may also permit developing countries to secure markets despite non-competitiveness of their manufactured exports because of low quality and/or high price. Straightforward price competition may be ruled out by the exchange rate policy being pursued by the country, while countertrade permits hidden price discounts (a form of *selective devaluation*).

(vi) In a world of rapid changes in environment – including changes in trade restrictions as well as economic factors – countertrade may be believed to *offer more certainty*, which may be desired by countries trying to plan their industrialisation, trade and payments in a co-ordinated way. Countertrade deals may be planned in advance and sales will be less dependent on the vagaries of the market. This seems to have been a prime motivation in Pakistan's recent decision to greatly expand the role of countertrade.

While these motives are varied, they have one important feature in common. They all arise from 'imperfections' in the world trade and payments system, i.e., from the fact that the free trade/perfect competition/fully employed model of the world economy, often assumed in trade theory, does *not* exist in the real world. For developed countries, the imperfections consist in the existence of oligopolistic companies seeking to increase their market share, and the depressed markets arising from recession and payments problems; for the developing countries, distortions and restrictions in the primary product market (some largely created by the developing countries themselves, e.g. in oil), some by the developed countries (the carve-up, for example, of the markets for bananas, sugar and bauxite), and restrictions on access to markets in manufactures in both developed and developing countries are a major underlying factor; the manifold restrictions on financial payments and exchange rates are a further important element. And for all countries lack of certainty lies behind many deals.

The fact that these deals arise from imperfections is very important to the assessment of countertrade, because it means it is quite wrong to take a free trade/full employment world as a model against which countertrade should be judged. Yet this is the assumed 'counter factual' in many assessments of countertrade.

4 COSTS AND BENEFITS

The major trade and financial institutions have taken a firm stand against countertrade. A report from the Fund,[13] for example, states that

> The Fund is generally concerned with their [countertrade deals] proliferation because they may be seen as undermining the objective of the multilateral trading system, the promotion of which was a basic objective for the setting up of the Fund, and also because they share many of the micro-economic disadvantages that are common in bilateral payments arrangements.

It has been reported by senior officials in a number of developing countries that the single most important factor constraining countertrade deals for government procurement and parastatals is the fear that this would jeopardise their IMF packages (see Kopinski, 1985). Clearly, this perspective is not fully accepted by many decision-makers – as indicated by the growing prevalence of countertrade. In most deals involving industrialised countries, the decision-makers are private companies, so that the existence of countertrade indicates private advantage, but does not necessarily reflect government perceptions of the social value of these deals. However, the Chairperson of the US International Trade Commission, summarising their recent study on countertrade, stated that it

> helped to maintain or increase existing levels of employment and plant capacity due to new business generated by such sales agreements . . . other benefits from countertrade include larger and more efficient production runs, lower unit costs, increased capital formation and the development of new technology (Ericson, 1985).

In Third World countries, there is near universal government involvement in countertrade deals. It therefore appears that many Third World governments believe the gains may extend beyond the private beneficiaries to the society at large.

From a Third World government perspective, the case *for* countertrade is that it permits a greater level of activity and a higher level of income in the short term than would be possible without it. It is also (implicitly) assumed that these apparent short-term benefits would not be offset by medium-term costs, although for countries in crisis a certain level of medium-term costs might be judged worth incurring for the sake of short-term gains.

In order to assess the costs and benefits of countertrade, it is necessary to consider therefore:

(1) Short-term consequences for levels of income;
(2) medium-term consequences for levels of income;
(3) Effects on organisation and use of resources.

The assessment is complicated: first, the variety of deals and motives makes generalisation difficult; what follows will tend to be selective, both in discussion and conclusions. Secondly, a single Third World country might gain (either in the short or medium term) although Third World countries taken collectively may not. Thirdly, as noted already, any assessment depends critically on the assumed alternatives. In the short run, this is less problematic since the alternatives are more or less known, but the issue is more complicated and controversial in assessing medium-term costs and benefits, since the framework of trade and payments will itself be affected by decisions made on current trading strategies.

Short-term Effects

If more or less perfect competition and free or open trade prevailed in the world, there would be a general presumption that countertrade deals would involve losses for one or other partner (except in very special and unlikely circumstances where both gain a terms-of-trade advantage over the rest of the world as a result of the deal because, as a result of the countertrade deal, there is a shortfall of the commodity and a rise in price in trade with the rest of the world (see Caves, 1974)).

In the normal case, prices are likely to diverge from market prices in such a way that one of the partners will gain at the other's expense, in terms of trade, by changing terms of trade compared with the free market price. In general, developing countries are not likely to be the gainers in such transactions when trading with developed countries – being normally in a weaker bargaining position and less skilled negotiators – so that if the terms of trade do change they are likely to be adverse to the Third World partner. There is some empirical evidence confirming this: for example, Jones states that 'the usual practice is for the countertraded export from a developing country to be sold at a discount', quoting one study which found an average discount of 12 per cent. However, another study showed that India improved its terms of trade in a deal with the USSR (Outters-Jaeger, 1979), but paid a higher price for imports in a deal encompassing Australia, Czechoslovakia and East Germany (*Financial Times*, 4 October 1984). Moreover, political circumstances can lead to improved terms of trade for the developing country, as with Cuban sugar. The likelihood of an adverse movement in the terms of trade has led a number of countries to exclude some hard currency exports from countertrade (e.g. Colombia with respect to coffee, Peru with respect to minerals and fish).

Within the South, the bargaining power may not be as unbalanced, but inequality in bargaining strength and negotiating ability may lead to a relative loss in terms of trade for the weaker partner. In addition, there may be heavier transaction costs than with normal trade. This clearly occurs when one partner does not want the items acquired and has to dispose of them subsequently in third markets. These extra transaction costs may be borne by one or other partner, or shared. Again it seems probable that the weaker developing country would bear disproportionate costs because of weak bargaining power. In one respect, developing countries may gain in terms of trade – that is, it may not pay as much interest costs on trade finance – but it is probable that such gains will be offset by other costs in the deal.

It has been suggested that export earnings would be more *stable* with countertrade than market transactions, which could offset any loss in terms of trade. However, empirical investigation of trade in Egypt, Ghana, India, Sri Lanka and Tunisia in the 1970s showed that stability was significantly greater with barter-like trade than multilateral trade only in the case of Sri Lanka (see Outters-Jaeger, 1979). But this evidence mainly concerns Eastern-bloc trade and not the more recent developments in countertrade.[14]

For most deals, then, the terms of trade are likely to be worse for the weaker (often Southern) partner than with market transactions. If markets were perfect, and a country could sell any quantity at the existing price, countertrade deals would usually not make much sense, the one major exception being where any market-generated foreign exchange would be immediately pre-empted for payment of arrears and debt servicing. But in all other circumstances, market transactions would be preferable. However, most countertrade deals occur precisely because market transactions at prevailing market prices are *not* an option, because of import restrictions, market-sharing arrangements, etc. In that context, deterioration in terms of trade may be accepted or even sought as a means of enlarging markets and/or of providing immediate import finance. The 'bottom line' as to the short-run effects of the deals on levels of income and activity is whether they increase or decrease the volume of imports to which a country has access. The generation of import capacity through countertrade depends on three elements – price, quantity sold and proportion of earnings available to finance imports. Ignoring the last factor, the issue is whether the terms-of-trade loss is compensated by more than proportionate increase in market size.

To analyse this, it is necessary to distinguish between primary products and manufactures.

Some primary product markets come near to fulfilling the perfect competition model: there are world markets to which any producer has access, and neither price nor quantity is likely to be significantly improved by countertrade deals as compared with market transactions. Countertrade deals may permit more retained earnings for exports, but otherwise will not have major advantages. But there are many other primary product markets where the world market is dominated by cartels – of producers or processing and marketing companies – or where industrialised country governments play a dominant role in determining price and quantity. In these 'dominated' markets, countries may gain a temporary or even permanent advantage by countertrade deals. Very many primary commodities fall into this category to a greater or lesser extent – sugar, bananas, bauxite, tin, oil, plutonium, wheat, are all examples where some governments' decisions (or those of a few companies) may significantly alter the market. In all 'dominated' markets, individual countries may have much to gain by countertrade. But collectively, Third World countries gain much less because to some extent increased market share by one country will be at the expense of reduced share of others, while if all Third World countries try to gain market share by accepting reduced prices, total foreign exchange earnings may fall. (The estimates of elasticities by Stern *et al.* (1976), Cline *et al.* (1978), and Godfrey (1985) show that many primary commodities have inelastic demand.) Where Third World market share exceeds the price elasticity of demand, output restriction and price appreciation would offer higher levels of foreign exchange in the short or medium term. Developing countries could avoid the fall in their overall earnings by co-ordinating production and sales. But problems of individual countries may overrule these collective considerations. This is especially likely with depressed demand or excess supply for exports, i.e. the conditions which encourage countertrade.

If Third World countries – or a relevant subset of countries – wish to collaborate to counter some of these effects, they should draw up a list of commodities where such a situation is believed to prevail and develop guidelines for policies towards quantities, prices, exchange rate and countertrade deals, which would be in the medium-term interest of countries individually as well as collectively.

While such considerations apply to many major primary commodities, there is still some room for manoeuvre in most commodities on aggregate market size, in 'dominated' markets. For example, the US strategic stockpiles may increase or reduce the size of world markets significantly; decisions on protection and production may influence the size of the Third World market for other items also produced by industrialised countries (sugar is the most obvious example); and in the planned economies the size of the market may be greatly changed by policy decisions. These exceptions – all occurring where pure market forces do not prevail – create room for countertrade deals which increase Third World earning capacity.

Although primary commodity markets appear to offer less potential for gains for countertrade than manufactures, market transactions (accompanied by much intervention, specially from industrialised countries) have been rather largely unfavourable to primary producers. Prebisch's thesis of tendencies to deteriorating terms of trade for primary producers has gained support from recent developments. A more interventionist approach by the Third World – of which co-ordinated countertrade could play a role – might therefore be worth pursuing.

For manufactures, where markets are evidently not perfect, worsening in terms of trade is an acknowledged means of increasing market share. Devaluation represents the most straightforward way of achieving this terms-of-trade deterioration. An overvalued exchange rate generally leads to both static and dynamic inefficiencies in the economy. In that context, the use of countertrade as a device for avoiding or postponing desirable devaluation may offer short-run benefits compared with maintaining the overvalued exchange rate and having no countertrade, but serious costs compared with correcting the exchange rate. However, there are circumstances when across-the-board devaluation of a magnitude sufficient to correct the disequilibrium is either undesirable or even impossible to achieve. For example, countries whose exports are composed to a large extent of certain commodities (e.g. oil, copper) may not want to change the exchange rate for these commodities, but may want to change the manufacturing exchange rate. Countries may wish to avoid the inflationary effects of major devaluations – which can be so large that the real exchange rate actually appreciates, following nominal devaluation.[15] In these circumstances, real devaluation of the magnitude desired may not be possible. Since 1980, countries in sub-Saharan Africa have recorded substantial and accelerating appreciation in their real exchange rate, despite a large number of nominal devaluations (World Bank, 1986).

Countertrade offers a way of introducing selective devaluation, in circumstances where a real change in the exchange rate across the board is not desired, for reasons such as these. In some circumstances, it can be a short-run device to permit gradual elimination of major disequilibrium, through successive exchange rate changes. However, if countertrade is used as a substitute for needed correction across the board in the exchange rate, it could result in resource misallocations and prolonged disequilibria.

Countertrade may be equivalent to a highly *selective* devaluation (being selective with respect to commodity, country and transaction). In addition, countertrade deals may bypass non-tariff import restrictions, such as quotas, especially in developing countries, where devaluation would not, and may also help in the export of low-quality products. Consequently, countertrade can be a valuable instrument for promoting manufactured exports, especially where there are problems with across-the-board devaluation, or there are non-tariff import restrictions, or if other competitors offer the inducement of countertrade in their trade deals.

These conditions are especially likely to apply to trade between Third World countries. The majority of developing countries have been facing foreign exchange difficulties in the 1980s and most countries have imposed tight import restrictions. Many also have adopted austerity measures to restrain imports. In Latin America GDP *per capita* fell by 1.0 per cent per annum from 1980–85; in Africa it fell by 2.6 per cent per annum. In Latin America imports (in current prices) fell by nearly 40 per cent from 1980–85, and by nearly 20 per cent in Sub-Saharan Africa.[16] Substantial levels of industrial excess capacity have emerged. Rates of capacity utilisation of one-half or less are quite common.[17] In these circumstances, shortage of foreign exchange is holding back imports, investment and output. Countertrade agreements may permit higher levels of output, employment and investment for both partners; in these circumstances the alternative is often not a market transaction *but no transaction at all*.

Effects in the short run: The analysis of the short-run effects has suggested that countertrade deals are likely to lead to terms-of-trade deterioration compared with market transactions for Third World countries trading with the North. Where this generates more import finance because it leads to a more than proportionate market expansion (trade creation), it is likely to be worthwhile. This may occur for a few exporters in some primary product markets which are already heavily 'distorted' by cartels and government interventions. For primary products, however, the effects on terms of trade should be carefully assessed before going ahead with the deals.

Deals involving manufactured exports from Third World countries are more likely to be advantageous than those involving primary products, offering higher levels of capacity utilisation, incomes and employment in manufacturing. It should be noted, however, that the majority of Third World countertrade deals do not consist of manufactured exports (see Table 7.2).

Medium-term Effects

On the whole, it may be assumed that most deals are perceived to offer short-term gains to both partners, or they would not be accepted. But is this at the cost of medium-term losses?

The medium-term losses result from reduced competitive pressures to trade on lines of comparative advantage, and to improve export efficiency over time. In this respect, the considerations are very similar to those often discussed with reference to import protection, except that countertrade does involve exports, and therefore generates more external pressures to increase efficiency than pure import protection. Some dynamic losses would be faced in countertrade – with respect both to allocational and export efficiency – compared with free trade. But against this there could be dynamic advantages of greater certainty and of learning generated by experience. In addition, the higher short-run levels of imports should permit higher levels of investment, sustaining medium-term growth. In both sub-Saharan Africa and Latin America, there have been sharp declines in investment in the 1980s: if these were reversed, this could do more for growth over the medium term than the possible negative allocational or efficiency effects. To the extent that free trade is not the real alternative, but rather no-trade and import protection, the dynamic effects of countertrade in promoting efficiency are likely to be positive.

From a broader perspective, much depends on what happens to the world finance and trading system as a whole. Some see the growth of countertrade deals as leading to the break-up of the multilateral trading system, with substantial losses for all countries. Others would see countertrade as a constructive and trade-creating response to a very restrictive trading environment. Multilateralising countertrade (for example, by payments arrangements among Third World countries) would then offer advantages of both trade and protection, with greater trade links between Third World countries, combined with protection against others (for some advantages of Third World trade, see Stewart, 1984). The recent emergence of agencies providing information to facilitate multilateral countertrade is a first step in multilateralising countertrade and shows the potential for such a move.

But again the relative merits of these alternatives depend on broader developments. If the industrialised countries resumed rapid growth and fairly open economies on the lines of the 1960s, the advantages of an open trading environment for Third World countries would become very strong. But if the circumstances of the 1980s were to become prolonged, options which limited Southern dependence on the North and increased Southern links in trade and finance would have major advantages. Countertrade offers one way of promoting South–South trading links; discriminating tariff or payments arrangements are other (possibly preferable) alternatives.

In practice, countries do not have to make once-and-for-all choices, but can and do switch as events develop (see Kopinski, 1985; Outters-Jaeger, 1979). Consequently, while the medium-term effects could be seriously disadvantageous in some circumstances, countries should be able to opt back into a freer market environment if they wish. Probably of more consequence than the medium-term effects on growth, however, are the effects on internal organisation and use of resources, to be considered below.

Organisation and Use of Resources

The recent history of countertrade deals suggests tendencies in relation to organisation and use of resources.

(a) *Organisation*. Countertrade deals tend to be associated with large companies (public or private). In the North, almost all transactions concern very large companies. In the Third World, the government (or government-appointed agent) acts as an intermediary, so the suppliers or consumers may be small companies. But, as with all administrative decisions, there are major economies of scale in dealing with a few large units as against many small ones. For the same reason, high-value products may be preferred to low-value ones. Institutional arrangements can be devised to offset the bias towards bigness. Where countertrade is intended to cover a large proportion of a country's manufactured exports (as in Pakistan), a conscious effort will be needed to devise institutional mechanisms so that small producers can participate as fully as large ones.

The large role of administration in countertrade also makes such deals susceptible to corruption. This was an explicit criticism of

Nigerian deals that led to a committee of enquiry in Nigeria which reported 'that former government officials and some private individuals have exploited the deals for their own financial gain'.[18] This is not a unique feature of countertrade but is a tendency associated with any administrative decisions involving large sums of money, especially where large companies stand to gain or- lose a lot from the deal. What countertrade does is to extend the area of corruption-prone decisions, so that special care is needed in this area.

(b) *Use of resources*. There is a definite pattern of resource use associated with countertrade – a pattern which may be a consequence of the bias in favour of large companies and high-value products noted above. In manufactures from the North, high technology items, and especially military sales, dominate. The ITC survey of 500 US corporations found that military-related offsets accounted for over 80 per cent of all sales agreements involving countertrade. Non-military items included computers, aerospace products, communications and electronics. Examination of all countertrade deals where the specific products were described in the *Financial Times* over a two-year period (1983–5) showed *no* basic needs-type products in any deal involving Northern manufactures.

Countertrade between North and South therefore tends to involve use of imports for military and high-technology uses and not for basic needs. To the extent that resources are fungible, this may not alter the actual pattern of resource use, but at times of great foreign exchange scarcity, and where countertrade accounts for a considerable portion of a country's trade, the countertrade pattern could seriously affect resource allocation in a direction which may be undesirable.

This feature of countertrade is less marked with deals involving Southern manufacturers, where consumer products and simple producer products often feature. For instance, jute textiles have been exported in countertrade by Bangladesh and simple textiles by Mozambique, as well as in a number of other cases. A detailed study of earlier deals (Jones, 1984) showed the main manufactured products exported by developing countries to be textiles, plastics and some wood products.[19] Processed foods are also a frequent component. In principle, and to some extent in practice, South–South countertrade could involve appropriate products (with basic needs goods, like hand-pumps, basic foods and small-scale machinery). But the potential bias in favour of large companies and high-value products would need to be offset.

5 CONCLUSIONS

Countertrade as an instrument of trade policy – covering a significant proportion of trade – is undoubtedly here to stay. The analysis in this chapter has suggested that it may offer Third World countries significant gains. But it can also be associated with significant losses. Thus neither blanket condemnation, such as that of the IMF, nor blanket approval is appropriate. Rather, countries should exercise careful surveillance over countertrade deals to ensure maximum benefits. To do so requires:

(a) Surveillance of the terms-of-trade implications of any deal, but especially deals involving primary products in those cases where hard currency markets are an option. The probable terms-of-trade loss – allowing for higher cost imports as well as effects on the price of exports – must be offset by identified gains which the country considers outweigh these losses.

(b) For primary products where the Third World supplies a significant proportion of total exports, policies should be co-ordinated among Third World countries. This requires calculations of price elasticities and consequent effects on Third World earnings resulting from price reductions and increased supply. Appropriate policies need to be devised for these commodities, including but by no means confined to countertrade. Countertrade must be incorporated in Third World community arrangements because otherwise it may provide a serious obstacle to their success.

(c) Manufactured imports need to be scrutinised not only for cost but also for type of product, making sure that the deals do not divert resource use in an undesired way towards military and high-technology items.

(d) The greatest potential benefits from countertrade arise where the deals involve manufactured exports from Third World countries. For these cases implicit selective devaluation can be a useful way of promoting exports, and countertrade may also bypass non-tariff barriers. Here too, countries should keep a check on the terms of trade. But, in addition, a conscious effort is necessary to ensure that the big-company bias is avoided and that the exports generated broadly follow dynamic comparative advantage. Otherwise the exports could involve negative value-added for the country concerned.

(e) South–South countertrade in manufactures is most likely to be trade creating, permitting higher levels of output, employment and investment than would otherwise be possible in current circumstances. In the medium term, regionalising or multilateralising these arrangements by payments arrangements among Third World countries may economise on scarce convertible currencies and permit specialisation and competition between these Third World countries. This is especially important for small countries where bilateral countertrade deals could lead to high costs and inefficiency.

Countertrade politicises trade, in part replacing the market by administrative mechanisms. This has potential costs, which include the biases arising from administrative decisions, the tendency towards corrupt practices, and the danger of becoming specialised in non-dynamic high-cost areas of production. But where the market offers poor terms and has failed – and promises to continue to fail – to allow countries to make full use of their resources, capacities and potential, the costs are often outweighed by the benefits. To maximise these gains, Third World governments need to be selective in countertrade, only making use of it where there are clear gains, and instituting mechanisms to help minimise distorting effects. The interest-groups involved – especially as countertrade grows in importance – may make this a difficult task.

Notes

1. See Banks (1983), Department of Trade and Industry (1985), External Affairs Canada (1985), OECD (1981, 1985), Outters–Jaeger (1979), Tschoegl (1985), Verzariu (1984).
2. Department of Trade and Industry (1985), p. 5.
3. External Affairs Canada (1985), p. 1; also see Jones (1984), p. 20.
4. See OECD (1985), Banks (1983), Cooper (1984), Grieves (1984), Eisenbrand (1985).
5. Barovick (1986) showed 5.6 per cent of US firms' exports and less than 1 per cent of their imports involved countertrade. OECD (1985) estimates 10 per cent of trade between developing countries and 30 per cent of their trade with Eastern Europe was countertrade. OECD (1981) estimated that, at maximum, 20 per cent of Eastern European trade with OECD countries was countertrade. Agarwala estimated only 2 per cent of Indonesia's imports (mid–1982 to January 1984) were countertrade financed. Dodwell (1986) estimates one-third of China's trade was countertrade.

6. *Business International*, 23 December 1983.
7. Including China and excluding other Eastern Trading Area countries (i.e. Albania, Bulgaria, Czechoslovakia, German Democratic Republic, Hungary, Poland, Romania, USSR, Mongolia, North Korea and Vietnam). Vietnam).
8. The deals reported in Table 7.2 exclude the ETA. The Soviet Union has exported oil in countertrade deals.
9. International Trade Commission Report (reported in the *Financial Times*, 11 February 1986).
10. Turkey has been categorised as a developed country in Table 7.2.
11. See, e.g., Waldmeir in the *Financial Times*, 5 June 1985. This will hold if the country has agreed to set aside a certain percentage of its hard currency foreign exchange earnings for payment of arrears.
12. See S. Griffith-Jones (1986).
13. IMF *1983 Annual Report on Exchange Arrangements and Exchange Restrictions*.
14. The effects on overall export earnings' stability depend not only on the countertrade deals but also on what happens to the rest of exports. In principle, larger variations in countertrade deals earnings could be offset by an inverse movement in market transactions, thus leading overall to greater (relative) stability of export earnings. Outters–Jaeger (1979) provides some evidence for this stability effect.
15. See Godfrey (1985) who shows cases where devaluation in Africa led to revaluation in real terms as a result of the consequent inflation.
16. Data from UN Statistical Office, IMF *World Economic Outlook*, April 1986.
17. For example, in Tanzania, rates of capacity utilisation in manufacturing were estimated to be between 20 per cent and 30 per cent in 1981 (see ILO/JASPA, 1982). See also Bautista *et al.* (1981) and Phan-Thuy *et al.* (1981).
18. *Financial Times*, 11 February 1986.
19. See also Agarwala (1986).

References

Agarwala, P. N. (1984) 'Trade Goes Over the Counter', *Far Eastern Economic Review*, 23 August.

Agarwala, P. N. (1986) *Countertrade policies and practices of selected Asian countries and their State trading organizations*, UNCTAD/ECDC/176/Corr. 1.

Avramovic, D. (1985) 'Commodity Problem: What Next?', mimeo (October).

Banks, G. (1983) 'The Economics and Politics of Countertrade', *The World Economy*, 6, 2.

Banks, G. (1985) 'Constrained markets, "Surplus" commodities and international barter', *Kyklos*, 38, 2.

Barovick, R. L. (1986) 'Study Confirms Growth of Counter-Trade', *Journal of Commerce*, 6 January.

Bautista, R. M., H. Hughes, D. Lim, D. Morawetz and F. E. Thoumi (1981) *Capital Utilisation in Manufacturing* (New York: Oxford University Press).

Caves, R. E. (1974) 'The Economics of Reciprocity: Theory and Evidence on Bilateral Trading Arrangements', in *Honour of Jan Tinbergen* (Basingstoke: Macmillan).

Cline, W. R., N. Kawanabke, T. O. M. Kronsjo and T. Williams (1978) *Trade Negotiations in the Tokyo Round, A Quantitative Assessment* (Washington, DC: Brookings).

Cooper, R. N. (1984) 'Why counter-trade?', *Across the Board* (March).

Department of Trade and Industry (1985) *Countertrade, Some Guidance for Exporters* (London).

Dodwell, D. (1986) 'Expertise in Short Supply', *Financial Times*, 11 February 1986.

Eisenbrand, L. (1985) 'Why is Counter-trade Thriving?', *Industry and Development*, 15.

Ericson, H. (1985) 'Firms Soften Handicaps with Counter-trade Deals', *Journal of Commerce*, 28.

External Affairs Canada (1985) *Countertrade Primer for Canadian Exports* (Ottawa).

Godfrey, M. (1985) 'Trade and Exchange Rate Policy: a Further Contribution to the Debate', in T. Rose (ed.), *Crisis and Recovery in Sub-Saharan Africa* (Paris: OECD).

Grieves, R. T. (1984) 'Modern Barter', *Time* (11 June 1984).

Griffith-Jones, S. (1986) 'Framework for analysing debt crisis management', mimeo (Institute of Development Studies, Sussex).

ILO/JASPA (1982) *Basic Needs in Danger: A Basic Needs Oriented Development Strategy for Tanzania* (Addis Ababa).

Jones, S. F. (1984) *North/South Counter-trade Barter and Reciprocal Trade with Developing Countries* (London: The Economist Intelligence Unit).

Kopinski, T. C. (1985) 'Global Perspectives on Economic Motivations, Opportunities and Risks for State Trading Organisations of Developing Countries Engaged in Counter-trade', paper for International Workshop on Counter-trade, Belgrade, 25–28 June 1985.

OECD (1981) *East-West Trade: Recent Developments in Counter-trade* (Paris).

OECD (1985) *Counter-trade: Developing Country Practices* (Paris).

Outters-Jaeger, I. (1979) *The Development Impact of Barter in Developing Countries, Synthesis Report* (Paris: OECD).

Phan-Thuy, N., R. R. Betancourt, G. C. Winston and M. Kabaj (1981) *Industrial Capacity and Employment Promotion* (Gower: Westmead).

Richter, S. (1982) 'Hungary's foreign trade with CMEA partners in convertible currency', *Soviet and Eastern European Foreign Trade*, 8, 2.

Sherwell, C. (1985) 'South-east Asia: Of Growing Importance in Obtaining Business', *Financial Times*, 7 February.

Stern, R. M., J. Francis and B. Schumacher (1976) *Price Elasticities in International Trade: An Annotated Bibliography* (London: Trade Policy Research Centre).

Stewart, F. (1984) 'Recent Theories of International Trade: Some Implications for the South', in H. Kierzkowski (ed.), *Monopolistic Competition and International Trade* (Oxford: Oxford University Press).

Tschoegl, A. E. (1985) 'Modern Barter', *Lloyds Bank Review*, 158.
Verzariu, P. (1984) *International Counter-trade: A Guide for Managers and Executives* (Washington, DC: US Department of Commerce, International Trade Administration).
Waldmeir, P. (1985) 'Lagos keeps the I.M.F. at Bay', *Financial Times* (5 June 1985).
World Bank (1986) *Financing Adjustment with Growth in Sub-Saharan Africa, 1986–1990* (Washington).

Part III

Balance-of-Payments Policies and Development

8 Restoring the IMF to its Old Purpose

John Spraos*

There is a conflict between what the IMF was meant to be doing and what it is doing. This is a problem which hovers above the immediate preoccupations of the Fund but which sooner or later must be explicitly addressed.

The IMF was meant to provide early stage assistance to countries in balance-of-payments difficulties in order to ease their adjustment process and encourage them to avoid precipitate or drastic action which would be unduly disruptive for other countries. Private sources could not be expected to finance such assistance to an appropriate extent because they could not translate into encashable profit the gain accruing to the international community from non-disruptive adjustment. The IMF, reflecting the international community's interests, could perform this role, thus enhancing the efficiency of the system, but only if its assistance was sought at an early stage and, therefore, only if its assistance was offered on terms attractive enough to encourage early resort to the Fund by member countries. Delayed resort allows imbalances to accumulate and fester and is destabilising.

The principle of early stage assistance is explicitly incorporated in the Fund guidelines on conditionality adopted in 1979, the first paragraph of which says:

> Members should be encouraged to adopt corrective measures, which could be supported by the use of the Fund's general resources in accordance with the Fund's policies, at an early stage of their balance-of-payments difficulties or as a precaution against the emergence of such difficulties.

What the Fund is actually doing is quite different. Its conditionality terms are, or are perceived to be, so disagreeable that countries need

*This chapter presents the personal views of the author and was written before he assumed an advisory responsibility in the Greek Government. It attempts to bring together, in a brief exposition, some essential elements which underlie the ideas set out at some length in J. Spraos, 'IMF Conditionality: Ineffectual, Inefficient, Mistargeted', (Princeton) *Essays in International Finance*, December 1986.

to be desperate to resort to IMF assistance. For middle-income countries, with a credit rating which for a time gives them access to commercial lending, this means that they come to the Fund only after they have sunk up to their necks in bank debt, at which point the creditor banks expect the Fund to play the role, if not of receiver, of creditor-appointed overlord. In that role, considerations of short-term or medium-term solvency override not only the long-term interests of the national communities of the countries concerned but also the legitimate interest of the international community in avoiding disruptive adjustment.

The Fund claims that the toughness of its conditionality terms is due to the fact that countries turn to it only after excessive delay and thus leave it with no option but to engage in drastic surgery. But given the Fund's duty to encourage early recourse to itself – and not by exhortation alone – the delays experienced are not something of which it can wash its hands.

Whatever the reason, the conditionality practices of the Fund, as they have developed over the years and as currently operated in the context of the international debt crisis, conflict with the role which the Fund was designed to perform of providing early stage assistance for balance-of-payments needs.

Ideally, the roles of tough solvency restorer and of provider of early stage assistance on terms which would encourage resort to such assistance should not have been mixed in one institution at all. But given that they have, an attempt should be made to keep the latter role distinct and to enhance its importance.

This could be done by reducing the intrusiveness of conditionality.

Conditionality takes, at present, the form of a package in which a number of policy instruments are specified – ceilings on credit, restrictions on the fiscal deficit and devaluation are dominant – timed targets are set for them (unless they are 'preconditions', in which case they must be satisfied in advance, as is usually the case with devaluation) and successive instalments of pre-agreed drawings on the Fund are made dependent on the attainment of these targets, which are known as 'performance criteria'. Instruments of policy which are not included in the performance criteria are subject to policy understandings which are sanctions-free.

The object of Fund assistance is the improvement of the assisted country's balance of payments. This is basically uncontentious, though views would differ about the speed with which the objective is to be attained. Yet no conditionality is attached to this genuine target of policy. Instead, as noted, conditionality is attached to the instruments of policy.

The targeting of instruments (such as the money stock) became popular even in national economic policy making for a time. But, unlike a target subject to IMF sanctions, target changing always remained at the discretion of policy makers and the discretion has been frequently exercised. This is as it should be. The commitment of policy should be to the policy objective – in the case of IMF programmes to the improvement of the balance of payments – not to the instruments of policy.

Instrument targeting does not get support from the IMF's own experience. As documented in internal staff studies, despite a firm targeting of instruments, a large minority of Fund programmes fail to be crowned by any improvement in the balance of payments, let alone adequate improvement. And the most obvious excuses do not help to account for this result.

The Fund has clearly something to learn from Franklin Delano Roosevelt, who once said:

> We will try something. If it works, we will keep it. If it doesn't, let's try something else.

But more central in the present context than the ineffectualness and weak logic of current conditionality practices is the fact that IMF specification and targeting of instruments is humiliating (because meddlesome in matters of national sovereignty) and divisive (because neglectful of profound differences about the effectiveness of instruments and the evaluation of their side effects). This practice is responsible for much of the disagreeableness of fund conditionality packages which makes the IMF untouchable, except in desperation, and frustrates the Fund's role as provider of early stage assistance.

A switch to conditionality hinged on balance-of-payments targets is urgently needed. It will not achieve miracles but, by concentrating on essentials and leaving the choice of instruments to the sovereign power, will make the Fund more approachable and will give it an opportunity to do what it was meant to do.

Such a switch need not imply less toughness; balance-of-payments targets can be made as tough or as soft as one likes. But it will probably require more subtlety of design, more contingent targeting (to allow for foreseeable exogenous events), more flexibility of interpretation (to take account, *ex post*, of unforeseen occurrences), more ingenuity in monitoring, less mechanical triggering of sanctions.

The Fund management will argue that this will introduce discretionary, and hence contentious, elements in the tests of compliance with conditionality terms. But this will not be new because the present tests are subject to discretionary waivers.

Conditionality attached to instruments, as hitherto, could remain for countries that, having availed themselves of the more congenial terms for IMF assistance proposed here, persistently fail to put their balance of payments in order (after proper allowance for exogenous adversities) and thus become deserving candidates for international receivership.

Thus a three-tier structure for stand-by credits will be created: the virtually condition-free first credit tranche will continue; the second tier will be interposed in which credits will be conditional on balance-of-payments targets alone; the present conditionality practices will remain as the third tier.

To be effective, the middle tier should be wide and attractive with, in particular, a more generous time dimension. It will need to be underpinned by a once-over increase in the resources available to the Fund. (This may or may not involve a transfer between creditors and debtors; it will depend on the interest rate charged.)

Some claim that there is too much international lending from private sources already and that it should not be added to by the IMF. This was never true for the poorest countries and since 1982 it is not true for the middle-income countries either. In any case, IMF lending targeted on the improvement of the balance of payments should not be put on the same plane as some of the low quality loans which have been made by commercial banks.

The addition of a middle tier of balance-of-payments-targeted conditionality is perhaps the least that needs to be done if what the Fund was meant to be and the benefits it was meant to yield are to regain ground lost to the different Fund which has now developed.

9 The Impact of Currency Devaluation on Commodity Production and Exports of Developing Countries*

Alfred Maizels

Since the sharp collapse in the world market prices of virtually the entire range of primary commodities exported from developing countries from their peak in 1979–80, a large number of these countries have faced an external financing crisis. This has been the case not only for the very poor countries which are heavily dependent on commodity exports and official aid flows for their foreign exchange availabilities, but also for the more economically advanced developing countries many of which had been heavy borrowers on the commercial banking markets, and were faced, as from 1981, with an unforeseen and unprecedented increase in interest rates on their outstanding foreign debts. The majority of such countries have been forced to reach agreements with the International Monetary Fund (IMF) as a condition for obtaining stand-by credits, and for the conclusion of agreements with commercial bank creditors for debt rescheduling.

These IMF agreements have involved strict 'conditionality'. Though the specific conditions set by the IMF may vary somewhat according to the circumstances of individual countries, they typically include ceilings on domestic credit expansion and on credit to the public sector, the reduction or elimination of domestic subsidies (including food subsidies), import liberalisation and currency devaluation.[1] The IMF views these and related measures as necessary to create a 'viable' payments situation, i.e. a current account deficit that can be financed 'on a sustainable basis by net capital inflows on

* This is an extended and updated version of papers prepared for use in the UNCTAD Trade and Development Report, 1984 and 1985.

terms that are compatible with the development and growth prospects of the country'.[2]

IMF conditionality has, however, come under increasingly sharp attack, not only by many governments which have had to accept unpalatable domestic economic and monetary policies, but also by professional economists on the grounds that conditionality, as enforced by the IMF, operates to undermine the basis for future economic growth by drastic deflation of domestic real income and increase of the net trade balance, which drains real resources out of developing countries in order to meet interest and amortisation on foreign debts.

It would be generally agreed that currency devaluation would be an appropriate policy response where an external payments deficit has arisen as a result of domestic inflation, which has raised the production costs of a country's exports to uncompetitive levels at the existing rate of exchange. However, it is abundantly clear that the balance of payments crisis which has confronted the majority of developing countries since 1981 has its origins in external factors, of which the severe economic recession in developed market-economy countries has been the central element, though no doubt inappropriate domestic policies have aggravated the situation in a number of developing countries.

Moreover, it cannot be assumed that the factors which have led to adverse shifts in the international economy will reverse themselves in the near future, since the purely recessionary effects of reduced aggregate demand appear to have been superimposed on structural changes of a longer-term character – including the unfavourable impact of new synthetic materials and of new technologies on the demand for primary commodities – which are likely to persist in the future, and which will necessitate appropriate structural adjustment policies in both developed and developing countries.

The magnitude of the external shock to the payments balances of developing countries, and the speed with which it developed, left little choice to the governments of these countries but to make further cuts in imports, even where previous payments difficulties had already resulted in a drastic pruning of imports to a bare level of essentials. To be sure, a certain number of developing countries were able to raise loans on the commercial markets in 1982, but the possibility of large defaults on existing debt after mid-1982 resulted in a sharp contraction of loans on offer thereafter. Some of the poorer developing countries, too, were able to cover a growing export deficit by increased receipts of concessionary finance. But the majority of developing countries, faced with an immediate and often overwhelming payments crisis, were forced to cut imports, rather than to consider the longer-term need for structural adjustment to meet the changed conditions of the world market.

A variety of mechanisms has been adopted to achieve the required import cuts. In many developing countries, imports were already subject to some form of licensing or exchange control, so that the existing administrative machinery could be quickly deployed to restrict imports still further. Other forms of direct impact on imports, such as requiring advance deposits at the Central Bank of a proportion of the value of imports, have also been used in some countries. However, the most commonly adopted mechanism has been the devaluation of the currency, either as an open devaluation covering all traded items, or as a partly concealed devaluation, in which multiple exchange rates discriminate against different categories of imports.

A currency devaluation can be expected to work on both sides of the balance-of-payments accounts. Its primary effects are to raise import prices in terms of domestic currency, thus causing a reduction in the demand for imports, and to reduce export prices in terms of foreign currency, thus stimulating demand for exports. However, there are also important secondary effects, which in some circumstances can largely frustrate the objectives of the original devaluation, as well as having undesirable depressing effects on the standard of living of the population.

One important secondary effect arises where the resulting fall in imports impinges on the availability of intermediate products and spare parts for domestic production, including production for export. An increasing scarcity of such imports has indeed adversely affected the potential for expanding exportable supplies in a number of developing countries and, in some, even resulted in an absolute contraction in export volumes. Apart from this adverse impact on the export effort, a country forced to cut back imports of goods essential for its productive activities would also be unable to take effective measures to promote structural adaptation.

Another important secondary effect of currency devaluation – particularly if it forms part of a wider package of measures which include reducing food subsidies – can arise to the extent that it accentuates existing inflationary pressures. To this extent, the price incentives to correct an external payments imbalance can be wholly or partly eroded, since the resulting domestic inflation may prevent the real exchange rate from depreciating. The recent experience of developing countries in this respect reveals a wide variation in the ratio of the rate of currency devaluation to the rate of domestic inflation, the latter rate depending on many other factors also including, particularly, the success of the monetary authorities in controlling the growth of the money supply. For 27 developing countries which are important exporters of non-fuel primary commodities,[3] all of which experienced currency devaluations between 1980 and 1984, the rate of devaluation exceeded the rate of domestic inflation in 19 countries, and fell short of the rate of inflation in the remaining 8 countries. Thus, difficulties in controlling domestic inflationary pressures were widespread, particularly for countries having to make severe cuts in imports.

As regards export earnings, the effect of a currency devaluation will depend essentially on whether the relative profitability of export production is indeed increased thereby, whether the short-term response of producers to increased profitability is positive, and whether, and to what extent, a country's exports are large enough to influence the price on the world market.

As regards producer response, it has sometimes been argued that peasant producers of export crops, in so far as they aim to gain a minimum level of real income, will expand production when prices fall, and reduce production when prices rise. However, empirical studies do not bear this out. They invariably show that commodity producers in both developed and developing countries, whether peasant producers or large estates or mines, react positively to changes in relative output prices,[4] so that it can be assumed that devaluation, when associated with an increase in relative profitability of production, will result in greater output.

As regards the impact of greater commodity output and exports on the world price it is convenient, to begin with, to consider the simplest case, namely, where a country's exports represent so small a proportion of world supply that variations in such exports have no impact on the world price. For such a country, faced with a decline in the world price of its commodity exports, a devaluation will improve its export earnings only if there results a greater rate of expansion in export volume than the rate of decline in the world price. In the short run, this export volume response is likely to be related to the level of economic development and the structure and organisation of the commodity export sector. The small and least developed countries, particularly those exporting mainly tree crops, are unlikely to make a quick response, though countries specialising in mineral exports or in perennial agricultural crops may well be able to do so.

For a number of primary commodities, however, the exports of one, or a few, developing countries are large enough to influence the world price. In such cases, the beneficial effects of a currency depreciation will be greater, other things being equal, the greater the price elasticity of external demand for the commodity in question.

It is this last condition which can cause acute problems for developing countries exporting primary commodities, since the external price elasticities of demand are typically very low, being in the range of –0.1 to –0.4 for a large number of such commodities.[5] Thus, if a devaluation, by increasing the profitability of production of export commodities in a situation of persistent over-supply in the world market, results in an addition to world supply, a further fall in the world price will result over and above the price fall which was the original cause of the external payments deficit. In such a situation the devaluation, far from promoting a movement towards external equilibrium, will have the perverse effect of exacerbating the original commodity market imbalance and of further reducing the export earnings side of the balance-of-payments account of the producing country.

A SIMPLE MODEL

The interrelationships involved can perhaps be seen more clearly with the use of a simple model. Given a commodity-exporting country j which, in an initial period, exports a quantity Q_{ij} of commodity i for which the world price, in foreign currency, is P_{wi}, and for which country j's 'normal' elasticity of supply is η_{ij}, we can write:

$$Q_{ij} = A\,(P_{wi} \cdot R_j)^{\eta_{ij}} \tag{1}$$

where R_j is the rate of exchange of domestic currency per unit of foreign currency, after deflation by the general level of domestic prices (i.e. R_j represents, in a sense, the 'real' rate of exchange).

The parameter η_{ij} can be taken as the supply response to price change in 'normal' conditions of weather and of availability of inputs.

In particular years, above – or below – normal weather conditions or input availabilities will affect supply response and so modify the magnitude of η_{ij}. As mentioned earlier, one possible effect of a currency devaluation is to reduce the availability of imported intermediates and spare parts for domestic production, and this could substantially reduce the degree of supply response in particular cases. For convenience of presentation, however, it suffices here to assume 'normal' input availabilities. Though an appropriate adjustment would be required to η_{ij} in the event of an import constraint on supply, this would not alter the main conclusions.

Assuming, further, a real currency devaluation which more than offsets an initial fall in the world price of a given commodity *i*, the consequential proportionate change in production in country *j* is given by the first differential of (1):

$$q_{ij} = \eta_{ij}\,[r_j - p_{wi}\,(1 + r_j)] \tag{2}$$

where small letters represent proportionate rates of change in the corresponding variables.

The assumption that $r_j > |p_{wi}|$ implies that the real price, in domestic currency, received by the producers of *i* has risen, and given also a rational response to this price rise (i.e. $\eta_{ij} > 0$), then q_{ij} is positive, and the supply available to the world market increases correspondingly. This, in turn, will induce a (further) fall in the world price by the proportion p^*_{wi}, where:

$$p^*_{wi} = -\lambda_j\, q_{ij}/\varepsilon_w \tag{3}$$

where λ_j represents the pre-devaluation share of country *j* in world supply of commodity *i*, while ε_w denotes the price-elasticity of demand for exports of *i* from country *j*. Substituting (3) into (2), we have:

$$p^*_{wi} = -\lambda_j \cdot \eta_{ij} / \varepsilon_w\,[r_j - p_{wi}\,(1 + r_j)] \tag{4}$$

Thus, the further proportionate fall in the world price resulting from a currency devaluation by a commodity-exporting country will be greater, the greater the excess of the real rate of devaluation over the proportionate initial fall in the world price, the greater the supply elasticity, the greater the share of the devaluing country in total world supply and the smaller the price-elasticity of demand. Where currency devaluation is, in effect, offset by domestic inflation, r_j will be small or zero, thus negating any direct devaluation effect, while where the producing country is only a marginal supplier to the world market, $\lambda_j \to 0$, and again there is no further significant effect on the world price.

Commodity-exporting countries which are 'price-makers' (i.e. where λ_j is significant) and for which r_j exceeds p_{wi} by a substantial amount are likely to suffer a fall in commodity export earnings as a result of devaluation. Foreign exchange earnings of *j* from commodity *i* (F_{ij}) can be expressed as:

$$F_{ij} = P_{wi} \cdot Q_{ij} \tag{5}$$

so that:

$$f_{ij} = \eta_{ij} \, [r_j - p_{wi} \, (1 + r_j)] \, (1 - \lambda_j/\varepsilon_w) \\ - \eta_{ij}^2 \, [r_j - p_{wi} \, (1 + r_j)]^2 \cdot \lambda_j/\varepsilon_w \tag{6}$$

where f_{ij} represents the proportionate (further) fall in foreign exchange earnings consequent upon currency devaluation. The first term on the right-hand side of (6) must be negative, so long as $\lambda_j > \varepsilon_w$, in which case f_{ij} must also be negative. This can be taken as the typical condition for commodity-exporting developing countries, at least for the first half of the 1980s.

If, however, $\lambda_j < \varepsilon_w$ (which corresponds to the case of a marginal supplier or a 'price taker'), the first right-hand term of (6) becomes positive, but this is not a sufficient condition for f_{ij} to be positive. In addition, it would be necessary for the first term to exceed the second term, i.e. for:

$$(\varepsilon_w - \lambda_j)/\eta_{ij} \, \lambda_j > r_j - p_{wi} \, (1 + r_j) \tag{7}$$

This condition is also likely to be met for marginal supplying countries ($\lambda_j \to 0$) for which the excess of r_j over p_{wi} is substantial since, though the world price is not significantly affected, such countries can raise their export earnings by increasing their share of the world market.

However, as already indicated, in a period (such as that since 1980) when developing commodity-exporting countries have generally suffered a drastic curtailment of their foreign exchange earnings as a result of sharp declines in world market prices of a wide range of their primary commodity exports, currency devaluation by a number of exporting countries more or less simultaneously involves both an increase in λ_j and a fall in ε_w, as compared with the case of devaluation by a single exporting country. In this situation, even a 'price-taker' country, supplying only a marginal proportion of the world market, is unlikely to increase its export earnings, since any increase in its market share would be more than offset by a general decline in the world price resulting from the devaluations of its major competitors.

The effect of currency devaluation on the world price of a given commodity, and on the export earnings of producing countries, is shown in the illustrative examples in Table 9.1, for different values of the supply elasticity (η_{ij}), the proportion of world supply coming from the devaluing countries (λ_j) and the increase in the real price in domestic currency in these countries $[r_j - p_{wi}(1 + r_j)]$. For simplicity, it has been assumed that world demand elasticity remains constant, at – 0.3, throughout. With a commodity facing an inelastic world demand, prices can fall dramatically as either η_{ij} or λ_j rises. A similar result would ensue if the magnitude of the demand elasticity (ε_w) were reduced. The corresponding falls in export earnings will always be considerably less than the rate of decline in prices but, even so, export earnings reductions of 15–30 per cent could ensue as a result of a substantial increase in the real domestic price, combined with relatively high ratios of supply to demand elasticities, and of the proportion of world supply in a devaluing country or group of countries.

Thus, while currency devaluation would be one appropriate policy measure, among others, for a country suffering from a current account deficit arising as a result of its internal costs and prices increasing at a faster rate than those of its competitors, in a situation where the external deficit is essentially a reflection of an external demand recession, devaluation is likely to have the perverse effect of accentuating the initial price decline and worsening the external deficit of the devaluing country. This perverse effect, which accentuates the instability of the international trade and payments systems, as well as harming the devaluing country itself, is all the more likely to occur the greater the number of countries forced to devalue their currencies, and thus the greater the proportion of world supplies coming from countries with devalued currencies.

Table 9.1 Illustrative examples of effect of currency devaluation on world prices and on export earnings[a]

Effect of currency devaluation on:		*Assumed value of* $[r_j - p_{wi}(1 + r_j)]$ 0.1	0.2	0.3	0.4	0.5
		(Percentage change)				
World price						
$\lambda_j = 0.4$	$\eta_{ij} = 0.2$	–2.7	– 5.3	– 8.0	–10.6	–13.3
	$\eta_{ij} = 0.4$	–5.3	–10.6	–16.0	–21.3	–26.7
$\lambda_j = 0.6$	$\eta_{ij} = 0.2$	–4.0	– 8.0	–12.0	–16.0	–20.0
	$\eta_{ij} = 0.4$	–8.0	–16.0	–24.0	–32.0	–40.0
Export earnings						
$\lambda_j = 0.4$	$\eta_{ij} = 0.2$	–0.8	– 1.5	– 2.5	– 3.6	– 4.6
	$\eta_{ij} = 0.4$	–1.5	– 3.6	– 5.9	– 8.8	–12 0
$\lambda_j = 0.6$	$\eta_{ij} = 0.2$	–2.1	– 4.3	– 6.7	– 9.3	–12 0
	$\eta_{ij} = 0.4$	–4.3	– 9.3	–14.9	–21.1	–28 0

[a] $[r_j - p_{wi}(1 + r_j)]$ is a measure of the rate of change in the real price received by producers, in domestic currency; λ_j is the pre-devaluation proportion of exports of country j in world supply; and η_{ij} is the price-elasticity of supply.
Source Based on equations (4) and (6), assuming $\varepsilon_w = 0.3$.

RECENT EMPIRICAL EVIDENCE

It is not easy to determine whether, in fact, recent currency devaluations have had the kind of perverse result indicated by the above discussion. There is little doubt that recent devaluations, including floating depreciations, have considerably raised the domestic prices of primary commodity exports in the majority of developing countries, but it must be borne in mind that the increase in import prices (in domestic currency) resulting from devaluation has tended to increase costs of production, so that the rise in nominal commodity prices does not necessarily indicate any increase in the relative profitability of commodity production.

An approximate indication of the impact of recent devaluations on the incentive to produce export commodities can, however, be obtained by deflating the rise in the domestic prices of commodity exports by changes in the appropriate indices of consumer prices. Since, however, one of the consequences of devaluation is to reduce real wages, which constitute a major cost in the production of most commodities, the probability is that wage costs and inputs costs generally will rise less than the cost-of-living index, particularly where devaluation is accompanied by a reduction in food subsidies. Thus, deflating commodity prices by indices of consumer prices is likely to give a downward bias to the resultant indicators of profitability.

An analysis on these lines has been made for 19 non-fuel primary commodities of importance in the exports of developing countries for the periods 1980 to 1983, and to 1984 (see Appendix Table A.1). For each commodity, separate indices were calculated for the change in the world price (in United States dollars), the exchange rate, the implied change in the domestic price, and the latter deflated by the change in consumer prices. In all, 56 country/commodity situations are covered, for each of which a currency depreciation was associated with a concurrent fall in the world price.

These calculations, which are summarised in Table 9.2, show that the deflated commodity price rose between 1980 and 1983 in 15 cases (or over one-quarter of the total), while between 1980 and 1984 the deflated price had risen in 24 cases (over two-fifths). A number of developing countries had to devalue their currencies substantially in 1984, including Argentina, Brazil, Ghana, Peru and Zaire. Generally speaking, countries with large currency devaluations were also those with relatively large domestic inflation though, in many cases (e.g. Argentina, Brazil, Ghana and Zaire) the rate of increase in domestic prices fell short of the corresponding devaluations. For almost one-half of the cases in which the deflated commodity price rose between 1980 and 1984, the rise was less than 25 per cent; for the other half, the mean unweighted increase was as high as some 70 per cent. The analysis thus indicates that where currency devaluation is substantial, a perverse incentive for producers to increase output in a period of excess supply may well be generated.

However, this approach – based on adjusting the movement in world prices by changes in exchange rates – is indicative of the *potential* for perverse supply reactions rather than of the actual extent of such reactions where they exist. This is because in many developing countries marketing boards, *caisses de stabilisation* or other mechanisms insulate the producer, to a greater or lesser extent, from price fluctuations on the world market. This is generally achieved by ensuring that the producer price rises, in terms of foreign currency, by less than the world price in a boom period, and falls, in terms of foreign currency, by less than the world price in a recession. But the movement in producer prices in terms of domestic currency will

Table 9.2 Indices of real domestic prices in developing countries for selected commodity exports, 1983 and 1984 (Indices: 1980 = 100)

	Under 75	*75–100*	*Over 100*	*Total*
		(*No. of cases*)		
1983	19	22	15	56
1984	15	17	24	56

Source See Appendix I.

depend heavily, also, on the extent of the currency devaluation, and the lag between the date of devaluation and the consequential adjustment in producer prices.

Relevant data for producer prices in developing countries are, however, available only for a limited number of commodities. For coffee, for example, prices paid to growers, deflated by the relevant consumer price index, fell by about 20 per cent from 1980 to 1983 in Brazil, Colombia and Indonesia,[6] compared with falls of 24, 31 and 11 per cent, respectively, in these countries as derived by the method used here (see Appendix I). For the period 1980 to 1984, the real price paid to coffee growers fell by 28 per cent in Brazil, and by 18 per cent in Colombia, compared with falls of 14 and 21 per cent, respectively, shown by the method used here.

For cocoa, deflated prices paid to growers in 1983 ranged from 72 to 96 per cent of the 1980 level for the five major producing countries[7] as against a range of 67–118 shown by the present method (apart from Ghana, for which the index was an unusually low 17). With the upturn in world cocoa prices in 1984, producer prices tended to lag behind, the indices for 1984 ranging from 52 to 92, as against a range of 58–147 for the method used here.

For raw jute, the deflated growers' price in Bangladesh, the principal producing country, rose by 27 per cent from 1980 to 1983, and by 123 per cent from 1980 to 1984, compared with increases of 5 and 89 per cent, respectively, shown by the present method.

For sugar, the present method gave a fairly close fit for the Philippines (an index of 79 for 1983, as against a deflated growers' price of 91 for that year, and 75 for 1984), but for Brazil there was an important discrepancy, as between the index of 47 for 1983 on the present method, and a range of 108–129 for the deflated growers' price.

Comparable evidence on producer prices for most other commodities is generally lacking. However, it would seem from the above comparisons that, apart from a number of cases where divergences are significant, the method used here should provide an acceptable general indicator of changes in real prices received by producers in different developing countries.

AGRICULTURAL PRODUCTS

For agricultural commodities, an assessment of the impact of changes in the real domestic price on supplies to the world market can be made by relating these price changes to the corresponding changes in planted or harvested areas, in production and in exports, of the commodities concerned. For those products for which the comparable data are available, the relevant changes are summarised in Appendix II. The data for planted or harvested area, production and exports have been converted to indices based on the averages of the years 1978 to 1980 to eliminate, in particular, variations due to climatic or other special factors in individual years. For the same reason, current production and export data are shown as averages of two calendar years, but for the cultivated area, where year-to-year shifts are not generally a major problem, separate figures are shown for 1983 and 1984.

Of the 28 commodity/country cases covered, the planted or harvested area rose by more than 10 per cent between 1978–80 and 1983 in 7 cases, was much the same (changes being within ± 10 per cent) in 15 cases, and fell by more than 10 per cent in the remaining 6 cases. For the change from 1978–80 to 1984, the corresponding frequencies were 6, 10 and 12 respectively. As was to be expected, changes in production and export of many individual commodities varied widely in relation to changes in cultivable areas, reflecting to a large extent variations in climatic conditions and productivity as well as, for exports, changes in stocks and in domestic consumption of food crops.

These changes are brought together with the corresponding changes in real domestic prices in Table 9.3, which shows the harvested or planted area in 1983 and 1984 both in relation to 1980–81 and to the 1978–80 average. For those commodities for which real domestic prices rose substantially, there appears to have been a significant expansion in the harvested or planted area, when the comparison is with the 1978–80 average, as against a marginal decline for other commodities. A similar result emerged for the

Table 9.3 Changes in real domestic prices, harvested or planted area, production and exports of selected agricultural products from developing countries, 1978–80 to 1983 and 1984

	1983 Compared with 1980		*1984 Compared with 1980*	
	Prices lower or risen by under 10%	*Prices risen by 10% or more*	*Prices lower or risen by under 10%*	*Prices risen by 10% or more*
No. of cases	21	7	16	12
Indices, 1980 = 100				
Real domestic price	82	151	78	136
Harvested or planted area[a]	98	110	103	106
Indices, 1978–80 = 100				
Harvested or planted area	98	119	98	117
Production	96	117	107	112
Exports	107	126	112	126

[a] 1980–81 average = 100.
Source Appendix II.

comparison between 1983 and 1980–81, but not for that between 1984 and 1980–81. For production and exports, the comparisons with the 1978–80 average also show higher growth for commodities for which real domestic prices increased substantially.

The relationship indicated by these results, that a substantial increase in real domestic prices is associated with an expansion in productive capacity, and with increases in production and exports to the world market, must be taken as only a general tendency, since it is not likely to apply in every case as the result of the operation of various offsetting factors. None the less, the general tendency does exist, even though the magnitude to date appears to have been relatively modest. For the period 1980 to 1983, the elasticity of harvested/planted area with respect to price was 0.20, on average, for the seven commodities for which real prices rose by 10 per cent or more, the corresponding elasticity for the 1980–84 period being 0.17 for a larger group of 12 commodities. It seems probable that if the rise in real domestic prices were to be sustained for a longer period, the response in terms of cultivable area could well be greater.

MINERALS AND METALS

For minerals and metals, a similar analysis of changes in productive capacity is not possible at present for the period since 1980. Changes in real domestic prices in any one producing country may, or may not, have an influence on decisions to invest in new mining or smelting capacity, particularly where such decisions are taken by transnational mining corporations. In any event, even if a decision was made to invest in new capacity following a rise in the real domestic price, the consequent capacity expansion could typically take seven to ten years before the additional output came on the world market.

Though world market prices of non-fuel minerals and metals have remained generally depressed since their peak in 1980, currency devaluations in the main developing producing countries were not large enough, apart from one or two exceptional cases, to result in any substantial improvement in real domestic prices.[8] None the less, output of the major non-fuel minerals and metals in developing countries have not fallen significantly below 1980 levels, while in some cases (e.g. aluminium), output actually rose. The main impact of the recession on world production has, rather, fallen on the mineral sector of developed market-economy countries, and particularly on that of North America. This has resulted partly because North American iron ore and copper mines are generally high-cost, and partly because many developing countries heavily dependent on minerals for their export earnings have been constrained to continue production and exports at previous levels in spite of lower prices, in order to maximise their foreign exchange earnings in situations of sharp deterioration in their external accounts.

CONCLUSION

Though a currency devaluation is an appropriate instrument, among others, to deal with a deficit in a country's external accounts due to its costs of production of exportables having risen out of line with those of its competitors, currency devaluation is likely to be inappropriate in a situation where the majority of countries exporting a particular primary commodity face large external payments deficits due to a recession in world demand for the commodity. In such a situation, currency devaluations by the producing countries – to the extent that real domestic prices and profitability of production are thereby enhanced – will have the perverse effect of stimulating production, of expanding exportable supplies and thus of adding further to the depressing influences on world commodity prices.

The statistical analysis described above has indicated that such a perverse effect appears to have been operating in recent years, at least for a number of important commodities and producing countries.

APPENDIX I

Calculation of Changes in Real Domestic Prices

The change in the real domestic price of commodity i in country j between two periods (0 and 1) was calculated in ratio form as:

$$P^1_{dij}/P^0_{dij} = (P^1_{wi}/P^0_{wi})\ (R^1_j/R^0_j)/(P^1_d/P^0_d)$$

where P_{dij} represents the domestic price of i in country j, P_{wi} the world price in US dollars, R_j the rate of exchange (domestic currency units per dollar), and P_d the domestic consumer price index, the superscripts indicating the relevant periods compared.

Table A.1 Commodities and countries covered by the calculation of real domestic prices

Commodity	*Countries*	*Proportion of world exports in 1980 (%)*
Agricultural		
Wheat	Argentina	10
Maize	Argentina, Thailand	12
Rice	Pakistan, Thailand	31
Cocoa	Brazil, Cameroon, Ghana, Ivory Coast, Nigeria	78
Coffee	Brazil, Colombia, Indonesia, Ivory Coast	49
Sugar	Argentina, Brazil, Philippines, Thailand	19
Soyabeans	Argentina, Brazil	14
Palm oil	Indonesia, Ivory Coast, Malaysia	72
Palm kernel oil	Ivory Coast, Nigeria, Malaysia	72
Linseed oil	Argentina	62
Cotton	Pakistan, Sudan, Turkey	11
Jute	Bangladesh, India	74
Sisal	Brazil, Kenya, Madagascar, Tanzania	88
Natural rubber	Indonesia, Malaysia, Sri Lanka, Thailand	93
Tropical timber	Indonesia, Malaysia, Philippines	39
Minerals, ores and metals		
Iron ore	Brazil, Chile, India	30
Copper	Chile, Peru, Zaire, Zambia	98
Tin	Indonesia, Malaysia, Thailand	78
Phosphate rock	Jordan, Morocco, Togo	48

Data sources for Table A.1: World market prices: UNCTAD *Monthly Commodity Price Bulletin* (various issues). Exchange rates and cost of living indices: IMF, *International Financial Statistics* (various issues). World exports in 1980: UNCTAD *Yearbook of International Commodity Statistics*, 1984.

APPENDIX II

Changes in real domestic prices, harvested or planted area, production and exports of selected agricultural products, 1978–80 to 1984

		Real domestic prices		*Harvested or planted area*			*Production*		*Exports*	
		1983	*1984*	*1980–81 (av.)*	*1983*	*1984*	*1982–3 (av.)*	*1983–4 (av.)*	*1982–3 (av.)*	*1983–4 (av.)*
		(*1980 = 100*)					(*1978–80 = 100*)			
Wheat:	Argentina	162	139	120	163	127	171	158	198	248
Maize:	Argentina	183	168	112	112	114	113	112	115	118
	Thailand	70	74	94	115	122	114	134	133	141
Rice:	Pakistan	67	60	101	101	100	107	106	97	113
	Thailand	59	54	105	106	109	105	112	151	169
Cocoa:	Brazil	90	110	110	128	133	117	116	107	94
	Cameroon	100	117	102	98	99	91	95	108	136
	Ghana	76[a]	77[a]	100	83	92	66	63	98	73
	Ivory Coast	118	147	123	106	113	109	102	132	145
	Nigeria	67	58	100	100	100	87	90	104	95
Coffee:	Brazil	76	86	105	97	105	107	124	139	150
	Colombia	69	79	97	90	88	119	113	86	93
	Indonesia	89	101	120	121	123	88	99	104	119
	Ivory Coast	122	151	105	110	80	108	74	106	93
Sugar:	Argentina	74	84	99	97	99	108	102	142	172
	Brazil	119[a]	119[b]	108	139	154	121	120	124	132
	Philippines	91	75	94	107	106	107	105	83	69

continued on page 204

APPENDIX II *continued*

		Real domestic prices		Harvested or planted area			Production		Exports	
		1983	*1984*	*1980–81 (av.)*	*1983*	*1984*	*1982–3 (av.)*	*1983–4 (av.)*	*1982–3 (av.)*	*1983–4 (av.)*
Soyabeans:	Argentina	226	200	123	143	162	126	165	66	91
	Brazil	106	114	104	98	111	118	129	95	151
Cotton:	Pakistan	94	89	106	109	116	104	117	180	124
	Sudan	88	80	96	94	98	118	140	88	116
	Turkey	113	118	102	94	116	105	115	85	56
Jute:	Bangladesh	105	189	81	78	72	81	74	120	121
	India	89	178	97	82	99	90	93	—[c]	—[c]
Sisal:	Brazil	83	91	107	108	112	112	105	74	99
	Kenya	93	98	98	89	89	130	130	128	119
	Madagascar	75	92	63	59	59	119	125	96	90
	Tanzania	55	56	101	52	54	62	50	56	43

[a] Based on actual average price received by producer (mean of range for Brazilian sugar).
[b] Assumed unchanged from 1983.
[c] Indian production of jute is almost entirely consumed domestically.
Source of Appendix II FAO *Trade Yearbook* and *Production Yearbook* 1980 and 1984, and sources listed in Appendix I.

Notes

1. For a recent detailed analysis, see Tony Killick, 'IMF Stabilisation Programmes', in T. Killick (ed.), *The Quest for Economic Stabilization: The IMF and the Third World* (Heinemann and Overseas Development Institute, London, 1984).
2. Quoted from, T. Killick, 'The Impact of Fund Stabilisation Programmes', in T. Killick (ed.), ibid.
3. These are the countries included in Appendix Table A.1.
4. For a recent study of agricultural supply responses, see Marion E. Bond, 'Agricultural Responses to Prices in Sub-Saharan African Countries', *IMF Staff Papers, Vol. 30, No. 4, December 1983*; see also F. G. Adams and J. R. Behrman, *Commodity Exports and Economic Development* (Lexington, Mass.: Lexington Books, D. C. Heath, 1982) for a summary of the available supply elasticity estimates.
5. See, for example, the summary of estimates of price elasticities for a variety of primary commodities in Adams and Behrman, ibid., Table 2–1.
6. International Coffee Organization, *Quarterly Statistical Bulletin*, Section V (November 1985), Table V–18. These prices refer to a comparison of March 1983 with September 1980, and so are not strictly comparable with the present calculations.
7. Gill and Duffus, *Cocoa Market Report*, No. 316, January 1985.
8. See Appendix II.

Part IV

Resources for Development

10 Development Economists for Arms Control

Jan Tinbergen

1 FROM REGRET TO ATTACK

The Pearson Commission recommended, in 1969 already (Pearson *et al.*, 1969), that industrialised donor countries make available for official development assistance (ODA) 0.7 per cent of gross national product (GNP). None of the large or middle-sized industrialised countries (whose experts were members of the Pearson Commission) followed this advice. In 1980 the Brandt Commission, in its first (Brandt *et al.*, 1980), and in 1983 in its second report (Brandt *et al.*, 1983) had to repeat the Pearson suggestion: a sad confirmation of the lack of interest of the industrialised nations. One of the consequences is that we are now facing, among many other problems, an enormous 'debt problem'.

Among the reasons of the lack of interest the armament problem probably is the most important. The mutual distrust of NATO and Warsaw Treaty (WT) countries has led to the unprecedented amount now spent on armament, already beyond half a billion (in the European sense; Americans strangely call this a trillion) dollars a year. Development politicians and economists have pointed out, clearly with regret, that a reduction of this crazy amount by 5 per cent would make available an amount that, if spent on development, would constitute an unprecedented improvement of what could be done to raise the welfare of the poorest countries. In fact it might have meant that the Pearson Commission's philosophy would have been applied. The development politicians and economists make this point – as observed – with regret. They hoped that decision makers in the armament field would change their minds.

Enough time has elapsed now to state that the developers' regret did not work out in the hoped-for way.

The time has come for a change in attitude: *from regret to attack*. The ways industrialised countries spend their resources constitute an economic problem, as long as the choice between various types of civilian goods and services is concerned. But why do we restrict our judgement as economists to civilian goods? Why don't we include military goods and services? Don't they affect, as other goods and services do, human welfare? Of course they do, in a very outspoken way, and very negatively. Capital losses as a consequence of the Second World War were many times larger than capital losses as a consequence of the Great Depression. Whereas the latter can be interpreted as a yardstick for the effects of a bad anti-cyclical policy, the former may be seen as a yardstick for the effects of the Second World War. As economists *we should no longer consider war as an exogenous process*.

2 MILITARY POLICY PART OF ECONOMIC POLICY

So, since military policy requires increasing resources which are withdrawn from other destinations and since military policy affects human welfare negatively – in the future certainly even much more so than in the Second World War – it has become our duty, as economists, to participate in the discussion on the optimal amount of military expenditures.

It was customary, in designing economic policy, to introduce *corrections* on the preferences of citizens. A clear example is schooling: up to a certain age we have *obligatory* schooling, irrespective of the children's and some of the parents' preferences. Another correction on the citizens' preferences is the policy with regard to *merit goods* and their counterparts (unhealthy or culturally undesirable goods). The former are supplied below their cost of production and the latter are, often heavily, taxed.

Military policy requires a *similar, critical, correction*. Often that policy is affected by phenomena of a special character. One is nationalism or patriotism. *Nationalism* contains some elements open to criticism and correction. In essence it implies the belief that our own nation is better – in whatever sense – than other nations. But this cannot be true simultaneously for two or more nations. So it needs correction.

Another phenomenon explaining some components of military policy is *sovereignty*. Sovereignty is believed by many to warrant control of a nation's welfare. This is a misunderstanding. A nation's welfare is partly determined by other nation's decisions. Again, a correction is needed.

A third determinant of military policy that requires correction is the expected level of *welfare during a war*. This expected level is low, to be sure, but not low enough. It is largely based on the experience of the last war through which a country has gone. But only on the experience of those who survived: the victims killed cannot speak. Moreover, technological development is rapidly changing and lowers welfare during a war.

The outcome of the corrections discussed probably makes war still less attractive than most people already expect. There may be good reasons to have recourse to alternatives more often than has been done in the past.

3 PEACE POLICY AT LEAST A TWO-COUNTRY PROBLEM

In contrast to what is usual in exercises in policy planning by economists so far, we cannot base a peace policy on a one-country model. War or peace are concepts in which *at least two* sovereign nations (or other entities) play a role. In the Second World War a very large number of nations were involved. Also in today's discussions about military policy a large number of countries and their governments take part. The main discussions may be those among the North Atlantic Treaty Organization (NATO) and the Warsaw Pact (WP), with more than twenty countries as members, but clearly many more may be drawn in, such as Afghanistan and consequently Pakistan and India, possibly a number of West Asian countries and even Central and Latin American countries.

None the less an important core of today's military policies can be analysed with the aid of a two-country model, since the armaments of the two *superpowers*, the United States of America (US) and the Union of Socialist Soviet Republics (SU) constitute more than half of total world armament, and the aims and means of the policies, civilian and military together, of the two alliances, of which the US and the SU are by far the largest countries, are determined to a considerable extent by the aims and means of these two superpowers.

The aims consist of two main preferences, to be called *traditional* war aims and *ideological* war aims. By traditional aims we mean those of national power and prestige. They were the aims of the majority of all wars in history and we indicated them as nationalism in Section 2. Power and prestige not only reflect nationalist attitudes, but in the past also resources such as land and mineral deposits owned, often in the form of colonialist exploitation. In the Second World War ideological war aims were added in much larger 'quantities': Hitler's 'national socialists' were anti-democratic and anti-communist and from 1941 on the traditional aims of nationalist revanche *vis-à-vis* the Western countries were partly replaced by the anti-communist aims *vis-à-vis* the SU. These ideological controversies play an important role in today's political programmes; in official propaganda perhaps even the main role. Yet, according to former West German Chancellor Helmut Schmidt, that role is less important than official statements suggest: in several respects present Soviet aims are similar to previous czarist Russian aims. A well known element in Russian policy has always been its aim to have easier access to ice-free ports and to the world oceans. The ideological aims at present may be briefly summarised as capitalism versus communism, but this brevity is inaccurate, since the social orders do not differ as much as these extremes. The US order contains some adjustments in the socialist direction – a modest social security system – and the SU order contains some adjustments into the capitalist direction – a modest private sector.

An essential feature of even a two-nation model is that there are *two levels of decision making* as a minimum: the level of the sovereign national governments and a possible level of 'united nations', where representatives of both nations decided on a common meeting, a 'security council' for military policy or a socio-economic council for traditionally socio-economic policy. Of course more levels exist within the sovereign nations, down to municipalities or even families and enterprises.

4 OFFENSIVE AND DEFENSIVE MILITARY POLICIES

Even though some weapons cannot be qualified by this distinction, a number of them can be considered clearly *offensive* and others clearly *defensive*. Fischer (1984, 1985) shows how important this well known possibility is. In the field of conventional weapons, tanks and battleships are clear examples of offensive weapons and anti-tank guns and mine fields are typically defensive. Also strategies can be offensive or defensive. An army that is not used outside its own country is defensive. So are anti-aircraft guns on fixed locations. In Fischer's terminology defensive arms produce security for their own country. Offensive arms produce positive security for their own country, but at the same time a negative quantity of security for the other country.

Missiles have become a very important category of arms and evidently they are offensive. There are various types. One distinction is long distance versus short or medium distance. The former, also called strategic, may for the first time, bring war into American territory. A second distinction is made according to the number of warheads mounted on them, from single-warhead to many. The latter are called multiple independently-targetable re-entry vehicles (MIRVs). A third distinction is between immobile and mobile missiles. The former are mounted in a silo and can be seen from reconnaissance aircraft or satellites. The latter are mounted on ships or trucks. Especially when mounted on submarines they cannot be observed from the air. As will be discussed in Section 5, the role of the various types in military policy can be very different.

Their *defensive counterparts* are not so clearly defined as in the cases of older types of weapons. Technologies of defence against missiles still are a subject under research. Some have been tried out, rather more by the SU than by the US. A defence system around Leningrad was tried out, but withdrawn again. Another, around Moscow, still exists and its existence is stated in the 1972 anti-ballistic missiles (ABM) treaty. This treaty limits such defensive systems to two for both countries and for the launchers used. According to American information the SU is experimenting with laser techniques for defensive purposes. The main point to make about defensive techniques is, however, that no satisfactory technology is known yet.

5 UNEXPECTED POSSIBILITIES

The importance of defensive systems has been shown by Professor Fischer's 1985 article. In it he shows, with the aid of a very simple model with two countries and two industries, producing civilian and military goods respectively, that in a non-co-operative game the countries may in their own interest decide to disarm or to stay at relatively low levels of armament from which they do not wish to deviate. The condition that must be fulfilled is that at least one country chooses a '*sufficiently defensive*' military policy and armament system.

What sufficient means can so far only be specified for the simplified technologies used in the model, however.

Some other indications of 'unexpected possibilities' are shown already in Fischer's 1984 book, especially in Table 8.1 (p. 97). In that table he illustrates by what factors the *stability of an equilibrium* of deterrence is determined. Stability means that neither of the two opponents wishes to change his position – assuming that technology is not changed. The table shows that strength (measured by the total number of warheads) *need not be equal at all*. It also shows that accuracy (the likelihood that a target is hit) is no guarantee for stability either. These two conclusions are unexpected for many military and political experts and illustrates the necessity to rethink part of the traditional theories. A third conclusion is that the mounting of many warheads on each missile ('MIRVing') considerably *destabilises* the equilibrium, and hence reduces security. This is an interesting example of the usefulness of integrating economic policy in the traditional sense with military policy. MIRVs have been introduced because they are cheaper in the limited economic sense. But since they lower security they must be rejected nevertheless, on the basis of our wider concept of economics.

6 THE DANGER OF FIRST-STRIKE CAPABILITY

The preceding argument seems to underline the desirability of a shift from an offensive to a defensive policy (called '*transarmament*' by Fischer). The resources spent by the SU on research in this direction confirm that conclusion. President Reagan's '*strategic defence initiative*' (SDI) points in the same direction. Why, then, is the SU terrified by SDI and opposes it in an almost desperate way?

The answer is that both sides fear, more than anything else – and rightly so – the possibility that the opponent attains *first-strike capability*, that is, the possibility to defeat, by a first strike, and almost riskless, the own country. This is what may happen if the opponent finds the defensive counterpart to missiles, especially if conventional weapons are used. (The use of nuclear weapons threatens the offender too, if with some delay.)

The fear for the opponent's first strike capability partly depends on the uncertainty about the opponent's aims. If the opponent is aware of the advantages it could derive from peaceful co-operation in the fields of trade and transfer of technology it may not want to use its first-strike capability. So it remains possible to follow a policy of peaceful co-operation and with its aid to reduce the danger of the opponent's first strike capability.

It is perfectly possible that the SU's fear for a US first-strike capability is unjustified. Communists do adhere to the theory that wars are caused by capitalism; they do not agree with Robbins (1939), who sees the causes of war in militarist and nationalist ideas rather than in business circles. But even if the US leadership aims at peaceful coexistence what matters is the SU theory; and it is well known that communists are doctrinaire.

7 COMMON SECURITY A NECESSITY

The dangerous unstable situation created by a race to reach effective defence against missile attacks before the opponent reaches it can be avoided only if the search for a defensive technology is *undertaken jointly*. Since defensive technologies contribute much more to security than offensive technologies it is in the interest of both countries, even if they do not like each other at all, to organise such co-operation. And in order to make such co-operation acceptable, it is better to behave in a business-like way and not unnecessarily to irritate the other. That implies that Western rulers do not continue to emphasise that they dislike central planning and that Eastern rulers do not continue to point out that they hate private enterprise. By now this is known. So let us discuss what agreement will warrant the search for common security – because without security there will be no possibility to establish, in our own member countries, the social order we think will make our peoples happiest.

The important point to add is that other approaches to find the best policy lead to the same answer. In Section 3 we found that, in a two-nation model, two levels of decision making are possible: the sovereign level of the nation or a higher level of 'united nations'. Let us try to answer the question which level of decision making is optimal, i.e. enables us to attain maximum welfare. In this attempt we have to be aware that our problem is one with '*external effects*', that is a military policy does not only affect the acting nation, but also the other one. If decisions are taken at the national level, the interests of the other nation may not be given the weight they have for the other nation. A combination of two autonomous decisions may not, therefore, maximise total welfare. A decision *taken jointly* holds better promise. For economists this can be made understandable by referring to the duopoly problem: two sellers in a market can maximise the total profits of both sellers by concluding a cartel, i.e. by joint decision making.

The level of security attainable by a joint search for it is called '*common security*' by the Independent Commission on Disarmament and Security Issues, presided over by Swedish Prime Minister Olof Palme (Palme *et. al.*, 1982). It is what they recommend. Apparently the two approaches we followed in this simple essay arrive at the same conclusion. Of course we should be aware of the tremendous switch in political thinking the proposed process requires. To give up part of a powerful government's sovereignty is very close to impossible. And yet this is the only road to survival.

8 A SHORT-TERM SOLUTION

Given the mistrust now existing between the United States and the Soviet Union, an unlimited co-operation in the search for defensive weapons to replace, in the long-run, the present mainly offensive arsenals, is illusory. More time is needed to establish the minimum of trust required for a joint venture in military research. Some forms of joint efforts exist in non-military research and a very modest beginning of open discussions on some military issues took place in the Standing Committee for Consultation, created under Article XIII of the 1972 ABM Treaty.

As long as the need for a joint venture is not yet sufficiently understood the best form of co-operation and arms reduction seems to be *continued adherence to some treaties concluded in the past* and the *conclusion of some new treaties*. More precisely, continued adherence to the ABM, the Non-Proliferation and the Strategic Arms Limitation Treaty (SALT) II, as well as the conclusion of a Comprehensive Test Ban, a ban on weapons in outer space and a Treaty on Peaceful Use of Outer Space may be a start. Reductions of the arsenals as discussed in Vienna, Stockholm and Geneva should be negotiated more seriously. There are some changes in attitude observable recently which give some hope.

References

Brandt, W. *et al.* (1980) *North–South: A Programme for Survival* (London: Pan Books).

Brandt, W. (1983) *Common Crisis* (London: Pan Books).

Fischer, D. (1984) *Preventing War in the Nuclear Age* (London and Canberra: Croom Helm).

Fischer, D. (1985) 'Weapons Technology and the Intensity of Arms Races', *Conflict Management and Peace Science*, 8, pp. 31–48.

Palme, O. *et al.* (1982) *Common Security* (New York: Simon Schuster).

Pearson, L. B. *et al.* (1969) *Partners in Development* (New York, Washington, London: Praeger).

Robbins, L. (1939) *The Economic Causes of War* (London: Jonathan Cape).

Part V

Multilateral Diplomacy for Development

11 The Confidence Factor in Multilateral Diplomacy*

Johan Kaufman

'The fostering of understanding and trust, in fact, is just as important as the actual reaching of agreement.' Masayoshi Ohira (Prime Minister of Japan), 'Brush Strokes', *Moments from My Life*, (Foreign Press Center, Japan, 1979, p. 118)

CONFIDENCE AS A NEGLECTED FACTOR

It is conspicuous that in the enormous literature on international negotiations the confidence factor is more or less neglected. It is mentioned in passing here and there, in particular in respect of political issues; it has not been systematically treated. Yet any negotiation, whether bilateral or multilateral, is bound to be heavily influenced by the amount of confidence one party has in the other. In terms of time sequence the following distinctions can be made:

— confidence in the way the counterparts prepare their position for the forthcoming negotiations;

— confidence in the degree of good faith with which the counterpart will conduct negotiations;

— confidence in that legislative or other organs will complete the necessary approval or ratification of the results of the negotiations;

— confidence that the counterpart will execute in good faith the results of the negotiations.

* I have made certain suggestions or observations in this chapter elsewhere: Johan Kaufmann, 'Decision-making for the New International Economic Order', in *Partners in Tomorrow, Strategies for a New International Order* A. J. Dolman and J. van Ettinger (eds) (Dutton, New York 10003, 2, Park Avenue); Johan Kaufmann, *Conference Diplomacy*, rev. edn (Nijhoff, Dordrecht, 1987).

In multilateral diplomacy the precise influence of the confidence factor is complicated because countries do not negotiate one to one but they negotiate in a great variety of configurations: one country *vis-à-vis* a group, a few countries as a group *vis-à-vis* a large group, one large group with another large group, countries grouped by a particular interest versus countries grouped by another particular interest, etc.

The confidence factor in all these positions can be put on a scale of say from one to ten: anywhere from very low to very high.

My argument is that the results of any negotiations are possibly almost as much influenced by the confidence factor as by the substance of the matters involved.

INTERNATIONAL SECRETARIATS AND THE CONFIDENCE FACTOR

The role of the international secretariat of an organisation is often of decisive influence on the degree of confidence the participants in that organisation will have in the organisation generally, and in the decisions both in the negotiating stage and when they are implemented. It is probably useful to distinguish between (a) the executive head of the secretariat; (b) its principal officers and; (c) the rank and file of the secretariat. Of these three the position of the executive head is presumably crucial. In relation to the executive head of the secretariat we must look at:

(a) The statutory role of the executive head. The constitution and other basic instruments of an organisation indicate the powers or functions of the executive head, his rights to take initiatives and his duties *vis-à-vis* the organisation and the membership. Alternatively, the constitution may be silent on the powers of the secretariat. In certain extreme cases there is no constitution and therefore limitations on the role of the executive head will follow from any decisions of the governing bodies and from gradually developed habits.

(b) The personality of the executive head. He may be a man of action exploiting every possibility for new initiatives and for strengthening his own position and that of the secretariat, or he may be more inclined to be an 'administrator' in the strict sense of the word.

If the executive head tends to use his powers as much as possible, he is likely to run into difficulties with one group of member states or another. This was the tragedy of Secretary-General Hammarskjōld, when he used as much as possible and for the best of things his powers in relation to the Congo conflict. It produced the opposition of the Soviet Union and its allies. On the other hand an executive head who limits himself to the role of 'administrator' in the narrow sense of the word, is likely to be accused of being 'weak' and for that reason may also lose the full confidence of many member states. A 'middle-of-the-road' approach may be the best way out.

The high officials directly under the executive head often determine the reputation of an organisation. Are they generally competent? Are they easily accessible to governments? Are they appointed on the basis of their competence, and not or not primarily on the basis of some geographic key of distribution, or of some presumed right for any one country to retain a particular position? The answers to these questions will be important for the degree of confidence which various countries have in the organisation. To a much lesser extent the same kind of consideration applies to the 'rank and file' of the Secretariat.

Sometimes an organisation is created with an in-built bias towards certain objectives. A typical example is UNCTAD, which was born out of the desire of developing countries to have a stronger voice and a 'body of their own' for dealing with problems of primary interest to them. As a result the Secretary-General of UNCTAD has so far always come from a developing country. Starting with Doctor Raúl Prebisch, they have never made it a secret that under the constitution of UNCTAD they felt they had to defend the interests of developing countries. This, however, became automatically a source for lack of confidence on the side of developing countries. Of course this lack of confidence differs from time to time, from subject to subject, and also, presumably, from Secretary-General to Secretary-General.

The total role which a secretariat can play can be argued to derive from the confluence of three factors: statutory role of the executive head, personality of the executive head, and the confidence which governments have in him. The net result may determine the 'intensity' of a Secretariat's activities, and can, in a very rough manner, be illustrated in the following way:

Secretariat 'intensity'

A *Statutory position of executive head*	B *Personality of executive head*	C *Confidence in secretariat*	D *Secretariat 'intensity'*
(1) strong	active	great	high
(2) weak	active	great	high
(3) weak	active	average	medium
(4) weak	passive	small	low

More specifically the effect of the degree of confidence in the Secretariat can be indicated as follows:

Confidence in secretariat		*Effect on negotiations*
High with some Low with others	}	potential clash
Low with all	=	consensus, but decision-making difficult in cases where secretariat support is needed (statistics, fact-finding, etc.)
High with all	=	basis for constructive action

CHAIRMAN AND THE CONFIDENCE FACTOR

In certain situations the degree of confidence a chairman inspires may be of considerable importance. His role is influenced by the following factors:

— his experience and intelligence, including his grasp of the rules of procedure;
— the degree to which he is successful in bringing opposing delegations or opposing groups of governments, around a negotiating table;
— the manner in which the chairman can operate as a team with the secretariat and also with the other members of his 'Bureau': the Vice-Chairmen and the Rapporteur.

The efficient chairman will permit time for informal negotiations which are indispensable to the success of a conference.

The chairman not only will promote informal consultations or negotiations; he will also on occasion take part in them, possibly as an informal presiding officer. At the annual sessions of the UN General Assembly the President frequently gets involved in behind-the-scenes consultations or negotiations on procedural or other points. In some cases a chairman will prefer not to preside over an informal negotiation himself, because this will give him a better opportunity to mediate by offering some wise suggestions at a point where talks seem to be headed for a stalemate. In other situations it may be inevitable that he chairs the negotiation himself.

CONFIDENCE WITHIN AND AMONG GROUPS

If one compares the present situation with that in 1960 the most conspicuous change in decision-making in the United Nations and also in other parts of the United Nations System, is the rise of the group system. Negotiating between individual countries or between small clusters of countries has — in particular in the economic field (much less in regard to political issues) — gradually been overtaken by negotiating between large groups. Of course, a closer look at the group negotiating system will divulge that there are small nuclei of countries who play a more significant role within these groups than others. However, what we are concerned with is the impact of the group negotiating system as such. Before 1964 there were already many examples of inter-group negotiation. In a formal sense, the group system — in the economic area — can be said to have started at the first UNCTAD Conference (Geneva, 1964). Prior to that conference, held at Geneva, 75 developing nations prepared a common point of view, specifically in regard to what they expected in terms of concessions from developed nations. During the Conference the group turned out to have 77 members, and it has been called ever since 'the Group of 77'. Its present membership is about 125. The developed countries came to be known as 'Group B' (after the name given to the group of developed countries for election purposes in the Annex to the basic UNCTAD resolutions). It is hazardous to generalise on the advantages and disadvantages of groups for the effective conduct of conference diplomacy, since each conference presents its own 'make-up' of groups. In analysing the behaviour of each group in a specific conference, one can come to a conclusion as to its effect on the outcome of the conference.

The positive effect of the group system would be a gain in conference efficiency especially if negotiating procedures between groups become an established routine, and communications between groups are made easier by the existence of such procedures. Moreover, in so far as statements by group spokesmen replace a large number of individual speeches, time is saved.

On the negative side it has become apparent that the willingness to aim at an acceptable compromise may be absent, and may have been replaced by a sort of group inflexibility which makes the negotiation of compromise agreements more difficult.

This is likely to occur where a 'demand-offer' type of conflict arises: a group of countries presents maximum demands to another group which tends to respond with minimum offers. This has been the unfortunate pattern of many North–South negotiations, including some of the more important subjects discussed at several UNCTAD conferences.

The more homogeneous a group is, the easier it is to formulate a common position. This common position will be generally arrived at fairly early in the negotiating process, in particular if preparatory meetings of the group have been held prior to the conference in question.

In the case of the Group of 77 they have managed remarkably to prepare common positions for each UNCTAD conference. However, it has become increasingly difficult to maintain this cohesive point of view during each conference. At the Fifth UNCTAD Conference a group of oil-producing Latin American countries rebelled openly against the Group of 77 point of view, according to which energy was not a suitable subject to be taken up by UNCTAD. Similarly, in Group B (developed countries) Australia at one point submitted a draft resolution on its own, without previous thorough consultation in Group B. Such individual actions are symptomatic of a lack of confidence that individual country positions will be adequately reflected in, let alone taken over by, group positions. Countries like the Netherlands, Norway and Sweden, with advanced positions on the new international economic order and on problems related to the Third World generally, have never felt quite comfortable in the formalised set-up of Group B. This led to the establishment of a group of 'like-minded countries', the kernel of which was constituted by the Netherlands, Norway and Sweden, with a somewhat less committed fringe which varied from meeting to meeting, and which included Belgium, Canada, Finland and occasionally other countries. The group of 'like-minded countries' never formalised its status and did not come forward with any rigidly formulated positions (if it had been possible to formulate these, which is uncertain) at any subsequent conference. As positions of individual countries or smaller groups of countries, such as the like-minded countries, tend to divert from what can be presumed to be the majority point of view of the group, confidence in the positions of the group as a whole, and in the action of the leadership of the group (or of those who represent the group at negotiations) becomes less.

If confidence in the group is high among its members decision-making is obviously easier at any conference requiring negotiations with other groups. Conversely if confidence tends to be low within the group, decision-making becomes more difficult. If there is dissension within a group, it takes that much more time to arrive at a common group position. The time factor then starts to play havoc with good intentions. If the group position is arrived at late in the conference timetable, time lacks for a thorough negotiation; tempers are running high, chances for failures are that much greater.

Summing up, it can be said that the degree of confidence which individual members have in their group as a whole can often be of decisive influence for the success or the failure of a negotiation.

TYPES OF ACTION IN MULTILATERAL DIPLOMACY AND THE CONFIDENCE FACTOR; THE ROLE OF THE ESCAPE CLAUSE

It can be said that the confidence factor always plays a role, latently or openly, at any time of multilateral diplomacy.

The confidence factor can be analysed by order of ascendancy of type of action sought from governments and/or from the international secretariat involved:

(a) the most simple type of action, often contained in resolutions of United Nations organs, is to request the secretariat to undertake an enquiry or a further study, or to set up a group of experts to analyse an issue further. In formal texts the request is usually made to the Secretary-General or whatever the name of the executive head of the organisation may be. Even such a relatively innocuous type of decision may occasionally stir up the confidence element. If a group of experts is to be composed by the secretariat there may be doubts whether the Secretary-General will appoint the right experts. The right expert to one country or group of countries is of course inevitably the wrong expert to another country or group of countries! For this reason one often finds in texts related to the appointment of groups of experts that these should be selected and appointed 'in consultation with governments'. In United Nations General Assembly resolutions this usually is interpreted to mean that the Secretary-General shall seek the agreement of either the various regional groups, and/or consult with the principal governments which have been involved in the process of negotiation leading to the resolution in question. Governments opposing some type of action will always prefer a questionnaire type of enquiry among member states over the appointment of a group of experts who might come up with some revolutionary thoughts. The experts usually find ways to make forceful recommendations, even if the mandate of the group is rather restrictive. Both types of action, the enquiry among governments, or the setting up of a group of experts (the two approaches can also be, and are occasionally, combined) signify delay in the action sought by some governments.

(b) A variant on (a) is the setting up of a group constituted by government delegates, with a specific mandate. If the governments to be members of a committee are to be appointed by the President of the General Assembly he will engage in close consultations with the regional groups, and endeavour to get an 'agreed slate' recommended by each group.

(c) A type of action sought very frequently from governments in United Nations resolutions is some sort of modification of their international policies. This may for instance relate to an increase in the transfer of financial and other resources from developed to developing nations (a perennial in UN resolutions for several decades), or it may refer to modifications in international trade policy, or more fundamentally it may have to do with basic changes in the structure of international economic relations. As soon as actions of this type are sought, the confidence factor comes into play more actively. Of course, the primary reason why certain governments will oppose this type of action is that, for substantive reasons, they are not prepared to let themselves be drawn into what looks like the beginning of a commitment, even though the text to be adopted is in terms of a non-binding recommendation. A recommendation can of course be gauged in different terms: the General Assembly may 'strongly urge' governments to do this or that, or, governments may be 'requested' to take this that action 'in the shortest possible time'. Many governments will be cagey in voting for such texts, even though they are legally not committed. A vote in favour is usually interpreted in the United Nations milieu as an indication that a government is willing to 'play ball'. An affirmative vote can be mitigated by an 'explanatory vote', in which a government will put on record express reservations on the action taken (ironically, in most UN organizations the text of such explanations of vote are not included in the summary record!).

(d) Even more pronounced opposition is provoked by texts of resolutions requesting a 'domestic policy commitment'. Of course, every international policy commitment has domestic policy consequences. 'Domestic policy commitment' is therefore construed, in this context, as direct commitments or recommendations related thereto, in respect of the modification of some important element of domestic policy, i.e. the structure of agriculture in developing countries, attention to be given by governments of developing countries to their poorest groups, the structure of industry in developed countries (i.e. its change to accommodate more imports from developing countries) the 'lifestyle' of the population in developed countries, e.g. to diminish conspicuous consumption and thereby free resources for developing nations. Recommendations of this type usually provoke severe opposition from many governments. Developing nations were vigorously opposed, when efforts were made during the seventh special session of the General Assembly dealing with economic development, to have them undertake some preliminary engagement of domestic policy actions. When Mr McNamara, President of the World Bank, and a well meaning group of Western European countries (mainly Scandinavian countries and the Netherlands) wanted more attention to be given to financial and other assistance benefiting the poorest groups within each country, they ran into vigorous opposition. The so-called 'basic needs' approach, which was also developed at the ILO World Employment Conference (1976) was received with an argument somewhat as follows: We, the developing nations, know very well how to deal with our poorest groups; many of us are of the opinion that a vigorous industrialisation programme is the best method to assist, and lift towards a higher level, the poorest groups, of our society; giving direct assistance to the poorest in our country is 'charity', and this is something we wish to control ourselves. Similarly, the developed countries did not wish interference with delicate domestic economic policy commitments, related to the structure of their trade, industry or agriculture. Reactions of developed countries have also been heavily influenced by difficult problems of unemployment and inflation.

(e) The actions discussed thus far are all 'non-committing' for governments (in the legal sense). Several types of decisions in international organisations do commit governments, for example certain decisions of the Security Council and those related to the budgets of organisations. Hence, governments will look at the financial implications of draft resolutions which are non-committing in other respects. The beneficial effects of some action may be considered by some countries to be less than the cost (economists would say: 'the opportunity cost'). In other words confidence in the beneficial effects of the action is insufficient to overcome financial hesitations.

The overall budget decision in each organisation is considered quite important. For anyone who has followed the proceedings of the Fifth (Budgetary and Financial) Committee of the General Assembly over a period of years, it becomes clear that overall confidence in the performance of the United Nations Secretariat is, whether one likes it or not, an important element in the United Nations budget decision-making process. This may come out into the open. In the corridors, however, lack of confidence not necessarily in the Secretariat as a whole, less even in the person of the Secretary-General, but more often in the particular secretariat component which is going to execute a part of the programme, will be heard as an argument for not supporting some particular activity, or occasionally the entire budget.

CONFIDENCE FACTOR IN RELATION TO THE INSTITUTIONAL FORMAT OF MEETINGS

Large Fora where Every Member has One Vote

Typical examples of this are the General Assembly, the UNCTAD Board and Conference, and more generally most voting organs in the United Nations system. In a situation where voting, rather than consensus-making is the usual method of decision-making, it is probable that if a majority is determined to impose its views by a vote, the minority will feel 'oppressed' and will be inclined to have no confidence in any negotiations preceding the vote, and in the substance of the text itself. This has been referred to as the 'tyranny of the majority'. Yet, if a vote is taken in accordance with the rules of procedure, and a majority votes for a certain text, it is difficult to regard this as a deviation from democratic procedures. In United Nations organs occasional hasty voting on important texts has created, rightly or wrongly, an amount of resentment with a minority. Some of the resolution texts emanating from the Group of 77 have been thus criticised. The criticism, as a generalisation, seems to be exaggerated, because there are many examples of important texts on which the Group of 77, although it had the obvious majority, showed patient willingness to engage in informal negotiations. Sometimes, some of the developed countries were not able to accept a compromise because they were apparently unable to get the necessary authorising instructions from their capital in time.

Fora with Weighted Voting

In the United Nations system the only organisations which have a system of weighted voting are the World Bank and the International Monetary Fund. Their decision-making is based on a system of consensus-making. Decisions are prepared in the Executive Board of each of the institutions, and then put before the annual meeting of the Governors of the Bank and the Fund. In practice, there seem to have been no major difficulties with this method of decision-making in the Bank and the Fund. Yet governments have argued that the system of weighted voting as it exists in the Bank and the Fund is outdated. While no member of the Bank or the Fund has proposed a replacement of weighted voting by a one country/one vote system, many have pleaded for a change in the weight of the votes, in order to take into account changed economic power relationships in the world of the 1980s. Some changes in the weight of votes at the Bank and Fund have been made and appear to have restored confidence of the states involved. Outside the Bank and the Fund, in some United Nations organs, there has been some pressure for a radical review of the weighted voting system of the Bank and the Fund. The consensus tradition of World Bank and International Monetary Fund decision-making is no doubt confidence-inspiring, and has overcome possible disadvantages of the weighted voting system in use at these two institutions since their establishment. On the other hand, there seems little doubt that the consensus procedure as applied at the Bank and Fund barely conceals the strength of countries with large voting power. Since developing countries know that the United States and others can block any proposals, they are in fact reluctant to pursue some of these, which are then elaborated in statements in and press communiqués of their own Group of 24 (which comprises developing countries, members of the Bank and Fund).

Fora with Qualified Majority Voting Requirements

In several United Nations bodies there is a requirement that for certain questions a minimum of two-thirds of the members present and voting is required. Under rule 83 of the General Assembly, for example, such questions include recommendations with respect to maintenance of international peace and security, the election of non-permanent members of the Security Council and of members of the Security Council and of members of certain other bodies, the admission of new members to the United Nations, the suspension of membership rights and privileges, and all questions which are budgetary. The General Assembly can decide, by a simple majority, that a question is 'important' under rule 83. In recent years, in most cases at the United Nations General Assembly, majorities on any given disputed question have been so large that the two-thirds majority could easily be reached. Often a vote by a two-thirds majority is preceded by a motion which proposed to declare a question an important question under rule 83 of the General Assembly. The vote on this prior motion is then a test case; if those who aim at a two-thirds majority lose this vote, they know that they will also lose the vote on the substantive matter itself. If they gain the motion to have something declared a two-thirds majority item, it does not automatically follow that on the substance they will be able to produce a blocking third (because several countries which have supported the procedural motion will go along with the apparent majority on the substance). A qualified majority requirement often forces governments with opposing points of view to continue negotiations aiming at a compromise consensus resolution. It can be said that on balance a qualified majority rule is confidence-building.

Fora with Restricted Membership

In the United Nations system as well as elsewhere there are numerous bodies which have a restricted membership.

A smaller or sometimes somewhat larger part of the membership of the organisation becomes a member of a committee or another organ, either as the result of an election, or on the basis of an appointment by the executive head of the organisation or by the president of its main deliberative organ. Almost nothing seems to cause more distrust, and lack of confidence, than the fact that a government is not represented on a particular body to which it attaches importance. The government feels left out of the negotiating process, and may in advance take a distrustful attitude of any results to come out of the particular body. Election fights to become members of restricted bodies are among the fiercest known in the United Nations system. If the Secretary-General or the President of the General Assembly is to appoint members of a body, he is often put under strong pressure from various countries.

The lack of confidence emanating from not being represented on a particular body, can partly be overcome by a procedure involving review by a larger (some would say higher) body, in which all members can participate. This time-proven technique could be more systematically applied in the United Nations and outside it. Thus the results of the Committee of the Conference on Disarmament (CCD), replaced in 1978 by the enlarged Disarmament Committee (as a result of the decisions of the tenth Special General Assembly Session on Disarmament (1978), were reviewed by the First Committee of the General Assembly. Yet the Disarmament Committee was formally a non-United Nations body. Similarly the work of restricted bodies in the economic fields, including ECOSOC, is critically reviewed by the General Assembly through its Second (Economic and Financial) Committee. A remedy for the lack of confidence in restricted bodies which may be worse than the difficulty itself, is to terminate the restrictiveness and to make them 'open-ended'. This is what has happened in several cases in recent UN history. Thus, the UNCTAD Board has been made open for membership by any interested member country.

Overlapping Fora

It is one of the significant characteristics of the United Nations that when a problem cannot be solved a new organ is created in the expectation that somehow this new organ will be better suited than the previous one to solve a particular set of problems. Thus when there was dissatisfaction with ECOSOC in the early 1960s, UNCTAD was created. Since 1964 UNCTAD does have some solid accomplishments, but at the cost of an enormous amount of resources, both human and financial. The 1977 General Assembly created a 'Committee of the Whole' which is supposed to assist the General Assembly with the following tasks:

(a) Overseeing and monitoring the implementation of decisions and agreements reached in the negotiations on the establishment of the New International Economic Order in the appropriate bodies of the United Nations system;
(b) Providing impetus for resolving difficulties in negotiations and for encouraging the on-going work in these bodies;
(c) Serving, where appropriate, as a forum for facilitating and expediting agreement on the resolution of outstanding issues; and
(d) Exploring and exchanging views on global economic problems and priorities; (General Assembly Resolution 32/174).

The Committee was born under a dispute separating those who would like to give the new committee maximal tasks, including the right to try to settle the fate of negotiations going on elsewhere (for example in GATT) and those who felt that the committee should be no more than a monitoring outfit, taking note and discussing, but not interfering with progress or lack of progress in negotiations elsewhere. This dispute has continued to plague the committee during its initial meetings in 1978 and 1979. The relationship of this committee to ECOSOC and to UNCTAD was unclear. Cynics called it 'Committee of the Hole' where problems disappear but are not solved.

Another example of what in principle is an overlapping organ was the separate creation of a preparatory committee for the Third Development Decade, starting in 1980. In this case there was a solid precedent, i.e. a similar preparatory committee for the Second Development Decade. The elaborate resolution of goals and various other measures for the Second Development Decade can be called a moderate success; it was the first time that the international community came up with specific economic targets accepted by most countries (although implemented by less). Yet, inevitably, the question arises whether such preparatory tasks might have been undertaken by ECOSOC or by an appropriately constituted committee of ECOSOC.

The World Food Council, which started its activities pursuant to a decision at the World Food Conference (Rome, 1974) overlaps with FAO organs and also with ECOSOC, if one accepts the wide United Nations Charter definition of ECOSOC's work. The World Food Council is supposed to decide on overall policies in the food area. One argument for its establishment was the likelihood that the Soviet Union would join this Council (which it did) while the Soviet Union had never joined FAO. However, as far as can be seen, the membership of the Soviet Union has made no difference to the World Food Council's accomplishments, which have been thus far modest. An interesting experience with what was not meant to be an 'overlapping body' was the CIEC (Conference on International Economic Cooperation, 1975–7). The CIEC, set up outside the UN because of the latter's slowness and cumbersomeness, composed of 27 countries (19 developing and eight developed), held out promise for concrete results. It has led to considerable clarification and to a special aid action for the poorest countries, but it did not solve basic problems. After the 'failure' of CIEC, attention was focused again on the United Nations as an overall mechanism for negotiating interlinked economic problems. The CIEC suffered from its onset of a deep suspicion and lack of confidence among many countries, in particular developing countries who were not members. The failure of CIEC to come up with concrete solutions has counted among the motivations for setting up the General Assembly Committee of the Whole whose fate has not been better than that of CIEC.

Intellectual Fora

Sometimes there are expert bodies in the United Nations system which come up with reports, so sophisticated and intellectual, that they produce a lack of confidence which higher political organs may put in them. Such reactions have occasionally been the fate of recommendations of the Committee on Development Planning (CDP) a body of individually serving experts who meet twice a year, and make recommendations on important issues on economic policy, especially as related to developing countries. The reports of the Committee on Development Planning do not seem to get the attention they deserve in such bodies as ECOSOC and UNCTAD since they are hardly discussed. Presumably, some of the things recommended by CDP were not 'popular' in the light of the general trend of ideas within, say, the Group of 77 or some other group. For some of the developed countries the mere existence of the word 'planning' in its name may have caused an in-built negative bias.

THE NEW INTERNATIONAL ECONOMIC ORDER AND THE CONFIDENCE FACTOR

What is the New International Economic Order (NIEO)? Superficially, the answer is easy: the NIEO is the Declaration and Plan of Action adopted at the Sixth Special Session (resolution 3202-S-VI of 1 May 1974), supplemented by the Charter of Economic Rights and Duties of States (resolution 3281–XXIX of 12 December 1974) and followed by resolution 3362 (S–VII) on 'Development and International Economic Co-operation' adopted at the Seventh Special Session of the General Assembly (16 September 1975). This, however, is a non-answer, both because of the vagueness of many of the precepts in these texts, and because a number of important governments did not accept, or only in part, the policy recommendations in these texts. In the case of the Sixth Special Session this non-acceptance took the form of a series of formal reservations.

The result of the Seventh Special Session, i.e. resolution 3362 (S-VII), has been described by the former Netherlands Minister for Development Corporation, J. Pronk, as 'a commitment to commit'. This is semantically, perhaps morally, true, but not legally. Without a time-frame, and without real agreement on fundamental objectives and principal means to achieve these objectives, the significance of the commitment was limited, and potentially negative, if frustration and anger over non-results led to negative action which made subsequent agreement even more difficult.

If there is no agreed definition of the New International Economic

Order, the negotiating process is obviously rendered more difficult. Every sub-goal has to be negotiated in cumbersome talks; simultaneously or subsequently instruments are tackled; often (sub-) goals and instruments get mixed up. On top of this, semantic and conceptual difficulties negatively affect the process of decision-making which more often than not becomes non-decision-making.

Of course in a more basic sense the lack of confidence which the concept of the new international economic order has left with some governments and people goes beyond any vagueness of definition. The most fundamental element of the lack of confidence among some large developed countries is no doubt due to the fact that they did not feel that it was possible to modify with a big stroke, in one or two international texts, the existing international economic system. The words 'new' and 'order' were in particular elements designed to inspire lack of confidence. The word 'new' because many elements of the present economic order were satisfactory to these countries, in particular the general principles of the capitalist marketing system. More fundamentally however, would be their objection against the concept 'order' which to them seems to indicate some sort of centralised global planning. This is precisely what these countries did not want. They want to proceed 'pragmatically' step by step. For the same basic reason they had for a long time objections against the integrated commodities programme of UNCTAD and against the worldwide Common Fund to be created. This had elements of world economic planning to which these countries were opposed. Interestingly, the UNCTAD Common Fund has finally been accepted, also by those who were first opposed. As of October 1987 the required number of ratifications has been reached. Opposition of the United States and others to the concept and proposed operations of the Common Fund continues to make it doubtful whether the Fund will ever start work. Yet, the intellectual argument that the nature of worldwide problems and the widely lip-serviced principle of 'interdependence' require worldwide solutions and worldwide management is apparently very slow in overcoming these elements of distrust of a philosophical and conceptual nature.

CONCLUDING REMARKS; CAN CONFIDENCE BE IMPROVED?

There can be no general answer to this question because the situation in each organisation is different, and because the nature of substantive problems combined with such things as the institutional format and the way in which governments approach problems, including the psychological factors of confidence in themselves and in the groups to which they belong and in other governments, are all factors which combine to produce a total confidence result.

Semantics and Definition-making

One aspect which we have not yet dealt with is that of semantics. It played a particular role in the case of the new international economic order.

Because there was no agreed definition of the NIEO, several countries objected vigorously every time the term NIEO, especially if preceded by 'the' rather than by 'a', and if written with capital letters, was used in some draft resolution. These objections, as a minimum, meant loss of time in reaching agreement and, as a maximum, blocked or rendered ineffective any decision-making. This problem has largely disappeared, after the United States accepted the term, although interpreted in a special way:

> The international economic order is a system of relationships among all nations. The process of change, therefore, must be through an evolving consensus that takes into account the economic systems, the interests and the ideas of all countries. Thus we are talking about a process, or a broad framework for dialogue and progress, as much as an 'order' (Statement by Ambassador A. Young, sixty-third session of ECOSOC, 8 July 1977).

Greater attention will have to be given to semantics. The United Nations is reluctant to try to engage in definition-making exercises. It took most of two decades for a Committee on the Definition of Aggression to come up with an acceptable definition of aggression, which turned out to be, because of its relative vagueness, only a pseudo-concensus, hardly agreeable to anybody. Thought might be given to the creation of an *ad hoc* committee on concepts and definitions, composed of a mix of scholars, practitioners and government delegates, from time to time enlarged with subject-oriented experts. To them might be tossed any problem of definition.

Of course, such an exercise might create delays, but perhaps not more delays than are at present encountered.

How to Involve Non-members in Restricted Bodies

The problem we have discussed above of countries feeling left out of a negotiating process can to some extent be overcome by an appropriate review by another, or a higher body. Also the restricted body could on occasion assimilate non-members for a particular subject (this is actually provided for in the statutes or rules of several United Nations organs), or there could be hearings where a non-member, without feeling relegated to an inferior level, could put forward his point of view. This procedure works in a satisfactory way in several parliaments, including the US Congress. It should be worth trying to develop a hearings procedure in the United Nations. The present system of statements 'for the record' by officially accredited observers of governments (who are non-members of a committee) is unsatisfactory; these statements rarely make an impact. A revised procedure might improve the confidence climate.

Changes in Policy

To overcome another confidence problem, i.e. that nations do not want to be abruptly confronted with changes in an essential part of their domestic or international policy, more attention should be given to the timing factor in relation to desired policy changes. The decisions of the Sixth and Seventh Special Sessions were without a time framework; developing nations wanted the fastest possible change, the developed countries seemed to play for more time. Elections and changes of governments contribute towards absorbing more time. In the case of draft resolutions calling for important changes in policies of governments, there should be an effort to negotiate agreed time-frames, intermediate between slowness and abrupt change, perhaps conforming to the old concept 'with all deliberate speed'. Governments and private organisations should endeavour to prepare public opinion for change, and of course take effective domestic measures.

Another way to overcome an important element in the reluctance against accepting changes in policies, could be to give more attention to the possibility of appropriate 'escape clauses'. The General Agreement on Tariffs and Trade, still in its way one of the more successful examples of international decision-making, continues to function, *inter alia*, because of its escape clause machinery.

An effort could be made, perhaps in the framework of the International Development Strategy for the Third Development Decade, to create machinery to relate targets agreed in principle to 'examination procedures' to which governments voluntarily subscribe. An effort should be made to define a fairly precisely defined 'escape clause' in relation to each target, and to apply agreed 'examination procedures' to the use of escape clause machinery. Care should be taken that the use of escape clause machinery is subjected to international scrutiny (as is done in GATT and in certain OECD agreements) so that a minimum of equitable burden-sharing is maintained.

Another 'timing' factor in the question of accepting policy changes is that most governments have distinctly short-term views often linked to parliamentary or presidential elections. This contributes to their reluctance to accept long-term policy changes. A few exceptions exist, such as the Treaty of Rome creating the European Economic Community, which did imply imposed policy changes over the longer term.

There should be an international effort where countries concert in convincing their parliaments to accept long-term commitments. OECD countries might work out joint long-term commitment procedures and then seek to convince Eastern European countries (perhaps through the Economic Commission for Europe) to join. A global long-term 'commitment' policy should be negotiated in a United Nations body and include OPEC and other nations, the final result being a 'global compact' in which everyone can have confidence.

Conference Procedures

To the extent that existing conference procedures are an impediment to successful results, and thereby become by themselves a factor causing lack of confidence, an effort should be made towards change. In particular, in many of the United Nations conferences, including the General Assembly, ECOSOC and UNCTAD, most of the time is spent on speech-making and not enough time on effective negotiating. Moreover negotiations, whether in groups or amongst small clusters of countries, usually start late, sometimes too late. There should therefore be a systematic effort to separate the speech-making process from the negotiating process. This was in fact done at the Seventh Special Session of the General Assembly where negotiating started right away, while the general debate in the plenary room of the General Assembly was still in full swing.

An interesting effort to separate negotiations from 'deliberations' has been going on for years in the disarmament field and has now been made explicit. The Conference of the Committee on Disarmament, transformed pursuant to the decisions of the tenth Special Session of the General Assembly (1978) in an enlarged Committee on Disarmament, has for years been the main negotiating body (of a multilateral character, outside the negotiations between the Soviet Union and the United States) in the disarmament field.

Pursuant to the tenth Special Session's decisions a Disarmament Commission, on which all United Nations members would be represented, was re-established (an old commission with the same name had not been meeting for a long time) with the specific mandate to be 'deliberative', while the restricted Committee on Disarmament would be 'negotiating'. It seems worth pondering whether such a separation of what in fact is speech-making and negotiations should be emulated in the economic field.

The Group System

To the extent that the group negotiating system, discussed above is an impediment to effective negotiations an old tool might be revived: from the start of a negotiating process there could be an effort to constitute, however informally, what used to be called a 'fire brigade': a small group of well intended countries, coming from all the relevant regional or substantive groups involved, would try to negotiate – *ad referendum* to their constituencies – an acceptable compromise solution. Such an effort is not guaranteed to succeed, but is a device which can help in certain instances. It does require that groups are prepared to have delegations, not acting formally on their behalf, undertake such a 'fire brigade' activity, keeping in mind the overall positions a group may previously have arrived at, but not rigidly forced to follow group positions in the compromise being negotiated.

* * * * *

By and large the gist of the argument of this chapter is not only that the confidence factor has been neglected, but also that specific attention should be given to 'confidence building measures' in the international process of trying to achieve a better global international system.

Index